4,50
7/24

Imagining
a Nation

Reconsiderations
in Southern African
History

Richard Elphick, Editor

Imagining a Nation

History and Memory in Making Zimbabwe

Ruramisai Charumbira

University of Virginia Press
Charlottesville and London

University of Virginia Press
© 2015 by the Rector and Visitors of the University of Virginia
All rights reserved
Printed in the United States of America on acid-free paper

First published 2015

9 8 7 6 5 4 3 2 1

Library of Congress Cataloging-in-Publication Data
Charumbira, Ruramisai, 1967– author.
  Imagining a nation : history and memory in making Zimbabwe / Ruramisai
Charumbira.
     pages   cm. — (Reconsiderations in southern African history)
  Includes bibliographical references and index.
  ISBN 978-0-8139-3822-6 (cloth : alk. paper) — ISBN 978-0-8139-3823-3 (e-book)
  1. Nationalism and collective memory—Zimbabwe. 2. Sex role—Zimbabwe—
History. 3. Sexism—Zimbabwe—History. 4. Zimbabwe—Race relations—History.
5. Zimbabwe—Colonial influence. I. Title. II. Series: Reconsiderations in southern
African history.

  DT2908C53 2015
  968.9—dc23
                              2015011672

For Emildah Penina Gotore Charumbira
Mai Vangu, 1940–2011, in memory
and Margaret James Kavounas, Auntie

The tradition of all dead generations weighs
like a nightmare on the minds of the living.

—Karl Marx, *The Eighteenth Brumaire of Louis Bonaparte*

Contents

Acknowledgments

The main idea in this book—history and its memory and memory and its history—started in another form in my 2006 doctoral dissertation at Yale University under the outstanding supportive supervision of Robert W. Harms, whom students affectionately called "Uncle Bob." During my graduate years I sought to understand why Nehanda-Charwe was the singular precolonial woman mentioned in much of Zimbabwean historiography. I researched women's lives before and beyond Charwe and wrote about them in my dissertation, "Forgetting Lives, Remembering Symbols: Women in the History of Zimbabwe." That dissertation was a diamond in the rough. In the many years since, I have broadened and deepened my thinking about history and memory and about colonial and postcolonial history in Africa and elsewhere, which in turn has produced a book far different from the dissertation. I did my best to heed Uncle Bob's advice to patiently polish an important idea so that it would be of value to more people than just me. I hope he believes that I have done so.

I am also grateful to other members of my committee: Glenda Gilmore, who introduced me to (African) American history and got me hooked; and Michael R. Mahoney, a historian of South Africa, whose graduate course Memory and Orality has borne fruit in chapters of this book based on oral sources.

My ability to research and write this book was made possible by the emotional and financial support of various individuals and institutions. The number of individuals and institutions has grown, yet none but I am responsible for the interpretation of the stories told in this book.

Financial support came from the following institutions: the Yale University Graduate School of Arts and Science, the Yale Agrarian Studies Program, the American Association of University Women (AAUW) Educational Foundation, the Luso-American Foundation, the Mrs. Giles Whiting Foundation, the Huntington Library, Denison University's Fairchild Faculty Development Grant, and the German Research Foundation for a research fellowship at the Bielefeld Graduate School in History and Sociology, in Bielefeld, Germany. At the University of Texas at Austin, I thank the College of Liberal Arts and the John Warfield Center for African and African American Studies for a start-up research grant, the Department of History for a Scholarly Activity Grant, the Center for Women's and Gender Studies for a new-faculty development fellowship, the Humanities Institute, the British Studies Junior Faculty Program, and the Office of the Vice President for Research for a Subvention Grant toward the publication of this book. Lastly, I am most grateful to Richard Elphick, a distinguished historian of South Africa and southern Africa and the editor of the Reconsiderations in Southern African History series, who believed in this project from the time I sent him the prospectus; together with Richard Holway, History and Social Sciences Editor at the University of Virginia Press, he mentored me through the process. To those two men, the anonymous manuscript reviewers, and all the staff at the University of Virginia Press, especially Anna C. Kariel, Morgan Myers, and Joanne Allen: you are precious.

The stories in this book were interpreted from sources gathered from archives in Zimbabwe, the United Kingdom, and the United States. I am eternally grateful to all the archivists and staff—the memory keepers— at those institutions, in particular Malvern Ndokera at the National Archives of Zimbabwe, whose superb research assistance from 2002 to 2006 helped me locate as many documents as possible related to the memory of Nehanda-Charwe; and K. Tonhodzai, who went beyond the call of duty to assist me with images. Also in Zimbabwe, I am grateful to the Zimbabwe National Traditional Healers Association (ZINATHA) for leading me in the right direction, toward spirit mediums, where I met with wonderful mentors, especially Sekuru Dhewa and Sekuru Mutiti. *Handina kukanganwa, ndichanyora gwaro renyu vakuru.* Lucy McCann, at Rhodes House, Bodleian Library Oxford, helped me find material for this book and for other projects as well. Dorothy Woodson's encyclopedic guide through Yale's African Studies Collection helped me while I was a student, and the value of that guidance has grown exponentially, years after the fact. Judith Ann Schiff, of Yale's Manuscripts and Archives Library, helped me understand—and years later, appreciate—Howell Wright and his collection. Carol Leadenham was an affirming professional presence at the Hoover Institution on War, Revolution, and Peace Library and Archives, Stanford University Library. And last but not least, I thank Paul Rascoe, African Studies librarian, and the wonderful Interlibrary Loan Services staff at UT Austin, who sourced material for me from near and far.

I am also indebted to many people who have mentored me and those who continue to do so formally and informally, including my former teacher David Levine, at the University of Toronto (OISE); and Roderick McIntosh, a Yale archaeologist of Africa who models the passionate pursuit of Africa's deep past and its relevance today. Also at Yale, I am grateful to the late Robin Winks, who encouraged me to study the West the way the West had studied Africa—minus the prejudice; Jonathan Butler, whose research seminar in European and American history taught me the importance of good historical research and comparative analysis; and John Demos, whose seminal course Narrative and Other Histories sustained my desire to write accessible history many years after the fact. Florence Thomas, Pamela Y. George, Pamela Schirmeister, Ann Kuhlman, and Elisabeth Mead all supported me as I learned how to deal with Yale and especially the U.S. Immigration Services bureaucracy regarding student visas. At Denison University, I am grateful to Toni King and John Jackson, of the Black Studies and Women Studies programs, whose resilience reminded me of the importance of continuing the struggle for social justice for future generations. Also at Denison, I am appreciative of the support and friendship of Don Schilling, Lauren Araiza, Trey Proctor III, and Isis Nusair. Isis read an early draft of the manuscript, offering me a nonhistorian's perspective.

At the University of Texas at Austin, I am grateful to all my colleagues for their collegiality and support in varying capacities over the years, especially Toyin Falola, Omi O. J. Jones, Ted Gordon, Tiffany Gill, Roger W. Lois, Sue Heinzelman, Frank Guridy, Juliet E. K. Walker, Laurie Green, Denise A. Spellberg, Leonard Moore, Susan Deans-Smith, Jorge Cañizares-Esguerra, Alison Frazier, Tracie Matsik, Madeline Hsu, Nancy Stalker, Pauline Strong, Yoav Di Capua, and Joan Neuburger. Jacqueline Jones offered intellectual support and remarkable mentorship. She read the manuscript in various forms, offering invaluable feedback and critique; her assertive mentorship fortified me as I searched for a publisher interested in this book's success and timely publication. I have also benefited tremendously from the support and role modeling of Ann Twinam and Philippa Levine, scholars of great accomplishment and integrity. That this book sees the light of day is also testament to the mentorship and support I got from Alan Tully while he was department chair. I am also appreciative of my colleagues who shared ideas and/or feedback on all or parts of the manuscript, especially Frank Guridy for his close reading and incisive questions, Hannah Chapelle Wojciehowski for her editorial eye and belief in the book's main ideas, Diana R. Berry, Catherine Boone, Robin Metcalfe, Robert Abzug, and Tatjana Lichtenstein, comrade and friend. Laura Flack and the rest of the staff of the Department of History have provided, and continue to provide, the best support anyone doing academic research and teaching could hope for. Farther afield, I thank those who afforded me feedback and/or opportunities to present my work, including Terence O. Ranger, Paul Berliner, Sita Ranchod-Nilsson, Luise White, James Giblin, Nancy Rose Hunt, Timothy Scarnecchia, Lynnette Jackson, and Rola El-Husseini. I also thank my many students, especially the undergraduates in my "History of Southern Africa" classes and the graduates in my "History and Memory" classes; their interest and their questions have made me a better scholar and teacher.

Family and friends nurtured me through the many years of researching and writing this book. All their names would fill many pages. Suffice it to say, Zvinotendwa/Ngiyabonga/Asante sana—Thank you all. I thank in particular Linda Christiansen-Ruffman, Margaret Conrad, Chioma Ekpo, Temitope Adefarakan, and NourbeSe Philip—who will be surprised by the Nehanda who emerges in this book; Margaret Waller, for support when I was a rookie; David and Ching Leung, of Toronto, in whose home I first jotted down my changing ideas on Nehanda, which are now a major part of this book; Fiona Vernal, for continuing to travel with me; Roger S. Levine, Thomas F. McDow, Brian J. Peterson, Jacob Dlamini, and Eric Allina, all intellectual children of "Uncle Bob"; Judy Norsigian and Geneva T. Cooper, whose feminist activism inspires action; the radical feminist Patricia McFadden, whose friendship and sisterhood have sustained my intellectual engagement with Southern Africa's history— and women within it; Dr. Gibson Mandishona and his wonderful daughter, the accomplished filmmaker Mary Ann Mandishona, for many years of friendship; Majella Lenzen, who continues to sustain me, as do Carlos Sasso and his fiancée, Bahar; and Monika Bokerman, who made my stay in Bielefeld a memorable one. The architect Reiner Lembke and his artist partner, Neele, welcomed me into their lives and home, so that I was able to write my first complete draft even as I mourned the loss of my beloved mother in the middle of that sabbatical year in Germany. Alice Prochaska and her husband, Frank Prochaska, of Somerville College, University of Oxford, whom I met at Yale, have remained wonderful mentors and friends. My friends in Austin, Texas, Pat Shirejian and her husband, John Przyborski, remind me that life is enjoyable when taken easy, and Teresa Robinson provides support when I am stranded. One of the benefits of being an immigrant is the opportunity to expand the definition of family, and it has been my singular privilege to be an honorary member of the family of Margaret J. Kavounas, "Auntie," and her husband, Edmond A. Kavounas, "Uncle Ed," who have loved and supported me as if I were one of their own. To them this book is also dedicated. My mother-in-law, Rita, my sister-in-law, Stephanie, and Uncles Erwin and Manfred† welcomed me into their family—language barriers notwithstanding. Lastly, I am grateful to my late father, Andrea M. D. Charumbira, who read to me when I was young and taught me the importance of intellectual curiosity; my mother, who taught me the importance of intellectual honesty and resilience and encouraged me to make the most of an education denied her; my siblings, Tsitsi Matilda†, Abraham, Isaac, Anamaria†, and Anatoria, their spouses, as well as all my nieces and nephews, were the representative audience I had in mind when I was writing this book. I hope they find it worthy. Most importantly, to the man who came into my life unbid, but right on time: *Ich liebe Dich*, Holger Ahlrichs.

I am grateful for permission to include parts of works by me previously published elsewhere. Parts of chapter 2 appeared in "Nehanda and Gender Victimhood in Central Mashonaland 1896–97 Rebellions: Revisiting the Evidence," *History in Africa: A Journal in Method* 35 (2008): 103–31, copyright 2008 African Studies Association. Parts of chapter 7 appeared in "Nehanda, Gender, and the Myth of Nation-hood in the Making of Zimbabwe," in *National Myths: Constructed Pasts, Contested Presents*, ed. Gerard Bouchard (New York: Routledge, 2013), 206–22.

A Note on Orthography, Language Use, and Historiographies

This book, like many before, relies on colonial archives to tell many of the stories contained within. Consequently, there are issues of orthography, language, and meaning that should be noted. However, rather than itemizing all those terms and issues here, I explicate them as they appear in the text. A few examples should be noted from the outset. I generally use the spelling *Mazowe* when referring to Africans' use of that name or when they are narrating their history in that district of colonial Zimbabwe, but I use *Mazoe* when citing directly from the colonial archives or when referring to settlers and their telling of the history of that district. This means that at times, though rarely, I use both spellings in the same paragraph to show the shift in perspective from African to settler or vice versa. *Black* and *White* are used as historical terms as well as analytical devices. I capitalize the terms when highlighting (historical) nationalists' uses of them as not just nouns but identities. On the other hand, I lowercase the terms when I am making an analytical point about those identities. The term *Shona*, for the majority of the people whose history is narrated here, is to a large extent a colonial construct. I tend to use the now standard spelling *Mashonaland*, though sometimes I use *MaShonaland* or, rarely, *maShonaland*, all terms referring to the land of the Shona peoples. The term *native* is sometimes capitalized, and sometimes not, to show the ways settlers thought of Africans or the ways Africans turned a sometimes derogatory term into something affirmative. I capitalize *Southern Africa* when referring to the political region and lowercase it when referring to geography.

Colonial misspellings of African names means that sometimes one person can have three or more names depending on the sources. For example, the names for Nehanda include *Nyanda*, *Nianda*, and *Neanda*, and

Kaguvi's names include *Kakuvi, Kargubi,* and *Kakubi.* The chartered company that administered the colony from 1890 to 1923 is referred to as the *BSAC,* the *Company,* or the *Chartered Company.* The frontier war of 1896–97 was perceived as one *war* on the British side but as *wars* on the African side, as responses to colonialism were less coordinated and mounted as one African army against one British enemy. Thus, I use both *wars* and *war,* depending on the perspective. Contemporary Zimbabwe has three official languages—isiNdebele, chiShona, and English. My translation of terms tends to be in all three language, for example, water/*mvura*/*amanzi* (English/chiShona/isiNdebele).

The term *pioneer* appears in various forms—*Pioneer,* "*Pioneer,*" *Pioneer Column, pioneer,* and "*pioneer*" (and their plural forms)—because it was a formal designation as well as a contested term among settlers; I also use it to present a postcolonial critique. *Pioneer,* "*Pioneer,*" or *Pioneer Column* refers to those men who were part of Rhodes's formally constituted imperial groups of 1890 and 1893. Sometimes I use "*Pioneer*" or "*Pioneer Column*" (and their plural forms) when quoting from sources or when analyzing these groups as a way to include the excluded African perspectives. I also use the lowercase *pioneer* or "*pioneer*" (and their plural forms) to highlight the elasticity of the term as well as its contestations by and among settlers who arrived before 1890 and also their supporters and descendants. The same contestations were made by settlers who arrived between 1890 and 1900, that is, those who experienced the war of 1896–97 but did not belong to the formal associations of the 1890 or 1893 groups. I also use lowercase *pioneer* or "*pioneer*" to include the excluded African voices and, again, to offer a postcolonial critique. Overall, my varied use of this term (and others) highlights the inherent contradictions of colonialism. It would be a disservice to smooth over the term's jagged edges for an easy narrative.

Lastly, I should highlight my engagement with certain literatures—in African or other histories. The "missing" historiography is not absent because it is not important; it is. In fact, I read widely and had to make choices (given page and word limits) about which scholarship most closely related to the issues discussed in this book. For example, there is important literature on gender and the nation that I do not cite in my introduction—like the pioneering work of Lynn Hunt on the impact of gender in the processes of national-identity formation in the French Revolution—but that does not mean that this book is not in conversation with that historiography. Nor does it mean that this book is not in conversation with the work of scholars like Beth Baron, who looked at women and gender dynamics in the making of Egypt, or with Zimbabwean and African historiography. My own work is in conversation with a wide variety of relevant historiographies, and the careful reader will note this in the text and the endnotes. I focus mostly on scholarship that allowed me to say something new without recycling the same issues or staking "new" territory in fields that have been convincingly dealt with by those who came before me. You are therefore invited, dear reader, to engage the thick forest and its entanglements (history), as well as the neatly manicured paths and park benches (memory) presented in this book.

Imagining
a Nation

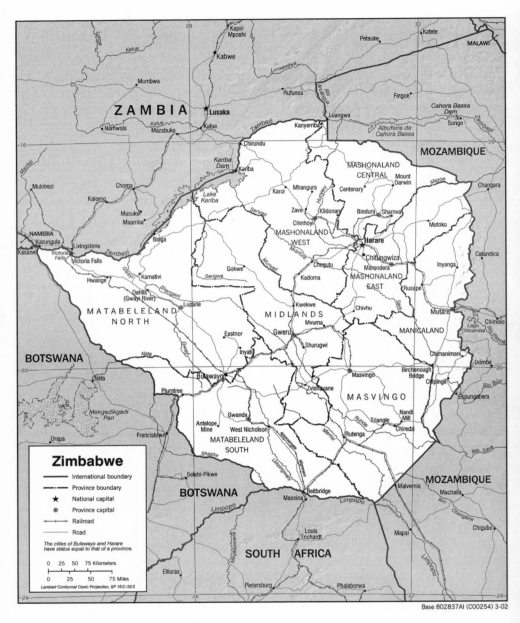

Contemporary map of Zimbabwe. (Courtesy of the University of Texas at
Austin Libraries, Map Collection)

Introduction
Musings

Nationalist memory projects, I argue in this book, are like well-manicured public gardens, complete with signs that read "Walk on designated paths," "Look, do not Touch," "Do not introduce alien plants." Public gardens and their maintenance are, in fact, instructive metaphors for thinking about memory and nation-building, as it is often the imagination of political and cultural nationalists that animates uses of the past for the present in a nation. Those nationalists act like avid gardeners, constantly manicuring the national image, insisting on the "proper" preservation of "indigenous" species by indigenous and cherry-picked outsider experts. Like uppity gardeners, nationalist memory makers often insist on narrow definitions of belonging, patriotism, and national identity. In such cases, dissenting voices are deemed unpatriotic and/or "intruders" planting "alien" seeds (ideas) that could destroy "indigenous" flora (the "pure" nation).

Since its founding as a colony in 1890, Zimbabwe has been dominated by political and cultural nationalists (mostly men) keen to turn the forest of that country's deep and recent past into a manicured garden of the present. Rather than seeing the past as a vibrant ecosystem, Black and White nationalists of Zimbabwe—like those of most modern nations—have been eager to cultivate an image of their country's past that resembles a native garden free of "weeds" and "alien" flora that might disrupt the nationalists' versions of history and who belongs.

This book is a history of the contested memories of what it meant to be Rhodesian/Zimbabwean as seen through the eyes of Black and White nationalists in the central and northern regions of that country since 1890. In it I critically examine the making of nationhood—its memory, meanings, symbols, rituals, and methods of inclusion and exclusion as expressed by cultural and political nationalists in a bid to lay claim to the power structures of the nation. To that end, this book is *not* a history of Zimbabwe; better books on Zimbabwe's history have been written. Rather, in this book I am interested in excavating the African nationalist context that converted Charwe wokwa Hwata, the nineteenth-century medium of the spirit of Nehanda in the Mazowe valley, into a "national" spiritual ancestor, Mbuya Nehanda. I juxtapose the spirit of Charwe as anti-imperialist ancestor to the spirit of the imperialist mining magnate and father of the famed Rhodes Scholarships, Cecil John Rhodes, a memory that animated settler nationalism, and ideological Rhodesians abroad, in praise of imperial conquest. Those two "ancestral spirits" of (colonial and postcolonial) Zimbabwe are the forests I venture into, in search of the sources of Zimbabwe's current postcolonial discontents.

Zimbabwe is now a paradoxical source of angst and pride among different types of people: The angst comes from those within and outside Zimbabwe who are scandalized by the abuse of power by the country's single postcolonial ruler and his political party–cum-government, who have shorted the ordinary people.[1] Pride, on the other hand, comes from those who argue that Zimbabwe is another Haiti, Mugabe another Toussaint L'Ouverture, pressed on all sides by erstwhile colonial masters (the British) in cahoots with other former colonial masters (Western powers) eager to perpetuate a neocolonial balance of power with Africa.[2] That paradox of angst and pride, I argue, carries grains of historical "truth."[3]

To say that former colonial powers have nothing to do with how postindependent Zimbabwe (and much of postcolonial Africa) turned out and how it operates today is at best naive or evasive. Conversely, to see African problems only through the prism of colonialism is to deny Africans their agency in both the positive and negative developments of that continent. As the subaltern and postcolonial studies scholar Partha Chatterjee observed of colonial states and the anticolonial movements, "The colonial state's power, we must remember, was the preservation of the alienness of the ruling group."[4] Equally, Chatterjee continues, "we have all taken the claims of nationalism to be a political movement much too literally, and much too seriously."[5] Thus the present book echoes Chatterjee's sentiments by analyzing some of the gendered founding myths of the colony/nation and those of the postcolony/nation. Rather than focusing on just the settlers or the indigenous people, this study takes into account narratives from both groups, showing that while history was vigorously contested, narrating memory, though accessible to everyone, was not always fair game when powerful ideologies, iconography, and institutions were at stake. Access to outlets of power in the (new) colony/ nation of Rhodesia/Zimbabwe privileged some citizens at the expense of others. This book, therefore, places an emphasis on exploring the liminal spaces between the binary of black/white histories and colonized/ colonizer. Those liminal spaces are the gray versions of history usually eschewed in public discourse in favor of simplistic narratives.

Rethinking Nehanda: Separating the Spirit from Its Medium

Similar to many African children born or raised in the heat of war in late 1970s Rhodesia, I grew up listening to tales of a woman popularly known as Nehanda. Her heroic resistance to British colonialism in the late 1800s was legendary, and it was impressed upon us to resist colonialism as Nehanda had. Bootlegged copies of her image were surreptitiously circulated like the image of a Christian saint in a land where that religion was forbidden. Such was her symbolic power—which extends to today, when a Google search retrieves thousands of hits. No one at the time, as I remember, ever said or seemed to know her real name or any other name for her; in fact, the story of Nehanda was confined to that colonial encounter. The people in the townships of my childhood in Bulawayo cherished the name Nehanda. She was a great female ancestral spirit who had finally come alive to help the living liberate themselves from oppressive white settler society. It was only later that I realized they could not have called her Charwe, her given name: Who has ever heard people call popes or Dalai Lamas by their birth names? Those "holy" men were known only by the names they assumed when they took ecclesiastical office. Charwe was no different. To many in my young days, she was (and to some still is) Nehanda—or Mbuya (ancestor) Nehanda.

Over the many years of thinking about Nehanda (Charwe) and, later, doing extensive archival research in Zimbabwe, South Africa, the United Kingdom, Portugal, and the United States, I have, naturally, come to a different understanding of the woman who inspired me (and this project) many years ago. The most important shift in my thinking was sociotheological, particularly with regard to how people thought and remembered spirits of the dead, especially how those spirits interact or interacted with the living in their societies. That shift in the meaning of spirits opened a space in my mind through which I had something of an epiphany about her: could it be that everyone—myself included—had and has been barking up the wrong tree, invoking Charwe's spirit as Nehanda's, when in fact it was and is Charwe's spirit that has gripped Zimbabwean historiography since her death in April 1898? I wondered whether scholars, the interested public, and I should really be thinking and talking about the spirit of Charwe, rather than that of Nehanda, in nationalist history and memory. After all, the memory of Nehanda was strongest among those African cultural and political nationalists who hailed from Shona-speaking regions, especially the northeast and central Mashonaland, regions where the colonial government was historically most nervous about the revival of a political Nehanda spirit.[6] Charwe as Mbuya Nehanda—ancestral spirit of the nation—became that nationalist and guerrilla movement's matron saint beginning in the 1960s and continued to be right through to the first decade of Zimbabwe's independence (see chapter 7).

The realization that most people were conflating the spirit of the legendary Nehanda—whose name, according to Shona oral tradition, was Nyamhita Nyakasikana—with the spirit of Charwe, the nineteenth-century medium of Mazowe, became very important to me as I broadened and deepened my analysis of the changing meanings of the past to the living. It became obvious that I needed to historicize the *imagined* ethnic memory of the original Nehanda (Nyamhita) among the Shona of northern and eastern Zimbabwe, as well as the nationalist memory of Charwe as Nehanda, the "national" ancestor deployed for propaganda purposes. That is, to my mind, the ethnic history and memory of the "original" Nehanda was an image from an agrarian past, rooted in the ideologies and rituals of the earth's cycles as understood and practiced by certain Shona peoples in particular geographic and cultural locations, while the memory of Charwe as "national ancestor" was an embellishment by a Black nationalist movement eager to graft shoots of an African past onto a White Rhodesian nationalist narrative that excluded African narratives in the history of the colony/nation's founding by European settlers. Because only the Europeans built it, the argument went, the nation belonged to them (alone) and their descendants, who were entitled to full citizenship by inheritance, but not to the "Natives."[7]

The intellectual freedom that came with separating the ethnic history and memory of the legend of Nehanda (the spirit) from the nationalist history and memory of Charwe (the nineteenth-century medium) allowed more light to filter into my mind, so I could rethink that storied but often misunderstood history. As more light filtered into my mind, I thought: What if, even though Charwe channeled the *mhondoro* (royal lion spirit) of Nehanda (as described in chapter 2), her own spirit as Charwe was not so royal a spirit and was perhaps an *ngozi* spirit? The Shona, among whom she was born, define an *ngozi* spirit as the spirit of a person who died a violent death, or was (unjustly) murdered, or died harboring feelings of vengeance for maltreatment by the living. Once dead, her or his spirit would seek revenge and/or justice among the living until appeased.[8] It occurred to me that the spirit of Charwe was (and is) unaccounted for in the historiography in its own right. To that end, in Shona cosmology, Charwe's spirit should be theorized separately, and perhaps as an *ngozi* spirit since she died contesting her death sentence.[9] Charwe's spirit (or life) should be historicized for its place in Black nationalist thought writ large.

On reflection, it was a plausible hunch given that the historical record (oral and written) shows that she was executed by hanging, a death she resisted but ultimately faced with a courageous rancor that left an indelible mark on all who witnessed the execution (see chapter 3). However, suggesting that Charwe's spirit may have been, or is, an *ngozi* spirit is sacrilegious and generates a vigorous debate, which I experienced at the British Zimbabwe Society's Research Days in 2010.[10] Counterarguments to my assertion that Charwe's spirit may have been, or is, an *ngozi* spirit adopted by the nationalist movement included one argument I thought quite useful: Since the British executed Charwe, the *ngozi* spirit would not, and should not, manifest among the (black) people of Zimbabwe; rather, it would or should seek revenge and/or justice among the (white) British, who executed her. As some people insisted to me at the break: "*Vele akwenzi!*" / "*Hazvi tomboite!*" / "It is impossible to think of such revered spirits as (possible) *ngozi* spirits!" The debate continues in this book as I show (in chapter 7) that there is evidence to support what started as a hunch for me, that she may be considered an *ngozi* because her next of kin accepted reparations from implicated families eager to appease her supposedly restless spirit. I emphasize the separation of the legendary Nehanda-Nyamhita from the nineteenth-century medium Nehanda-Charwe so that we can reevaluate nationalist history that has the urge to have it all fit neatly in rows, like clipped shrubs in a well-manicured estate garden. If Nehanda-Charwe does and does not shine as the heroine of everyone's imaginations, then I will have done my part in telling and showing the tectonic rupture of colonialism, especially African people's agency given the circumstances. In this book, therefore, it is the history and memory of the spirit of Charwe wokwa Hwata, the guerrilla-made "Comrade Nehanda"—not the legend of Nehanda Nyamhita Nyakasikana—that exercises the mind.

Looking Away: The Resurrection of Rhodesian Identity

The turn of this project toward more than just an understanding of African nationalism manifest in the memory of Nehanda-Charwe in Zimbabwe's history was also engendered by the rise of postimperial and postsettler nostalgia. This was evident on the Internet and in memoirs mourning the loss of idyllic Rhodesian childhoods and lives on farms and in urban centers with nannies, garden "boys," and country clubs. The imperialist and white supremacist Cecil Rhodes became a visionary founder, again. The imperial nostalgia, to borrow a term from the anthropologist Renato Rosaldo, seemed suddenly to make it not only possible but permissible to leap over the mess that was colonialism and its inherited racial and economic privilege to this moment of victimhood at the hands of Robert Mugabe and his minions.[11] The international community, especially the media, was animated to document and broadcast the plight of "white farmers" and the gross human rights violations going on in Zimbabwe in the first decade of this century.

The "white farmers," for their part, were media savvy and documented their plight through pictures, blogs, memoirs, and other forms of memory keeping.[12] This created an awkward situation for those wanting change in Zimbabwe, for not to rightly condemn state violence against a section of society was to be on the wrong side of history. On the other hand, not speaking about the historical privilege that begat the present was to elide the structural violence of colonialism. What also complicated the international, especially the Western, community's response to the white farmers' plight was that in the early 1980s the same international community (and its media) had whispered about gross human rights violations in Zimbabwe when the then newly inaugurated prime minister, Robert G. Mugabe, ordered and/or allowed state violence to be unleashed on the people of the Matebeleland North, Matebeleland

South, and Midlands Provinces in the name of national security during the "Gukurahundi" era.[13]

Internal fights for power among the new ruling elite in independent Zimbabwe, as well as apartheid South Africa's fear of a new "communist regime" in Southern Africa, fed the ethno-based violence that saw tens of thousands of people killed, maimed, and psychologically traumatized for life in the name of fighting the "dissidents." These internal and external bifurcated memories of Rhodesia and of Zimbabwe were of interest to me as it was obviously a country whose citizens had deeply fractured ideas about the past shaped not only by the citizens of that country but by outsiders as well.

The valuing of "white" lives over "black" lives invoked a colonial past that had nurtured the memory of a nation focused on singular ethnic or racial histories rather than of the nation at large. Given this juxtaposition of black and white histories, whose narratives of memory sought to control political and economic power, I became interested in why it was that histories of victimhood seemed to be the ones with the most saliency in Zimbabwe, with so little invested in histories of critical engagement across ethnic and racial lines. Why, I wondered, were ordinary people mostly invested in "their people's" history at the expense of a larger, more inclusive history of solidarity and/or contestation? What use is history if it only serves those in power and their minions? What use is memory if all it does is reinscribe patriarchal, racial, and ethnic notions of nationhood that exclude other forms of progressive politics, liberation, and equal citizenship by and for all citizens? What use is history to Zimbabwe if Rhodesia was for Rhodesians (read whites) and Zimbabwe is for Zimbabweans (read blacks)? Thus, rather than being a history of how the rulers marshaled state power and physical violence on the ruled, this book is about ordinary people's investment in the soft power of individual, social, and collective memory that created and perpetuated exclusionary national myths. That soft power promised ordinary people access to real power in the economic and (public) political arenas. The stories told in this book, therefore, question the value of history when all it does is celebrate uncomplicated pasts and an uncontested present by both the rulers and the ruled.

Conceptual and Theoretical Frameworks: Imagination, Memory, Gender

The concept that drives my interpretation and analysis in this book is *imagination*, which highlights the symbiosis between the process (history) and its products (memory and the nation). I mean imagination in the philosophical and psychocultural and sociohistorical sense to signify that the living have not always made up or invented the past outright; rather, they often have embellished the remembered past. As the philosopher-historian Paul Ricoeur put it, "We have nothing better than memory to signify that something has taken place, has occurred, and has happened *before* we declare that we remember it."[14] In this sense, this book is less about "traditions which appear or claim to be old [yet] are often quite recent in origin and sometimes invented"[15] than it is about the clutching of real historical events and personalities to insist on the right of one's existence at the expense of another. Therefore, imagination, as argued in this book, is about the *politics of remembering,* the power embedded in "true" history, from which black nationalists and white nationalists selectively chose narratives to construct an exclusive colony/nation.

The politics of memory that this book describes and analyzes shows the importance of history to society, even at the expense of the rational present. That politics also shows how memory, like a religion, evokes strong emotions because history is the irretrievable past, and its interpretation is at stake. The reason historical memory evokes such intense emotions is that it is a flash, a snap of things past, things that cannot (and often could not) be repeated in the same way by the same people, ever. That uniqueness "has to do with the privilege spontaneously accorded to historical events among all the 'things' we remember. The 'thing' remembered is plainly identified with a singular, unrepeatable event."[16] Memory, then, becomes the signifier of a past. Memory is the method by which the living stamp their claim and presence on the landscape of the past and in collective consciousness, creating traditions around which societies rise and fall as a "people." As Margaret Atwood astutely observed, "The past no longer belongs only to those who lived in it; the past belongs to those who claim it, and are willing to explore it, and to infuse it with meaning for those alive today. The past belongs to us because we are the ones who need it."[17] History became the mirror; it was the object the living used to assert their ownership (memory) of the past and their right to the present.

Imagination as described in this book, therefore, is not invention. It may sometimes read as if the two were interchangeable, but I use them differently: imagination places a premium on remembering things past, however distorted, while invention places a premium on the totally made up, however plausible. That is, imagination is about a remembered past, even when all that remains is a shard of evidence from the past, whereas invention is about a past in which not even a shard of evidence exists but in which whatever is "remembered" is presented as ancient tradition. This might seem like an overemphasis on semantics, but I insist on the clarity of definitions because I agree with the historian Alon Confino's argument that "the notion of memory [is often] *more practiced than theorized,* and has been used to denote very different things."[18] In fact, as Confino has it, the untheorized "term 'memory' is depreciated by surplus use,"[19] and unless scholars of history and memory clarify their conceptual framework and methodology, the undefined overuse of the term will mean that we all continue to participate in what I call memory-sticker labeling. In this book, therefore, imagination is not only about the preservation or fossilization of things past but "also about searching for it, and 'doing' something" to remember the past. Imagination is about the processes of remembering. In fact, Ricoeur reminds us that "the verb 'to remember' stands for substantive 'memory.' What the verb designates is the fact that memory is 'exercised.'"[20] The emphasis in this book, then, is on the exercise of those "substantive memories," especially the liminal spaces between history and memory, between the colonized and the colonizers, and between black and white imagine-nations, which share a geographic space and a political entity called the nation.

The second concept that anchors my interpretation and analysis here is memory itself, memory as exercised by the individual, by the social group, and by the larger collective, the nation. *Individual memory* is to be understood as divisible and indivisible from the social and the collective. It is the individual who remembers in social and collective settings. That is, each form of memory is a subset of the others, or each is a concentric circle within or encircling the others, with individual memory at the center (and sometimes at the margins)—with contestations simultaneously radiating in all three circles and in all directions. For example, colonialism produced individual, social, and collective memories for the colonized; that is, the colonized—as expressed in this book's latter chapters—experienced colonialism individually through, say, personal humiliations or privileges. They also experienced colonialism socially, as members of a particular ethnic or other group, as well as collectively as Africans, the "Natives" in colonial history. Although Ricoeur's philosophical hermeneutics is steeped in the western European philosophical traditions (which might raise an eyebrow for understanding African history), I find it instructive and illuminating when conceptualizing and interpreting personal, social, and collective memories as invoked by African people experiencing a rupture in a Western-oriented world that irrevocably changed their lives. Conversely, Ricoeur's philosophy is also instructive for understanding how Europeans were becoming African even as they tried to deny it.

Individual memory as conceptualized in this book puts a premium on the self. As Ricoeur noted, one of the best historical examples we have in written form is Saint Augustine's classic autobiography, *Confessions*. Augustine's kind of remembering was about "one person's memories," which "cannot be transferred into the memory of another, it is a model of private possession."[21] Thus, as witness memory, individual remembering is personal possession; it is the primary memory of the moment of (social) experience, which cannot be displaced from the one who experienced it. Yet, paradoxically, the same person can and does have secondary memory of the event as having happened in the past, and therefore his or her memory is subject to change depending on the sociocultural context of (re)telling. *Social memory,* by contrast, is about remembering as defined (and contested) by and within a group or groups. The philosopher-sociologist Maurice Halbwachs best theorized social memory that ripples into the collective and from individual memory when he said that memory is a social activity, because "one does not remember alone."[22] In fact, Halbwachs delineated three key social groups: the family, class, and religion. But what Halbwachs called collective, I call social, and I reserve the term *collective memory* for a larger definition that includes individuals and social groups with competing memories, namely, the nation.

If individual memory is the concentric circle at the center, then the social is the immediate circle with which the individual shares memory, and both are within a larger circle that may or may not share their social and individual memories but is bound together with them by history.

Thus, sources and examples of individual memory in this book include memoirs and oral life stories. Examples of social memory include the making of local heroes through medal awards and memorial plaques on the one hand and the reclamation of African landscapes through names embedded in precolonial history on the other. Collective memory is expressed in the competing narratives of the meaning of the colony/nation itself—was it (Southern) Rhodesia, or was it Zimbabwe? Who were the "real" founders?

In this book, therefore, I focus on selected case studies of individuals and groups in central Zimbabwe to tell how "history's epistemological claim," though the reason for memory's existence in the first place, was often "devalued in favor of memory's meaningfulness" in the collective present.[23] In other words, although the history of the nation was complicated, cultural and political nationalists often insisted that their version of history (their memory) was the actual history that everyone had to adopt when thinking about the founding/making of the nation. Memory became more important than history, because nationalists sought to make their versions of history stand in for "true" history rather than presenting them as an interpretation thereof.

Memory as told in this book, therefore, is what human beings, as social beings, made of the past to validate their existence in a place once called (Southern) Rhodesia, and now Zimbabwe. Memory was present in the minutiae and large arcs of colonial life that individuals and groups remembered and insisted upon—creating a new history in the process. By showing the short and long arcs of parallel histories and memories in colonial and postindependent Zimbabwe, this book illuminates some of the sources of the deep and wide chasms between the Blacks and Whites of Zimbabwe today. The hope is that the people of that country and elsewhere will pause before using the past—and the people thereof— as crutches because the living are too lazy to speak "unspeakable things [still] unspoken" about Zimbabwe's past in the present.[24]

While this book primarily engages the gendered nature of parallel memory in the making of Zimbabwe, especially its masculine variety, this does not mean that other important categories and questions of historical analysis are not at stake. Race, for example, is right in the middle of it, as is ethnicity, but rather than stating the obvious in narrating a racialized and ethnicized history of colonialism, I have chosen to focus on unpacking ideas about a nation that the colonizers tried out on themselves and on the colonized. Here I lean on the psychiatrist-philosopher Frantz Fanon's articulation of colonialism in his classic text *The Wretched of the Earth*. Fanon's psychoanalysis of colonialism's impact on the mind of the colonizer and the colonized is central to understanding a postcolony's tortured relationship with its past. By Fanon's telling, the colonial process was a violent one, and it produced "the native, an oppressed person whose permanent dream [was] to become the persecutor."[25] Colonialism and racialized nationalism produced perennial servants and masters, poisoning the very soil (the country) in which the seed of nationhood was supposed to flourish.

Lastly, this book uses gender as a concept that helps us understand the historical processes that shaped the remaking and reinforcement of sociopolitical relations between women and men, but especially men and men—the colonizer and the colonized. My definition of gender is not only the standard Western binary of female and male sociopolitical relations; it is also an expansive definition that includes the gender bending of historical processes—of women doing "male" things, and vice versa, among other variations. To that end, I lean on feminist scholarship that has broadened our definitions of gender as historical processes. That scholarship insists that gender is varied in place and time and cannot be held as a constant over time—not even in a single society. That scholarship includes the works of the anthropologist Ifi Amadiume, the postcolonial theorist Chandra Talhade Mohanty, the historians Elsa Barkley Brown and Jeanne Boydston, and the sociologists Patricia McFadden, Oyèrónké Oyewùmí, and Leslie McCall.[26]

The feminist scholarship that informs this book has an abiding interest in the idea that gender is not only about women's place in society nor only about men's dominance. Rather, gender changes over time; it is not static, just as any other historical process that historians are interested in is not static. So rather than putting gender on a pedestal, where it is the constant variable, narrowing the range of historical experiences, historians will enrich our understanding by embedding gender alongside other processes and experiences. As the historian Jeanne Boydston puts it, "The primaryness of gender in any given situation should be one of our questions, rather than be one of our assumptions."[27] Gender, therefore, rather than being the static binary category of analysis, I argue in this book, should be studied as a dynamic historical process "always nested in, mingled with and inseparable from the cluster of other factors socially relevant in a given culture. Deploying gender as a category of analysis [and not as a historical question of analysis] disguises this process of reciprocal constitution and implies for gender an independent quasi-scientific causal status."[28] Thus, even though this book is focused primarily on men's memories of how Rhodesia/Zimbabwe was made, my gender articulations are grounded in feminist philosophical, sociological, and cultural theories of history and memory to make sense of the masculine nationalist manicuring of history.

While very few women advocating women's rights and women's place in society appear in this book (which may lead to questions about my feminist assertion), I insist on feminist and gender analyses as a strategy for writing a holistic history that transcends the binary nature of most gender theories. By bringing a feminist lens to understanding black and white (male) nationalist articulations of nationhood in the history and memory of Zimbabwe, I highlight the ways Black and White women were excluded and included in the dominant nationalist narratives of their ethnic and racial groups. This helps us understand why nationalist victories were not always emancipatory for women—or for men seeking other ways of expressing their masculinity than domination. Thus, I think of myself as a historian whose task it is to engage society for the sake of both the past and the present. My interest in writing a gray history of Zimbabwe's contested founding is invariably tied to my birth in that country, and especially my ability to see it from a distance—both in time and in space.[29] Nelleke Noordervliet persuasively argued the same when she said that "the historian should be the first to take an active part in society and to defend, wherever necessary, the rights of the people of the past."[30] This way, history remains in vigorous debate with the present, and not only as an academic pursuit by professional historians. Furthermore, Noordervliet reminds us, "if knowledge of history is essential to good citizenship [then] changes and crises force us to ponder what was right and what was wrong about the way we've shaped society up to now,"[31] and it is the historian's task to hold up the past so it can be studied more closely. What concerns me here is the past in its own right and as understood by the then living.

My obligation as a historian, therefore, is to engage society, to invite a presence and conversations about the garden of "national history" that we often leave to career politicians and/or career historians. The past is not about neatly manicured narratives of black or white Zimbabwe or anywhere; rather, it is about understanding an unmanicured past with its tangles, clearings, and balanced and competing ecosystems, which have the capacity to illuminate the present so obsessed, with manicured versions of history. The past is not captive to the present, nor is the present enslaved to the past. The two can or ought to coexist in symbiosis, as this book and many it references show. Most importantly, this book reminds us that it was not always the rulers who remembered the violent past as national myths: ordinary people also shaped the way we know and understand that past. It behooves historians, then, to engage as broad a spectrum of society as possible so that those same ordinary people can begin to engage with one another and with the past, which so deeply shapes the present.

Historiographical Considerations

This book builds on three sets of historiographies/scholarship of regional, conceptual, and theoretical relevance. Rather than recounting those historiographies here, I will only highlight the key issues I have regarding each and then engage them more fully in relevant chapters. The first set is the historiography of premodern Africa, particularly Zimbabwean historiography of the period.[32] This historiography is important for two reasons: First, it shows the Africa-has-a-history-too phase in African historiography, an important intellectual moment in dismantling Eurocentric notions of the hierarchy of knowledge. Second, the focus was on countering assertions of influential Eurocentric thinkers such as the British Oxford professor Hugh Trevor-Roper, who argued that the study of African history was nothing but the study of "unrewarding gyrations of barbarous tribes in picturesque but irrelevant corners of the globe."[33] What that brilliant counterhistoriography often missed, at least in its Southern African variety, was the importance of a gendered analysis of history as shown in Paul T. Zeleza's statistical essay "Gender Biases in African Historiography."[34]

The second set of historiographical works this book builds on is imperial and colonial history by the colonizers (and their allies) and the colonized (and their allies). This is the historiography of settlers writing about themselves and those who occupied the colonies. In addition, there is the historiography written by Africans and Africanists as more of them gained Western intellectual tools to counter the hegemony of colonizing epistemology. Settler writing is grounded in "pioneer" histo-riography, which spawned many travelogues and autobiographies with descriptions of "having roughed it in the bush" to create a colony from scratch for the British Empire. African and Africanist historiography fo-cused on African kingdoms and their great men, and as with the first set, much of it focused on men, with little on women's history. When and where women appeared in the historiography, they were usually the "ex-ceptional" and/or privileged women, which accounts for the intense in-terest in Nehanda and Charwe. The importance of African and Africanist historiography is that it had an immediate impact on the African nation-alist movements, like the ones that propelled Zimbabwe's political liber-ation in 1980. The historian, this second set reminds us, is implicated in the making of national myths, in questioning them, and in obfuscating or shedding new light on the nuances of the past.[35]

The third set of scholarship that I learn from, build on, and contribute to is the field of memory studies. I come to the study of historical mem-ory sharing Richard Roberts's sentiments that "interest in history and memory is not new to the methodological and epistemological concerns of Africanists who have been at the forefront of this field since the origins of the academic field of African history nearly fifty years ago."[36] My debt to multiple traditions of African historiography on historical memory is evident in this book. Here I rekindle old debates and light fires for new debates about the paths less taken in African (colonial and postcolonial) historiography.

The Archives, Methods, and Other Ways of Telling Stories

In my attempts to show and tell the past as grayer than the cultivated black and white versions of Zimbabwe's nationalist imaginings, I ulti-mately relied on archival resources in three countries: Zimbabwe, the United Kingdom, and the United States. In Zimbabwe I used mainly the National Archives of Zimbabwe, in Harare; in the United Kingdom, the National Archives of the United Kingdom, London, and Rhodes House Library, Oxford; and in the United States, the Manuscripts and Archives Library at Yale University and the Hoover Institution on War, Revolution, and Peace Library and Archives at Stanford University. Though I visited many archives, including some whose material did not make into this book, it made me rethink how most historians of Africa

and the Global South have to live with the reality that archives have selective memory; they do not fully represent everyone.

The archive (in its singular and plural forms), while an important
site of ephemeral memory through its manuscripts collections, excludes
those with less power in producing material to self-represent in history
and memory. That, however, does not make the archive less important;
in fact, the archive is guarded because of its potential to contain traces
of individual or social or collective memories. As Ricoeur observed, "The
archive presents itself as a physical place that shelters destiny of the documentary trace. But the archive is not just a physical or spatial place; it is
also a social one."[37] As will become clear in this book, the archive is implicated in the stories memory tells; its ability to be everything to everyone
means that the archive illuminates as it obfuscates.

Given the multiplicity of historiographies and time periods and the
wide primary source base that I utilize in this book, my methodology
is, by definition and necessity, interdisciplinary. Holding gender as the
main tool and question of analysis, especially the masculinized versions
of history, my methods vary as demanded by each chapter's primary
source materials. And when conventional methods do not meet the
demands of the task at hand, I invent my own methods to deepen my
analysis. For example, my writing method, with few exceptions here and
there, tends toward the narrative, blending the imaginative with analysis.
By imaginative I do not mean inventing fiction and passing it for historical fact. Rather, I mean writing this history from the very broad archival research I have done for this book through my own eyes and leaving
enough room for debate and conversation about the past's presence in
our lives today. My major writing method in some of the chapters gives
primacy to the voice of the past by embedding substantive quotes in italics. Thus, rather than indenting long quotes as is conventional when citing primary sources in greater detail than a few lines, I use italics in order
to resist the temptation toward sound-bite quotations, and especially the
appetite for presentism, a perennial problem in memory studies. True,
the impetus for writing this book was a present conundrum, but narrating a history of the current crisis (in Zimbabwe) need not be presentist.
Thus, by embedding the sources equally and in juxtaposition to my analysis in the text, I attempt to give the past a fair hearing, as it were, so
that the reader does not always have to take my word at face value. This
writing method not only allows me intellectual flexibility to achieve a

narrative flow but helps me resist the urge to be the past's sole overseer and adjudicator, especially for Africans with very few self-produced materials in the archives—or access to them. My writing method is thus a deliberate invitation to the reader to engage and/or contest my readings of those same sources.[38]

The employment of a narrative writing method in most chapters also means that my analysis is both conventional and unconventional. When no conventional method could help me make sense of a critical source (a court transcript), as happened in one of my cases in chapter 2, I decided to invent my own method of reverse translation in order to make sense of that source, which, as written, did not make (historical) sense. The document was important for understanding why, generations later, people remembered the event of that court trial so differently. Inventing my own methods where necessary opened my mind to trying new ways of interpreting old sources—using different tools, old and new, to arrive at the desired goal. Thus, for chapter 5, rather than faithfully reproducing oral-history transcripts I found at the National Archives of Zimbabwe, I edited them down to short self-portraits that let the storyteller tell both his personal and familial histories, which could be understood as part of a social and collective memory. Allowing those men to tell a bit more of their own stories, interspersed with my own analysis, lets the reader get a sense of the fault lines of African masculine history, keen to remember the forefathers at the expense of the foremothers.

I was also compelled to weave the sources into my analysis, especially in chapters 3–7, by the fact that sometimes historians write books that appeal only to other historians in their specialized field, instead of writing for a wider audience to enable an engaged civic discourse. Granted, one cannot write for "everyone," and the "ordinary educated reader" may be a myth, but I think it is worth trying, as, ironically, most historians complain that the general public is ignorant about the past—especially Africa's past. How can it be otherwise, when all that intellectual labor ends up as lamps under bushels rather than invitations to informed and engaged public discourse?[39] Noordervliet's exhortation about the value of historical knowledge to all of society rings even truer and is worth repeating to underscore why I chose the writing methods and strategies I did for this book. "Knowledge of history is essential to good citizenship," she writes. "Changes and crises force us to ponder what was right and what was wrong about the way we've shaped society up to now."[40] I see writing an accessible history book as my intellectual, professional, and civic duty to engage those who do not or cannot visit the archives themselves so that they do not have to settle for the crumbs or glimpses of the past as told by one historian to other historians with access to the archives. Rather, I chose to include in some of my citations satisfying slices and chunks of history, instead of crumbs, to allow the reader substantive material to contemplate and engage so that he or she might contest my analysis more critically.

In addition to eschewing convention in some of my writing methodology, I place emphasis on themes and issues that illuminate the evocation of memory in the making of colonial and postcolonial national identities, rather than on a chronological account of who remembered what, when, or how in the making of Zimbabwe from 1890 to the present. Memory, after all, is rarely linear progression. In fact, people often keep snapshots of the past that, when they are prompted, they then tell as a narrative, movielike, with flashbacks. Thus, rather than drawing a straight line of memory from 1890 to the present, I chose to focus on case studies that illustrate what I consider key moments and/or turning points in the manicuring of (colonial and postcolonial) Zimbabwe's founding stories by political and cultural nationalists, both African and settler. The cases presented in each chapter, therefore, though tied together by the dubious thread of "ancestral" memory as constructed by nationalists, can also be approached as one would heritage sites or national monuments. To that end, my writing has a tour guide's approach to the presentation of Black and White nationalists' "sites of memory" and thus tends to be less tethered to a strict chronology.[41] However, the chapters do follow a rough chronological sequence, so that there is a narrative flow, with both the minutiae and long arcs of history and memory clearly visible.

Lastly, my choice of the personalities, events, source material, and ephemeral sites of memory in this book, though carefully made, was still, like all memory, selective. To my mind, my selections best illuminate the contingencies that produced a complex history of national myth-making not only in Southern Rhodesia and Zimbabwe but also abroad, where Rhodesian meant an ideological rather than a national identity and Nehanda resonated in the African diaspora as a resistance icon for different groups. My selection of particular persons and moments in Zimbabwe's history (and not others) is intended to show that memory in a postsettler and postcolonial society need not always be a litany of wrongs, or a denial of past injuries, or empty triumphalism in the name of history. Rather, this study shows that though nationalist declaratives want(ed) us to believe in the black and white versions of Zimbabwe's history, gray was sometimes the dominant version. The case studies this book show-cases highlight the making of a colony/nation in its sobering and trium-phant moments, moments that allow for another understanding of the dysfunction of nations founded on citizens defining themselves through the denial of "Others"—the perennial settler-and-native paradox that the historian and anthropologist Mahmood Mamdani so eloquently theo-rized.[42] I also chose the particular case studies in each chapter to illus-trate the seeds of parallel "national memory" planted at the founding of the colony/nation in 1890 and its terrible fruits to date.[43] Some of those bitter fruits remain unresolved as more wrongs and injustices pile on old unresolved events, haunting Zimbabwe deeply.

The study of memory analyzed in this book, therefore, is an evocation of a "spirit of the times" showing how people held on to the past—for better or worse—as they tried to make sense of their present. Thus, it is worth remembering that the memory of the spirit of Charwe as Nehanda evoked in this book is that of particular African ethnic individuals and groups who have invoked her memory as "national" history since her death in 1898. Charwe wokwa Hwata and Cecil John Rhodes's first appearance in history in the late 1800s was, to borrow from Marx, a tragedy—in the sense that their life choices produced tragedies for the people involved.[44] Charwe and Rhodes's appearance a second time in nationalist memory was a farce, because, as this book shows, nationalists chose the extreme versions of those historical figures in order to construct "purely" black or white versions of history. The spirit of Rhodes may not have been vision-ary, and the spirit of Charwe may not have been a possessive, malevolent *ngozi* casting for revenge in the land of the living. However, the evocation of the spirits of the dead to whom wrong was done or who did wrong but are no longer here to speak for themselves is a fascinating opportunity to study the living's continued aspirations for meaning in their lives today.

Now, let us begin.

1 Far from the Tree

Appropriations of Ethnic Memory and Other Frontier Encounters

The celebration of conquest typical of settlers in most colonized societies calls attention to the contestations and tensions between history and memory that reinscribed the wounding of those humiliated by colonization.[1] In this chapter I read the oral tradition as much as I do the landscape and the colonial archive in order to tell the continuities and discontinuities of African history and memory before and during the moment of "permanent" colonial encounter. The chapter therefore offers a historical context for understanding how Black nationalistic imaginings of Charwe as Nehanda from the 1950s were not a first, but a mutation of a longer, if varied, history. It also shows that settler memory was keeping up the tradition of upholding the idea that the British Empire was still the mightiest—it could still occupy and conquer "Natives" elsewhere. Thus, rather than focusing on how nationalists "invented" the past, its heroines, and heroes wholesale, I am more interested in how they often embellished the bare bones of history with their nationalistic imaginations to create larger-than-life varieties of the originals.

First, the chapter briefly presents the legend of the "original" Nehanda and its mutations before 1890 to show how Charwe, the woman today famously known as Nehanda of Zimbabwe, was not the originator of the name or the title Nehanda.[2] Also, Charwe was not the first Nehanda medium in the Mazowe valley, as detailed below. It is therefore important to keep in mind that Nehanda's power (and that of her mediums) came from older African historical epistemology that understood the world as feminine, governed by forces of fertility in nature.[3] Indeed, life itself was wrapped around the (goddesses or) female spirits that kept the cycles of life in balance.[4] Second, this chapter shows how history and memory circled each other during the frontier war of 1896–97 in Southern

Rhodesia, when settlers consciously and unconsciously erected real and symbolic sites of imperial memory on African landscapes in the Mazowe valley and elsewhere in the colony. History was being made on a landscape once sacred to some, now a new site of memory for others. The frontier war fought on that landscape simultaneously raised monuments to imperialism, while forgetting the history of Africans who had lived there centuries before.

The Original Nehanda, Nyamhita Nyakasikana, and Other Nehandas of Mazowe

Thirty miles north of Zimbabwe's capital, Harare, is a valley of rugged mountains and fertile land that has attracted generations of wanderers in search of secure water patterns and rich soil that could enable their agrarian societies to thrive. The current people claiming autochthony (original settlement and land ownership) are descendants of the northern Hera people, a confederacy of dynasties founded by two brothers and a nephew—Gutsa, Shayachimwe, and Nyamhangambiri. As in the kinship systems of most Niger Congo peoples, a highly structured kinship was remembered and maintained through a sophisticated totem (*mutupo*) narrative that served political, social, cultural, and economic functions, including practical ones like specifying who could marry whom to avoid incest.[5]

Charwe was born about 1862 of the Hwata people in the Mazowe valley, a dynasty founded by Shayachimwe.[6] Like many young girls of her time, Charwe grew up, got married, and had children. Things changed at the peak of her womanhood, when she became the medium of the spirit of Nehanda, a revered spirit of rain and land fertility among northern, central, and eastern peoples we call the Shona today.[7] To be a medium of the spirit of Nehanda, therefore, was to hold a position of significant religious and political power in an agrarian society in which life revolved around the seasons of earth and sky. Once Charwe became a medium of a significant female spirit, she followed in the footsteps of other women of the Mazowe valley who had held that politico-religious office, which afforded them a social and economic status not available to many women. The prestige came from being the *gombwe* (superior, or senior, medium) of a *mhondoro* (royal lion spirit) of an old dynasty's founding mother or father. *Mhondoro* were prestigious spirits, and their mediums, whether female or male, were treated like royalty. Being a *gombwe* was therefore different from the "common" mediumship (*svikiro*) of familial and local clan spirits.

Oral traditions and archaeological evidence suggest that among the Shona, mediumship of human spirits was a religious experience confined to familial and clan structures.[8] It turned into public office as family groups and clans settled and grew into larger ethnic groups of different families and clans, creating dynasties and kingdoms-cum-nations that aspired to legitimate their political and economic power, reminiscent of small empires. Among the Shona in older times, both women and men were revered and remembered by the living as founding ancestors in totemic praise poems and songs.[9] The dead, as royal (or ordinary) ancestors, were believed to make their presence tangibly felt through spirit mediums, people so chosen by the dead spirits. The dead, it was believed, chose their mediums without interference from the living, and those mediums were accepted through an authentication process administered by long-practicing and respected mediums. Once confirmed, the medium acquired gravitas that could not be nullified by the living; only the spirit could nullify that position by choosing another medium, which usually meant the (premature) death of the current medium. The reality, as we will see, was a little more complicated than that, for spirit mediumship, like all human institutions accredited with the power of the (dead and) beyond, was as human as it was said to be divine.

One oral tradition of the history of Nehanda Nyamhita Nyakasikana, the original Nehanda, tells that she hailed from northeastern Mashonaland.[10] Nyamhita's mother and brother, the tradition says, had her participate in the dynastic ritual *kupinga pasi*, laying claim to the land through ritual incest, against her will.[11] She was appalled by what had happened, and rather than stay in Dande, in her territory, known as Handa (see figure 1), she vanished into a small hill and was later reported as living south of her territory. It is worth noting at this point that the etymology of *Nehanda* is a geographic location in Dande named Handa. The article *Ne* is the honorific possessive denoting ownership (of territory or otherwise) in central and northeastern MaShonaland, therefore, *Ne* = (owner) of Handa (in other Shona regions people use the articles *Va* or *Wa* or *Nya*, hence some colonial spellings that use *Nyahanda, Neanda, Nianda,*

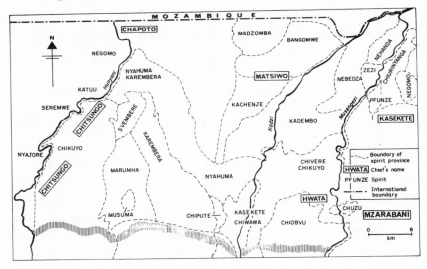

Figure 1. "Original" Nehanda territory, shown in the top righthand corner. (Lan, *Guns and Rain,* 33, with permission from the University of California Press)

or *Nyanda* for *Nehanda*). Indeed, the name Nehanda makes a compelling little piece of history of a term that in memory means a person, when its origin meant a place, a (sacred) site of memory on a hill.

To this day, the oral tradition continues: the hill in Handa bears the imprint of Nyamhita's disappearance and is called Gumbi ra Nehanda. After she died, her spirit split into two: The first was Musuro wa Nehanda (Nehanda's Head), a spirit that remained active within Dande ensuring the continued fertility and vitality of that region as well as retaining a place of sociopolitical and cultural power in society for women who were its mediums. The second spirit, Makumbo a Nehanda (Nehanda's Feet), manifested in the south among the people of the Gumbo dynasty, near Domboshawa, where she had settled. By the time Nyamhita died, she was venerated by many in that dynasty and region of central Mashonaland, including Mazowe and Chishawasha—important sites of history and memory in this book. She was known by many as their *Ambuya* (ancestor), a great rainmaking spirit, a spirit of fertility (human and otherwise).[12] The Gumbo dynasty later moved further south into what is now Gutu (Masvingo Province), and their former area, near Domboshawa (central Mashonaland), was settled by the Hwata dynasty, among whom Charwe was born. Interestingly, it seems that the second spirit of Nehanda, Nehanda's Feet, not only stayed in the Domboshawa area but also became part of the Hwata dynasty's own history and memory of belonging to a land the dynasty had just settled, having emigrated from VuHera (now Buhera), an area to the southeast. Paradoxically, the Gumbo took the tradition of the spirit of Nehanda with them to Gutu—which makes sense, for who would not want such a spirit of rain and fertility as they migrated in search of better lands and opportunities? That may explain why around the Great Zimbabwe (also in Masvingo Province) there has been a (contested) tradition of a Nehanda or Nehandas, some recently documented by the anthropologist Joost Fontein in his ethnography of communities in the area.[13]

The spirit of Nehanda and its mediums, as highlighted above, is a history that captures both the history of a woman who once lived (Nyamhita) and the memory of a spirit (Nehanda) still circulating among the living in memory through its female mediums not only in its original place but also in multiple sites around Zimbabwe. In a way, Nyamhita's history as Nehanda is a compressed history of religions that, like all religions, are "manifestly cultural products . . . [that] serve human and cultural ends."[14] Nyamhita, then, may be translated into an unsatisfying (and some will say false) analogy of a Jesus who became the Christ or a Siddhartha who became the Buddha. That is, Nyamhita's life may have radically changed gender, class, and ethnic realities in her society such that other women wanted to be her mediums—if not to be her.[15]

I chose the historian David P. Abraham's rendition of the Nehanda oral tradition not only because its content is rich in detail and has an ear toward memory told as history but also because it closely resembles some of the histories and traditions recorded by the Portuguese from the mid-1500s about women's place in the African societies they encountered in southern Africa.[16] Thus, though there is no definitive version, oral or written, of who Nyamhita was and how her spirit as Nehanda moved from the Dande valley to the Mazowe valley, it is indisputable that the name Nehanda still has resonances in both, as well as around Zimbabwe. The fruit of Nehanda's memory certainly fell far from its original tree, and wherever it fell, it adapted to its new environment—much as Christianity did over time and space. That memory of Nehanda was the power transferred to Charwe, as medium, when the British arrived on the scene in the Mazowe valley in the late nineteenth century. Thus, by the time Charwe started practicing her mediumship in the mid-1880s, the name and tradition of Nehanda was well established in the Mazowe valley thanks to several mediums who had preceded Charwe, perhaps since the early eighteenth century, such that the place was known as Nehanda's.

The recorded mediums of Nehanda in the Mazoe valley immediately before and after Charwe were Chamunga, Damukwa, Chizani, Charwe (ca. 1862–1898), Mativirira, and Mushonga.[17] The British traveler Walter Montagu Kerr, who passed through those lands in 1884–85, wrote that he saw in the distance "a chain of craggy mountains, stark upheavals spire-like rocks whose wild recess concealed Neanda, a large Mashona town."[18] Among those "craggy mountains" was the sacred Shavarunzi, at which Nehanda mediums of Mazowe practiced; and when they died, they were often buried there. Thus, Shavarunzi was a sacred site for rituals of rain-making. It was also a site of memory, because of the Nehanda mediums buried there. The burial of those women on that mountain had particular significance because among the Shona, dynasty founders, kings, and chiefs were buried in mountain caves, making their burial sites important places of remembrance and pilgrimage for their descendants and those who believed in their powers to heal, guide, and bring about rain and prosperity. Shavarunzi's status as a site of memory was equivalent to that of many old and new religious sites considered sacred in other cultures and traditions, for example, the Bodhi Tree in India, the "Holy Land" in the Middle East, or Wounded Knee in South Dakota.[19] Burial on Shavarunzi accorded very few women significant status in a society in which most women had lost or were losing power and influence, except in positions like mediumship of founding or royal spirits. In memory, however, Charwe became the one and only Nehanda. The Mazowe valley, not the Dande valley, became the new site of memory associated with the power of Nehanda in postcolonial Zimbabwe.[20]

The spirit of the legendary Nehanda-Nyamhita—the spirit of rain and fertility—as represented by its mediums, also called Nehanda, may have been the initial focus of African nationalists in their fight against colonialism, as illustrated by David Lan's ethnography *Guns and Rain*. However, unlike Lan's study, this book focuses entirely on nationalists' imagined Nehanda, transfigured into the warrior woman Charwe to fit the "modern" reality of a guerilla-cum-nationalist movement seeking relevance. By focusing on the history and memory of Charwe in her own right—rather than on Nyamhita and Charwe, as Lan did—this book calls

attention to the importance of studying Charwe's life and legacy in nationalist thought and ideas that shaped a sense of ownership of the "new"
nation, Zimbabwe, at independence in 1980. Thus, rather than tread-
ing and recycling the same ideas expounded upon by scholars such as
Terence Ranger, David Beach, David Lan, and David Martin and Phyllis
Johnson, among others, I move the historiography forward by centering
Charwe's importance in nationalist thinking and claiming Rhodesia as
Zimbabwe, a Black nation. I ask: How did Charwe become people's an-
chor as they tried to turn individual, social, and collective African history
into a useable memory to claim a right to citizenship in a nation constituted without their participation and consent in Berlin in 1884–85?[21] Despite nationalist rhetoric, this book insists that the contested Rhodesia
that was to become Zimbabwe did not exist in that shape or form prior
to 1890. By positioning Charwe at the center of white and black nationalist discourse, we can name the vandalism of British colonialism, while
asking why the nation has become *the* category, rather than a question,
in the historical analysis of African history.

Gendered Occupation and Its Contestations

The Mazowe valley came into the purview and control of the British Empire in the nineteenth century, as Portuguese power was waning in western Europe and globally.[22] The hold-your-nose-as-you-pass-by attitude
toward the Cape Colony on the part of the British and most western European powers racing for the Far East changed in 1867 when a gleaming
stone that turned out to be a twenty-one-carat diamond was found along
the Orange River. March 1869 turned up an even more fantastic find,
an eighty-three-carat diamond, and by the 1870s the diamond rush was
in full swing (fig. 2). In the field of competition that was the diamond
rush was a young man by the name of Cecil John Rhodes (later known
to admirers and detractors as CJR or simply Rhodes). Rhodes had tried
his hand at farming with his brother, Herbert, but it had not suited him.
When the diamond rush ensued in earnest, Rhodes decided to try his
luck at the enterprise, which changed his life and the course of history for
millions of people in the Southern African region. It also altered the for-
tunes of the British Empire. Rhodes not only made money in the diamond
fields; he also built alliances with equally ambitious young men, forming
a monopoly company, De Beers Consolidated Mines, which bought off

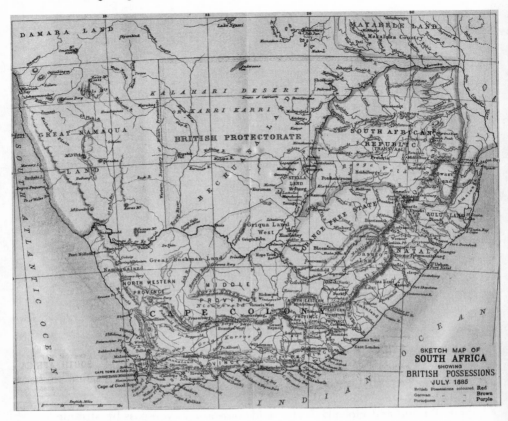

Figure 2. South Africa, 1885. (http://www-users.york.ac.uk/~ad15/SAmap
1885.htm)

competitors and small-time miners. This meant that the British-owned
company had control over the production and pricing of diamonds on
the world market from that point on.[23] That control allowed new funds
to be sourced for colonial expansion north of the Limpopo River into
the Southern African interior, and by Rhodes's reckoning, all the way to
Cairo, Egypt. Thus, while this book focuses on Rhodes's dreams for and
in Southern Rhodesia, it is important to keep in mind that his imperial
ambitions in Africa were much larger.

Another unexpected turn for Rhodes and the British Empire was
the 1886 discovery of vast gold deposits in what had become the Boer
Republic of the Transvaal. Here again, Rhodes was able to consolidate
his wealth and power as he, along with many hitherto unknown young

men, became fabulously wealthy and influential. With that wealth came larger-than-life imperial ambitions that led Rhodes and his associates to establish the British South Africa Company (BSAC), which gained a royal charter in 1889.[24] The charter allowed the BSAC to colonize lands in the African interior on behalf of the Crown. From late 1889 to early 1890 the BSAC board of directors allowed Rhodes to outfit a group of some two hundred men willing to march north across the Limpopo River and stake a claim on some lands for the British Empire. That group comprised young men eager to strike it rich in the same way that Rhodes and his business partners had in the diamond and gold fields of South Africa. Some of those young men were sons of the well-to-do in the Cape Colony and London, chosen to garner support for the imperial project—especially in the event that war broke out and the occupying forces would need to be rescued.[25] Having sons worth rescuing was Rhodes's strategy for making sure influential families in the Cape and in Britain were in on the project of imperial expansion. However, some of those who signed up for Rhodes's project were experienced men who wanted to journey north, as the prospect of land ownership—paid for by the BSAC—was irresistible. Rhodes's men were organized into two corps, the Pioneer Column and the British South Africa Police (BSAP). Their primary and official guide was Frederick Courteney Selous, a European old hand at hunting and trekking in the African hinterland.[26]

The BSAC board of directors instructed the Pioneer Column to march north of the Limpopo River, skirting the Ndebele kingdom-cum-nation of King Lobengula to the west. The history of occupation of what became Mashonaland later gathered the myth of being a piece of empire won without a single penny from the (British) taxpayers, or a single bullet fired. What memory forgot, of course, was the cost to African lives altered by that occupation. To marching settlers, the Ndebele kingdom had been the threat they most feared because of the history of its founder, Mzilikazi ka Matshobane, a renowned general who defected from King Shaka's Zulu army (with a band of followers whose numbers swelled as they trekked north) to form his own new nation, the Ndebele.[27] Another Rhodes pioneer column, of 1893, later learned that the Ndebele kingdom, though still viable compared with other forms of African political governance in the new colony at the time, was not the same formidable one of Mzilikazi. It was much reduced in power after the contested ascendancy of his son, Lobengula, as Ndebele king.[28] The story of the Ndebele kingdom, though not dealt with in this book, is important to briefly note here because it was invoked and remembered differently, especially by blacks and whites who had interacted with or lived among the Ndebele between the 1850s and 1890 and those who had fought the 1893 and 1896–97 wars with or against them.

The Pioneer Column began the final leg of its journey north in June 1890 from the British Protectorate of Bechuanaland (today's Botswana), traveling into the hinterland without much military incident. They arrived in what was to become Mashonaland three months later, on September 11. The next day, September 12, the Union Jack was hoisted with much pomp and ceremony, and the place was named Fort Salisbury, South Africa, in honor of then British prime minister Robert Arthur Talbot Gascoyne-Cecil, third Marquess of Salisbury.[29] It is telling that the capital got its name before the country did, and especially that, as in many colonies, the settled spaces that became towns and cities usually had *Fort* as part of their name—Fort Victoria (present-day Masvingo), Fort Salisbury (Harare), and so on—signifying the occupiers' conscious preparation for resistance once the occupied people realized what was going on.

After the September 12, 1890, official occupation of Mashonaland, the cultural differences between Africans and the British-sponsored settlers became fraught with tensions as more prospectors settled in places like the Mazowe valley and competed with the autochthons for resources and ownership of the land. Since it had become British territory, most prospectors did not respect the local leadership, and that heightened tensions. The Africans were puzzled by the uncouth behavior of the newcomers, as many in central Mashonaland remembered the Portuguese, who, for all their faults, had often tried to engage the local leadership. The colonial occupation by the Portuguese centuries earlier had ended with Rozvi resistance pushing them and their African puppet governments out of their lands.[30] British-sponsored colonialism—unlike its older Portuguese cousin, which had begun as friendly, turned sour, and then turned friendly again—had started off on an arrogant note, and it did not help that it was a business venture for the BSAC focused on the bottom line.

Disrespect for African customs sometimes proved fatal, as in the interesting case of a French-born naturalized American settler, one Guerolt, "who reportedly died at the hands of Chief Chiripanyanga in the Hwata Hills in the Mazoe Valley."[31] Guerolt's death led the colonial administration in Southern Rhodesia to marshal full force against the Africans rather than engaging them in diplomacy. The administration burned villages and shot Africans who "resisted or fired [back]," leaving seven Africans dead, while others were taken into BSAC custody.[32] The death of a white man had colonial officials in the Cape Colony (who had the last word on Southern Rhodesia's administration to the London Office) concerned, as it spelled potential disaster for prospective investors in the BSAC as well as prospective settlers. For the colonial project to succeed, the Cape Colony office thought, it was important to keep a lid on tensions like those that had led to Guerolt's death, while punishing Africans who resisted colonial expansion.[33]

As colonial power was coercing young and old men into oppressive labor conditions (a process Africans tellingly gave the gendered term *chibharo*, "rape") in the name of collecting taxes in the new colony, the African chiefs were caught between a rock and a hard place.[34] Those chiefs who resisted colonial rule, including supplying cheap labor to the settlers, were often replaced by unentitled chiefs, who acquired power and influence. This worked well, since the British favored "clean" colonialism, otherwise known as indirect rule. The colonial government made life difficult through coercive legislation like the Native Pass Law of 1892, which curtailed Africans' freedoms and rights in the land of their birth.[35] That law flattened social, political, economic, and cultural differences between and among Africans with the word *Native*, making the chief, the spirit medium, and the commoner all subject to the power of the local (European) district native commissioner (DNC) and his African policemen, who often acted with impunity.

Erasing African Memory, Making Settler History in the Mazowe Hills

Between September 1890 and December 1895 an increasing number of settlers entered Southern Rhodesia as it became a recognizable colony on the map. This influx of settlers and the increased appropriation of African land for European settlement not only bred resentment but also laid the foundations for insurrection.[36] The occupation of Southern Rhodesia consolidated and ruptured preexisting African alliances, as colonial racialized identity meant that anyone deemed white had a "state of right" in the colony,[37] and those deemed "natives" were coerced into giving up their rights to land, labor, and livelihood. By the mid-1890s, Africans had moved from informally registering their discontent to organizing themselves by geographic and/or social alliances so as to put up a fight for their lands and way of life. Some Africans, however, saw new opportunities for power and upward mobility in the new colonial state and did not hesitate to take advantage of them. Beginning in March 1896, formal and large-scale insurrections began in different parts of the colony, and the Chartered Company responded to those insurrections differently: for some the response was negotiated settlement; for others it was scorched-earth policies.

In other areas, like central Mashonaland, however, the war did not begin until June of that year, because the Mazowe valley and central MaShonaland in general still held promise for great gold deposits on the scale seen on the Witwatersrand in the Transvaal (South Africa). More importantly, many imperialists, including ordinary ones, thought Mashonaland had more settlers and was therefore safer from harm, a reality that proved fatal for some, as we will see in the story of the telegraphers. Reports in the colony's major newspaper, the *Rhodesia Herald,* often touted the Mazoe District as an economic and mining hub, and news from the district appeared as "Mining Intelligence," rather than regular news reports. Syndicates with digs in the area were numerous, and of different European origins, including the French South Africa Development (FSAD) and the Anglo-French Syndicate, as well as varied German, American, and Portuguese interests.[38] The strain of European settlement, harsh colonial laws, and natural disasters such as the devastating drought and the imported livestock disease rinderpest, which wiped out innumerable herds of cattle in southern African in 1895–96, put pressure on Afro-European relations even where Africans and Europeans had done business together in relative, if contentious, ease.[39] However, the fact that Europeans had the upper hand in those dealings left Africans feeling shortchanged in the land of their birth.

The Mazowe valley attracted a lot of Europeans because of its beauty and mineral and agricultural prospects. Once there, most Europeans did business with the local people, including chiefs and spirit mediums of repute like Charwe.[40] Francis G. Phillips, a British prospector born in Cornwall, wrote in March 1857 that "the district of the Mazoe may be described as a labyrinth of mountains, whose summits are on a level with the plateau on which Salisbury is situated. Looking down amongst the mountains from the edge of the plateau, the country presents a magnificent appearance."[41] Phillips was a thirty-five-year-old man who, like many of his British and western European contemporaries, dreamed of becoming rich in the goldfields of the African interior. In the Mazoe, Phillips found not only a magnificent view but also very keen businesspeople, especially the women. The men, Phillips observed, *offer rice or anything they have to sell, [but] the women reserve the option of selling. . . . The women are good at driving a good bargain. If, however, they have made up their minds not to part with their bargain, and there may be only a bead's worth difference, they will carry their stuff away again even if they have 30 miles to carry it. I have found them with few exceptions, to rely upon what I have promised, and indeed, they take one to his word. If one promise is made with them and not fulfilled, all further confidence is lost forever. . . . Therefore, it is well if you make a promise with these people to keep it if you don't want their ill will.*[42] That sense of business integrity, with no written agreement or contract, made a deep impression on people like Phillips as they were learning how best to maintain business relations with the Africans while quarrying for gold. The judicious and keen business acumen women displayed also tells us that in Nehanda-Charwe's home area, fair business practices, especially among women, were important in maintaining good relations with the outsiders, who they thought had no long-term plans for settlement.[43]

Charwe, as a senior spirit medium, also knew many of the Europeans in her district and had done business with some of them, including the district native commissioner of Mazoe, Henry Hawkins Pollard. As late as April 1896, Charwe still engaged Pollard; in fact, she had agreed to Pollard's request for some young men to accompany him north of the colony, where, he said, he wanted to pursue some business ventures. To Charwe's chagrin, it turned out that instead of only pursuing business ventures in the north, Pollard had taken those young men to scout for the BSAC. Pollard did not let on that he was fearful that African resistance to settler colonialism would spread and was on a mission to warn other settlers along the way that they might need to laager at town centers for protection. Pollard's BSAC mission to the north and northeast was aimed at avoiding incidents like the murders of Guerolt and the Nortons, a British settler family that had acquired vast tracts of land thirty miles west of the capital, Salisbury. The killing of the Nortons, including children, was a clear indication that the Africans considered Europeans enemies and that relations had soured irrevocably.[44] Pollard, also known to the Africans as Kunyaira, traveled north at the end of the rainy season in April 1896. Pollard's nickname was consistent with African cultural norms then (and now) of using meaningful nicknames as forms of inclusion, exclusion, derision, endearment, and disguise.

An understanding of Pollard's African nickname is important to the story because it tells of his positionality within and among the Shona people in the Mazowe District. Pollard's nickname and story is also pertinent here because, as we will see in the next chapter, his death was central to the British pinning a crime punishable by execution on Nehanda-Charwa. The word *kunyaira* can be translated in several ways. For example, Pollard walked with pomp and/or a sense of self-importance (*ku kunyaira*), and this nickname marked him as a despised commissioner—which he was in some circles. Alternatively, the nickname also meant that some Africans saw Pollard as a negotiator or ambassador (*ku nyaira* or *munyairi*).[45] Since he was the district native commissioner, he (probably) was fluent in chiShona and could translate for (or between) the Africans and the (English-speaking?) European prospectors doing business in the Mazowe. He was also the go-between for the bureaucratic business of BSAC administration at the local level. Most importantly, Pollard/Kunyaira had a working relationship with Nehanda-Charwe, discussed above, and that made his position rather precarious. Either way, Pollard's nickname tells us that he worked both sides of the color line, but knew which side his bread was buttered on, by spying for settlers using African young men supplied by Nehanda-Charwe for intelligence gathering. Although nationalist memory makers would later manicure Pollard's business relationship with Nehanda-Charwe, his nickname tells us that those who lived the history in the late nineteenth century were very aware that the frontier was a place of complicated entanglements and uncomfortable alliances.[46]

Pollard was reported missing in June 1896, and the news had the Mashonaland civil commissioner, Hugh Marshall Hole, alarmed and anxious. Hole's anxiety came from the realization that if Pollard, who knew that part of the colony and its local language well, could disappear, then no settler was safe among the Shona, whom settlers patronized as "cowards," without the mettle to fight for themselves. Pollard's disappearance, according to Hole, was proof that the Shona could not be trusted.

That distrust was exacerbated by the fact that some of Pollard's African policemen had "joined the rebels at the commencement of the rising, and have ever since taken a prominent part in the rebellion."[47] The search for Pollard was activated in central and northern Mashonaland and included the recruitment of neighboring districts' native commissioners (NCs) as team leaders. The fighting Africans, for their part, kept up the military pressure in the hope that their guerrilla tactics would yield positive results, reclaiming their land and way of life from what was clearly an aggressive occupier.

Hugh Marshall Hole may have been the typical naive colonial bureaucrat who believed his own myth that the Africans of central Mashonaland had no notion of their own self-interest or fighting gumption and were grateful to have British protection against other Africans. Hole's colonial attitude was the kind that settlers liked to invoke, as it included enough disdain for the "native" to allow them to keep the distance between citizens and subjects, to paraphrase Mahmood Mamdani. In fact, Hole's active participation in the 1896–97 war produced a colonial archive that would later become an important site of memory wrangled over by his widow (Mary/Molly) and the National Archives of Rhodesia. However, at the time, settlers on the ground, especially district NCs, did not share Hole's illusions African contentment with colonial occupation. For example, while A. C. Campbell, the native commissioner for Salisbury, shared Hole's settler anxiety about living in a colony at war, in his quarterly report of January 1896 he wrote, rather candidly for a colonial bureaucrat, about the Shona's "attitude towards the white men" in central Mashonaland. From experience, Campbell had learned that "although the attitude of Mashona is apparently friendly, there can be little doubt that we are looked upon by them as necessary evils who must be endured as there is no way of giting [sic] rid of us."[48] "The Mashonas," Campbell continued, "firmly believe that we will leave one day as they suppose the gold seekers of old [the Portuguese] did. . . . That we have settled here for good they do not believe for a slight instant."[49]

Campbell's report, which also appeared in the *Rhodesia Herald*, opened doors for an avalanche of articles variously titled "Our Native Troubles" or "The Native Question" in the same newspaper. Some expressed colonial denial that the Shona could revolt against Europeans, a sentiment best captured by one reporter who commented that "our policy of neglecting the native question of Mashonaland because the native question

of Matabeleland required attention is bearing its rich crop."[50] In that reporter's opinion, though the disappearance of Pollard and the murder of
the Nortons—after whom the town of Norton was named—was cause for
concern for settlers in Mashonaland, "we do not see sufficient evidence
in the murders to conclude that anything like a general or even a partial
rising is contemplated." The real fear, he wrote, was that should an insurrection break out, "the native labor supply would be threatened."[51] As
we will see in later chapters, deaths like the Nortons' and disappearances
like Pollard's became important reminders of the pioneers, who it was
said braved great difficulties to settle a new colony for the empire. Over
time, however, many forgot that some of the pioneers were more focused
on the bottom line than on who died in the name of settling a colony for
future (white) generations.

That the Mazowe valley went to war in June 1896, when other districts in central Mashonaland and regions in the colony had gone to war
earlier in the year, is worth noting, as it speaks to the complicated nature
of African and European relations in that area, as noted earlier. The flip
side of that late entry into the 1896–97 war by central Mashonaland was
that the colonial justice system treated prisoners of war from that district differently (often with little accommodation) than it did prisoners
from other parts of the colony.[52] In districts that had gone to war earlier,
notably Matebeleland, armistices yielded positive results, but in central
Mashonaland armistices seemed more like a strategy to buy time while
waiting for military reinforcements from South Africa and Britain than a
way to end the conflict. This was borne out once reinforcements arrived,
for then the colonial strategy was an all-out scorched-earth policy, a policy that later fed the memories of settlers commemorating the occupation of a colony.

The insurrection in central Mashonaland went on for about a year
and a half, from June 1896 through December 1897. It was during this
time that stories of Charwe's power as Nehanda migrated from African
mouths into European ears, slowly building a profile of a "witch" leading
an army—an African Joan of Arc. The commanding officer of the British
forces in the Mazoe District, Edwin Alfred Hervey Alderson, noted in
his report that the Mazoe valley was "a very fertile district in more ways
than one [as in it] were members of truculent natives." The natives were
"truculent" because it "was in this district that the celebrated doctoress

Nyanda [*sic*] lived and held court."[53] Alderson had encountered her personally when she attended a *dare*, a body of judicial or executive authority, for armistice negotiations in the Mazoe in 1896, which, however, yielded little peace, and the war continued into the following year.[54] Charwe's presence at the armistice negotiations indicates her importance to the people not only spiritually but politically and diplomatically as well.

The insurrection of June 1896 in central Mashonaland reanimated the legend of Nehanda-Nyamhita through its medium Charwe among the Shona of that region, eager to protect land entrusted to the living by the dead (ancestors) for the yet unborn. The chief native commissioner (CNC) of Mashonaland wrote a report noting the importance to the Shona during the war of the memory of major ancestral spirits, especially Nehanda-Nyamhita, who was prominent in a pantheon of mostly male ancestral spirits and their mediums. According to that report, there were key spirits and mediums important to the Shona that the British needed to know about, for example, a man named Gumboreshumba, who was the medium of a "common hunting spirit." Gumboreshumba, like Charwe, was commonly known by his title or by the name of the spirit he channeled, Kaguvi, rather than by his own name. Kaguvi was on the military officers' wanted list, but he did not evoke as much fear as Nehanda, who loomed large in the CNC's report. The difference between Kaguvi and Nehanda was that prior to the war Nehanda-Charwe had been "by far the most important wizard in Mashonaland," as evidenced by her receipt of tribute and gifts from many chiefs who acknowledged her powers to bring rain and land fertility.[55] Those same chiefs participated in the insurrection of central Mashonaland, and many worked with her, gathering and storing loot taken from fleeing or murdered settlers. Charwe did not hold her position as Nehanda, the CNC understood from his Shona informants, because of her own personal power and charisma; rather it was because her "title of Nianda is the name of the spirit which she has inherited. Her proper name being Charukwe [Charwe]." Since Kaguvi-Gumboreshumba was later to accuse Nehanda-Charwe and VaMponga (another female medium on whom there is very little information) of "starting the rebellion," the CNC's report lends weight to the idea that Nehanda-Charwe was a woman of stature in the Mazowe valley—and no poor saint. It also underscores the power of the memory of the legend of Nehanda-Nyamhita among the Shona of central Mashonaland beyond the Hwata dynasty, and Charwe herself as the memory of Nehanda-Nyamhita resonated with many people beyond the Mazowe and Dande valleys, as discussed at the beginning of this chapter.

The CNC's report thus suggests that though Nehanda-Charwe was later to deny her involvement in the uprisings, she was implicated by the power of her ecclesiastical office and her title as Nehanda. The position of being a Nehanda put her in the line of British fire, as imperial and settler forces sought to break African lines of communication that used Charwe's Mazowe location as a command center for communicating with others in central Mashonaland, especially Kaguvi-Gumboreshumba. The loot gathered and stored in Mazoe, the CNC's report continued, included numerous rifles, some of which were obsolete, goods and gold valued at one hundred forty pounds sterling, as well as seven hundred pounds sterling in cash that was still unaccounted for, as the Africans did not reveal its whereabouts for "fear of the spirit which [Charwe] possesses that the Natives are afraid of giving any information thereon."[56] This history will become important as we try to understand how and why the memory of Charwe vacillated between the image of a determined warrior woman averse to all things European and that of a hapless (female) victim caught in the claws of the British Empire with the complicity of African men.

Colonel Alderson oversaw some of the worst atrocities in the Mazowe Hills, and one of his men, Captain Horace McMahon, who shared his imperial ambitions, was assigned to scour the Mazowe Hills, throwing dynamite into caves. McMahon wrote vivid and triumphant reports of destruction as he and his regiment went "up the hills, burn[ing] several villages and mining some important caves, [including] the cave of the famous witch doctoress Nyanda [Nehanda] who was reported to be the cause of most of the discontent prevailing in the district and whose capture [we were] most anxious to effect."[57] For McMahon, it was imperative that the imperial and settler forces destroy the sacred caves, especially the ones associated with spirit mediums like Charwe, for to "destroy [the cave] completely [was] to show the natives that the white man had little respect for Nyanda's power."[58] The significance of some of those caves for Africans, as already mentioned, was that old royalty was buried in them, giving those environmental spaces their sacred power as African sites of memory. One can imagine the sheer horror when dynamite was ignited and exploded, causing unimaginable damage in a cave full of adults and children. Some survived and lived to tell the tale, as illustrated in one oral history in chapter 5.

Ironically, the destruction of African sacred spaces created new sacred spaces for the Europeans, who saw the area as their own, dignified by the valor of men like Alderson and McMahon. The destruction of the environmental landscape was a way to mark the triumph of one and the defeat of the other, and it did not help that Nehanda-Charwe was gone when "her cave" was blasted. By abandoning her sacred space, and her general area of jurisdiction, she unmasked the dubious nature of ancestral power and rituals purported to be able to protect fighters from bullets and dynamite. If the war brought out the worst in the colonials and settlers, it also brought to the fore the contrived nature of autochthons' ancestral power and their mediums. Rallying around mediums of powerful spirits like that of Nehanda did not save the people of the Mazowe valley—or anywhere else in the colony—from suffering heavy causalities from the weapons of mass destruction administered by the colonial authorities.

The status of Charwe as medium of Nehanda in the Mazowe valley, as well as the status of other mediums, was greatly compromised by the war. Charwe and her fellow senior mediums—especially the influential Gumboreshumba, medium of Kaguvi, a man whose territorial spirit was in Chivero and Zvimba and districts east of Salisbury—were faltering, and seemingly losing faith in the ancestors' ability to see them through the war successfully as the Africans took more fatal casualties than the Europeans, who had explosives and canon fire. The African ancestors, then, were being debated as Charwe sought counsel with the other mediums and chiefs in the Dande valley, seeking assurances from the land of Nyamhita, the original Nehanda, as it was obvious that things were not going well in central Mashonaland. On the other hand, she obviously had to protect herself, as some of her own people had passed on intelligence information about her whereabouts, and the colonial bureaucracy was building a profile for wanted posters that were never made. Charwe's profile as a person of interest was cemented by the fact that Pollard had disappeared (in June) after visiting Charwe's homestead. Thus, the convergence of some Africans' rejection of the politico-religious position she held and European suspicions of a "witch" leading an insurrection—Joan of Arc–like—made Nehanda-Charwe not only a target for imperial and settler forces but also a perfect candidate for mythological tales of a warrior ancestor in memory, generations later.

This chapter shows, albeit briefly, the memory of the legend of the spirit of Nehanda, from which Charwe derived her power as medium. Also highlighted is some of the history of contact between Africans and settlers that laid the foundation for autochthon and newcomer nationalist founding myths in that part of the Rhodesian colony. Though clearly a black-and-white history of the colonized and colonizer, this history shows us some gray areas as well. Prime among them was Nehanda-Charwe's working relationship with Pollard and other Europeans. Intelligence information on Nehanda-Charwe supplied to colonial bureaucrats by Africans who served them or who gave that information, perhaps under duress, complicates the narratives of ancestral heroes and victims. Lastly, the power of cannon fire not only ruptured the memory of the African world in colonial Zimbabwe but erected a new site of memory for British history in an African landscape. If enforcing African history and memory through spirit mediumship had been Charwe's prestigious role in an African society as a Nehanda before 1890, the British entry into the interior of southern Africa radically changed that history. Nehanda-Charwe's arrest and trial, as discussed in the next chapter, shows the deep psychic wounds the colonized were dealt—and the debasement of the colonizer wielding violence on another.

2 War Medals, Gendered Trials, Ordinary Women, and Nehandas to Remember

In most societies, origin stories are usually stories that involve "elements of recollection,"[1] making blank-slate beginnings rather rare. The sociologist Paul Connerton argued that blank-slate beginnings, while the aspiration, are often very difficult to achieve in many societies, especially those seeking a radical break with the past. Connerton used the case of the leaders of the French Revolution, who found themselves reverting back to traditions—the very ones they had revolted against—when confronted with the "trial and regicide of Louis XVI of France" before there were any new rules.[2] In the colonies, I would argue, a similar, if incomparable, situation arose in which the British, those champions of the abolition of the slave trade and slavery, found themselves reverting back to the same bigotry and violence of slavery when establishing colonies in Africa (and elsewhere).

This chapter continues where the previous one left off, highlighting a few more key historical moments that later became foundational in nationalist thought. Mahmood Mamdani's articulation of the grind between the colonizer and the colonized that created citizens and subjects at the founding of African colony nations in the nineteenth century is instructive here. By Mamdani's telling, because colonialism enforced racialized citizenship and ethnicized or tribalized subject status, at decolonization the settler and the native were (almost) unable to coexist as citizens of a new nation. The memory of that nation's founding was embedded in a history that celebrated the triumph of the colonizer (the citizen) and the defeat of the colonized (the subject) as the defining identity of settler and native in the colony.[3] The historian John Sutton Lutz argued in a similar vein when writing about how autochthons and settlers often told different stories of colonial beginnings, or what he calls "first contact" stories.

"For settler peoples," Lutz argued, contact stories are "origin stories, the explanation of how immigrants 'got here,' an opening paragraph of a long rationale for displacing indigenous peoples." On the other hand, "for indigenous peoples, colonial origin stories are a prologue to the process in which the world was turned upside down."[4] The history of how the nation was founded as told in this chapter, then, was a matter not only of nationalist creativity but also of the lived reality of the colonized. Taken together, that creativity and those experiences reiterate the idea that all beginnings are premised on recollections, but in a colonized society some of those experiences were unprecedented, and people grasped at the straws of the past to make sense of the present.

Keeping British War Traditions with Medals for "Conspicuous Gallantry in Action"

When we left off in the previous chapter, Nehanda-Charwe (among others) was on the run for her life in late 1897 from the Mazowe. That scenario buoyed the British victors, some of whom were seeking recognition as heroes and/or for the fallen in the 1896–97 war. Frederick Carrington, the imperial commanding major general in Southern Rhodesia—Alderson and McMahon's boss, proud of their trails of destruction in the Mazoe—was compelled to write to his superior (High Commissioner Rosemead in the Cape Colony) updating him on the situation in the colony. Carrington dispelled rumors of white annihilation and chaos north of the Limpopo River as reported in some newspapers. The general war situation was tough on many fronts, Carrington informed his superior, but all was under control on the frontier, even as there was still much happening there.[5] The most important message in Carrington's dispatch to the high commissioner was his desire to express and "recommend [for] favorable consideration the services of the officers, non-commissioned officers, and men noted in the attached list, for gallantry in action, meritorious work, keenness and soldierly qualities worthy of the highest traditions of the service."[6] Though it is a military tradition to award medals even as a war is ongoing, the process is worth unveiling, as it was at once history and memory intertwined, and sometimes it concealed more than it revealed of the processes of history and memory making by the people still waging war while awarding medals.[7] For Carrington, it was important to boost the morale of men still fighting the war against "the Native Rebels."

The institution of a tradition foreign to the land in which it was being administered ensured that those settlers who inherited the colony, and their descendants, would always invoke the names of those honored with medals for their feats of gallantry. Those so honored would be the focus of remembrance of the new gentry and aristocracy in a colony eager to sink its European roots in African soil. The medals and those so honored would indeed be the "opening paragraph" of how ordinary Britons became more than just subjects of empire, but citizens in an African colony.

By invoking "tradition" to justify the awarding of medals to individuals for acts of "conspicuous gallantry in action"—as his list of men was entitled—Carrington turned individual acts in war (history) into shared heritage for the settlers (memory). He turned the individual officer's and soldier's experience of the war into a collective one, acknowledged by Queen Victoria's War Office. The individual local soldier and the imperial army officer so honored rose and fell with the strength and/or weakness of the empire. Just as the empire depended on the "soldierly qualities" of its individuals in the army, the individuals depended on the empire to validate their service and their belonging to the (British) nation and its global empire. Carrington's desire to have his men awarded higher office and medals called for the celebration of empire in the individual, and the individual in the empire. In this exchange of medals for service, the liminal space of individual and collective memory converged, if briefly and uncomfortably. By celebrating the imperial individual male, the medals were revivifying the virility of an empire eager to penetrate deeper into the southern African hinterland.[8]

War awards, though often ephemeral and individualized sites of memory, were also collective in that they were made of the same metal and generally minted at the same time, yet they were pinned to an individual with a name and a family of his own. War medals, then, were the materiality of history to be retrieved in the future, reminding one and all of the colony's founding myths and heroes. War honors and medals certainly had their place, but as Ricoeur reminds us, "What [people often] celebrate under the title of founding events are essentially acts of violence legitimated after the fact by a precarious state of right. What was glory for some was humiliation for others."[9] The British imperial project, the literary historian Robert H. MacDonald astutely observed, was pursued to solve problems at home rather than abroad; it was also "tied to a sense that British government was good government, and the rest of the world would be better under British rule."[10] Thus, the war medals Carrington wanted for his men were meant to legitimize that claim of good British governance, and those so chosen were obligated to live up to its ideals.

Carrington listed his men who deserved awards and honors chronologically, beginning in March 1896, when Matebeleland had gone to war (with the settlers), ending in a negotiated settlement. "The List" would have additions and appendixes by the war's end in 1897. It also generated disagreements over who could be listed for which award from the queen and who could be outsourced to the local authorities for awards in the colony. Casting aside chronology, I focus on the significance and meaning of Carrington's list, which is divided into two broad categories: "Conspicuous Gallantry in Action" and "Gallantry in Action and Other Good Service." The first category is striking for the number of lower-level officers and foot soldiers personified by that beloved symbol of colonial memory, "The Trooper." The four Troopers on the list had distinguished themselves by giving up their lives for their comrades. Others had given up their horses to wounded comrades, tending them alone and bringing them to safety, while some had brought in bodies of the dead rather than leave them in enemy hands. The Trooper was the symbol of the empire shedding blood for the new colony of Southern Rhodesia.

The Trooper was also, however, an ambiguous figure, at once of the empire but not of it, a dilemma captured well by the South African (white woman) writer Olive Schreiner in her allegorical novel *Trooper Peter Halket of Mashonaland*, on the 1896–97 wars in Rhodesia published in 1897. The novel opens with a photograph of a lynching of three African men on one tree. About nine European men stand gazing at the dead men, posing with the "strange fruits" hanging from the now colonial trees of Southern Rhodesia.[11] The Trooper was also the adventurer in search of opportunity. He was the witness of colonial men loving African women before the empire arrived, the foot soldier of empire when it arrived, and the lynching man when the empire came calling with its promise of new gentry status based on his "race." The Trooper was imperial history's eyewitness on the ground, and the colony's memory when the ceremony of celebrating gallantry was over. This was the man who (had) made the empire proud.[12]

The second category of Carrington's list was made up of mostly officers and career military men, majors who commanded forces that fanned out throughout the colony quelling resistance against settler society, the

BSAC, and anyone white—or black—deemed to be working for the "other" side. The native commissioners made Carrington's list for their part in "obtaining information through native channels" or for showing "much personal courage in dealing with rebels occupying caves."[13] Once drawn up, the list went through the processing phase, in proper bureaucratic fashion. The first hitch came when the War Office wrote to the high commissioner intimating that "the Officers of the Local Forces brought to notice for their services during the recent campaigns in Matabeleland and Mashonaland did not hold commissions." For that reason, "Lord Lansdowne [the secretary of state for war] regrets to say the statutes of the Distinguished Order render them ineligible for appointment." Lansdowne recommended, however, that rather than their services not being memorialized at all, the Local Forces be "appointed Companions of the Order of St. Michael and St. George." The native commissioners' awards were outsourced to "the local authorities in South Africa."[14]

Remembering the war through the awarding of medals was controlled by London's War and Colonial Offices, which insisted on the definition of key terms for qualification to each medal and honor. It was a matter of quality control, a subjective process of deciding who could and who could not be awarded a medal. The secretary of state for war reminded South Africa that Carrington's list included a Trooper nominated for the Victoria Cross—one of the most prestigious of war medals for nineteenth-century colonists—who could not be awarded it unless further evidence of his qualification could be produced. The "qualification for the Victoria Cross is 'conspicuous bravery or devotion to the country in the presence of the enemy,'" the under secretary of state reminded South Africa.[15] The irony is that the Trooper in question, one Henderson, was the first on Carrington's list, nominated because he had been cut off from his patrol with a wounded comrade. Henderson had nursed his fellow Trooper for two days and one night, had given the other his horse, and had alone brought both of them to safety (in Bulawayo).[16]

The fact that the officers on the ground saw Henderson as deserving of the honor, while those in higher office did not, is a conflict that speaks to the social construction of memory, in which class interests clashed as those in power sought to preserve their privilege by opening the gate to upward mobility only so far. Halbwachs captured this reality well when he wrote that the European nobility, in an effort to preserve its class interests, often "prevented a plebeian from entering the nobility."[17] That way, they would minimize the confusion about who the "truly noble, and the recently ennobled" were.[18] Carrington's list was seen by the higher-ups as failing to discriminate the truly deserving from the merely deserving. For those in power, British imperial war medals were too precious to be "indiscriminately" awarded—running the risk of being cheapened and/or misremembered.

Carrington's list honored the "highest traditions" of military service in the British Empire, but it was also a memorial document that sought to ennoble the Troopers, who were poised to be the new upper middle class and landed gentry in the new colony. The foot soldiers of empire would have the chance and the artifact to claim belonging, and their descendants would have the chance to claim autochthony based on the sacrifices of their real and fictive progenitors. Again, this was Britain's version of ancestor hierarchy, with only elite males guaranteed a place among the pantheon of ancestral founders and, by extension, ancestor veneration in the history of that colony. The irony was that in the end, the already commissioned officers who did not settle in the colony in large numbers benefitted the most from the awards process, especially those in the category of "gallantry in action and other good service."[19] That category included three men who had distinguished themselves in the Mazoe valley, dealing with Nehanda-Charwe and her people. Native Commissioner Nesbitt, captain of the local Mazoe Patrol, was held up as the savior of the beleaguered settler community in the Mazoe valley.[20] The other two heroes cited as worthy of awards were Captain McMahon and Lieutenant Colonel Alderson, both of whom we encountered in the previous chapter as they traversed and scarred the Mazoe valley with their dynamite, blowing up caves and lives.[21]

What the spoils of war did was to starkly distinguish the losers and winners after the war. Though there were African "friendlies," who had supported the imperial war effort, the postwar era saw the emergence of racialized and stratified master-servant and patron-client relations, which shaped the later history of the colony and the postcolony. The intended and unintended consequences of that racialization and stratification were that they planted and nurtured very poisonous seed for race and ethnic relations in the colony. Worse still was the place of women, especially African women, who found themselves hemmed in by laws that sought to domesticate them, making their lives synonymous with everything "primitive."

Traumatic Juridical Beginnings:
Reversing the Language of Translation

While Carrington was busy hustling London for medals for his men, the hunt for Charwe in central Mashonaland was continuing with renewed vigor, led by the new native commissioner for Mazoe, Edward T. Kenny. Kenny was a former translator who replaced Henry Pollard as administrator of the Mazoe District. Right from the start, Kenny tried to get his African captives, mostly women, to talk, but he was generally unable to get any useful information out of them. After Pollard went missing in June 1896, Nehanda-Charwe and Kaguvi-Gumboreshumba separately disappeared from their usual abodes. In August, Kenny heard news that Kaguvi-Gumboreshumba had with him a "large body of his followers," which Kenny hoped would slow Kaguvi-Gumboreshumba down, so he could be captured. However, Kenny later noted with disappointment that they had all escaped before he could get to them.[22] Two months later, an exultant report in the *Rhodesia Herald* announced news from Kenny that "two Native Department messengers have succeeded in capturing two of Kakubi's wives in the Mazoe District."[23] Kaguvi-Gumboreshumba himself was still on the run, with African messengers and policemen of the Native Department in hot pursuit. About a fortnight later, on October 27, it was reported that Kaguvi-Gumboreshumba wished to surrender. A *Rhodesia Herald* report announced that "Kakubi has had enough of it; the war doctor desires to join his lady following who are with the Mazoe NC. The authorities expect Kakubi's surrender any moment."[24] Kaguvi-Gumboreshumba's desire to surrender was induced by the capture of the women in Kenny's custody. As the African police insisted to Kenny, "Had Kagubi's women not been captured, [he] would not have surrendered." Kaguvi-Gumboreshumba's surrender was also strategic, as he knew those women were not really his wives but war loot, with less loyalty to him and his cause, as would become clear at his trial in March the following year. Kenny was delighted by Kaguvi-Gumboreshumba's arrest, and to show his appreciation to (and of) his African police, he made a recommendation reminiscent of Carrington's list of "gallant men." Kenny requested of Taberer, the chief native commissioner of Mashonaland, stationed in Salisbury, that the African police "who captured Kagubi's women be awarded some small bonus for their able work." Kenny went on to suggest that another bonus be extended to those same fellows in the event that they captured Nehanda-Charwe, who was still on the run.[25]

Buoyed by the successful capture of Kaguvi-Gumboreshumba, Kenny led "those able men" in pursuit of Nehanda-Charwe. "I am leaving here under cover of darkness tomorrow night to arrest 'Nyanda' and also if possible 'VaMponga' who are in my district," Kenny informed Taberer. Kenny, the self-assured colonial bureaucrat, wanted to arrest those two prominent women because they were "keeping a lot of *my* natives from surrendering."[26] Since Kaguvi-Gumboreshumba's surrender had been anti-climactic for Kenny, the capture of Nehanda-Charwe and VaMponga was important for his credentials and for his career in the colony's bureau-cracy. For Kenny, "'Nyanda' is the more important of the two," and he would do all in his power to capture her.[27] Taberer's support (as CNC) added imperial weight to Kenny's keen interest in arresting Nehanda Charwe, an interest shared by many a settler as the insurrections tapered off at the end of 1897. At that point, Nehanda-Charwe was considered "more dangerous to the peace of the country than even Kagubi would be," suggesting that Kaguvi-Gumboreshumba, now held in police custody, had talked and thereby validating the intelligence gathered from other Africans up to that moment. The intense interest in capturing Charwe pointed to the importance of Nehanda in Shona memory in general and to Charwe's central role in the insurrection in Mazowe.[28] By the time she was captured, in December of the same year, the fighting had all but ended in most parts of central Mashonaland, as most leaders had been arrested or executed and the vast majority of people had been trauma-tized, maimed, or killed by the firepower marshaled by British officers like Alderson and McMahon.

Once Nehanda-Charwe was in police custody, Kaguvi-Gumbore-shumba publicly reiterated his position that he had not started the war. He made that statement during his preliminary examination when, after dismissing witness testimonies against him and positioning himself as a peaceful man, he demanded that "Nyanda, Goronga, and VaMponga be brought in[, because] they started the rebellion."[29] However, since nei-ther he nor Nehanda-Charwe was charged with insurrection, it seems that the issue of who had started the war was never pursued by the colo-nial government, as there is little else by way of evidence to illuminate Kaguvi-Gumboreshumba's accusation that Nehanda-Charwe had led the insurrection. That statement also hints at the philosophical difference

Figure 3. The Capture of Nianda and Kakubi, October 1897. (NAZ/Image 3729)

between those two leaders regarding war strategy—and perhaps its meaning, considering that Kaguvi surrendered and Nehanda was captured by Kenny and his African policemen. What is important to note here for later reference is that Kaguvi-Gumboreshumba was implicated along with the colonial machinery, as he testified against Nehanda Charwe and other key figures in central Mashonaland, yet generations later he emerged in nationalist memory as a hero on a par with Nehanda-Charwe.

Not only were the Africans subjected to a new juridical process of arrest, custody, and preliminary examination but they were made to stand in line to be photographed to "prove" their capture. An image showing the capture of Nehanda and Kaguvi (fig. 3) was produced by the BSAC as a powerful propaganda tool for a beleaguered Chartered Company, which was seeking to assuage the anxieties of investors in Europe and prospective settlers in the colony. The BSAC used that image to good effect to announce "the arrest" of Nehanda and Kaguvi. However, this image is problematical when juxtaposed to contemporary documents. For example, the title includes the date "October 1897." But as stated above, Kaguvi-Gumboreshumba surrendered on October 27, 1897, and Kenny, who left under the "cover of dark" on a mission to "capture Nianda," did not get to her until mid-December 1897. She was reported as arrested on December 18, 1897, suggesting that the photograph depicting her arrest might be unreliable evidence.[30]

On January 11, 1898, Frank Spurrur, acting for the clerk of the court, prepared a supporting document for the preliminary trial of the Africans held in custody for alleged involvement in the insurrections of 1896–97 in central Mashonaland that killed Pollard.[31] Among those indicted were "Wata [Hwata], Nianda (*female*) [Nehanda-Charwe], Gutsa, and Zindoga," charged with the murder of Henry Pollard. All four were committed for trial on January 12, 1898, by the acting magistrate of Salisbury Township, Cecil Bayley.[32] From the record of the preliminary trial we learn that Nehanda-Charwe was thirty-six years of age at the time of her arrest. Most interesting was the notation for occupation: "Without a trade or occupation." Obviously, mediumship of a high Shona spirit did not count as an occupation for colonists, whereas the German Jesuit prison chaplain, Francis Richartz, was accorded a title and salary for his occupation as a Catholic clergyman.

The indictment against Nehanda-Charwe read: "On the twentieth of June 1896, at the Mazoe District of Salisbury, Nianda kill and murder [sic] Henry H. Pollard, alias Kunyaira, in his lifetime a native commissioner there residing."[33] Bayley read that statement to her, and she was probably standing across from him, handcuffed. Responding to the charge laid before her, Nehanda-Charwe said: "I heard that Kunyaira [Pollard] had come and they went and brought him to me so we ran away we did not go close to him at all that's all I have to say they did not bring him up to the [homestead]." The whole process, the evidence suggests, was carried out with as much procedure and as much of a paper trail as possible. However, the record does not indicate whether her statement about not getting close to Kunyaira was contested. The preliminaries ended with the prisoners "signing" the documents. Since Charwe and others were nonliterate in terms both of reading and writing and of the British (colonial) judicial system, she (or someone) "authenticated" the documents by scratching an X for her signature as acknowledgment that she understood the charge against her. The colonial bureaucrats Joseph Bottle and Frank Spurrur signed as witnesses.

Nehanda-Charwe's statements at the preliminary hearing (and the trial itself, discussed below) are not easy to understand, because they carry conflicting messages. Unlike previous scholars who did not puzzle over the cryptic nature of her testimony, I am curious why her testimony is the least clear of prisoner and witness accounts and testimony at those important trials in the colony's history. To try and get at the cryptic meaning of those court documents, I will apply my own meth-odology of reverse translation to the English document we have in the archives, translating it into chiShona. That way, I can offer another way of understanding what might have been lost in translation (granted, my reverse translation utilizes twenty-first- and not nineteenth-century chi-Shona). The historiography, especially the works of Ranger and Beach, while acknowledging the skewed nature of the colonial court, picked the parts that made sense. By 1998 Beach's research had led him to make a "gender" argument for Charwe, for in revisiting the evidence, he wrote, he was surprised to realize that Charwe was "an innocent woman sur-rounded by men who were united by a desire to see her hanged."[34] Al-though Beach's attempt at gender analysis is commendable, he did not present a thorough gender analysis of all the evidence and all the actors. His article reads as though for him, Charwe's biology as a female among (African and European) males, rather than the racialized construction and reconstruction of power in that frontier encounter, was key. By only "raising the possibility that [Charwe] could be seen as a kind of victim in a gender-oriented sense for all her accusers were men,"[35] Beach's argu-ment, to my mind, leaves Charwe's testimony out in the cold. A full gen-der analysis would have revealed the collusion of African and European patriarchy, as well as the emasculation of African men at the hands of their British overlords. Moreover, by arguing that "all her accusers were men," Beach overlooked the critical detail that Kaguvi's accusers and wit-nesses against him were mostly women, as detailed below.

My reverse-translation methodology, therefore, is an attempt to "give" the defendant (Charwe) her Shona language back, in the hope that it may illuminate her mind and what was at stake in that colonial court of (in)justice. Giving Charwe her Shona language back, as it were, also means that we glimpse the historical figure—the image from the past, to borrow from Ricoeur. By approximating a voice for her, we get a woman who was no mere invention of African nationalists from the 1940s on. Understanding the trial from Charwe's point of view and language means that we take note of little things, like the fact that she referred to Pollard as Kunyaira—that African nickname discussed earlier—signifying an en-counter that settler nationalists and African nationalists would later try to omit in the racially divided memory of how Rhodesia was made since 1890. As we will see in later chapters, settler nationalists attempted to erase African contestation and resistance to colonialism, opting for the narrative in which Nehanda-Charwe was a symbol of settler triumph over "native barbarism." By contrast, black nationalists elided Charwe's European encounters but embellished her "performance" at the trial to create a larger-than-life anti-imperialist heroine. My gender analysis of Kaguvi's and Nehanda-Charwe's trials, therefore, is a departure from a historiography mainly focused, among other things, on faith in the archives, on chronology, and on colonial judicial procedure. My analysis is focused on the notions and meanings of "the rule of law" on a colonized population waking up to the depth of their defeat by the British.

To return to the first part of her statement in her testimony at the preliminary hearings, Charwe said: "I heard that Kunyaira [Pollard] had come and they went and brought him to me." That statement confirms that she had known (about) Kunyaira and that she first saw him on the day they brought him to her.[36] More significant is the fact that she said they brought Kunyaira to her, yet she did not refer to anyone else in that first part of the statement. Even the translation here—with chiShona honorific pronouns, which pluralize in the second or third person—would not be confused. Thus, in chiShona she might have said: "Ndakanzwa kuti Kunyaira awuya, ndokubva vamuunza kwandiri." It could well be that the translator misunderstood *Takanzwa* (*We* heard) and translated it as *Ndakanzwa* (*I* heard), as well as *Kwatiri* (to *us*), translating it as *Kwandiri* (to *me*). But this would be most likely if Nehanda-Charwe had spoken with a Shona accent that the translator was not familiar with; had a lisp; or had nasal congestion resulting from the use of ritual snuff (tobacco), making her *T* sound project as an *Nd* sound and thus difficult to understand and translate if one's ear was not used to it. It also could have been none of the above, or a combination of two or, most unlikely, all three. All of these are highly likely, and other than the lisp, linguistic, and nasal-congestion possibilities, the plural could also have been honorific if she meant that Kunyaira was brought to her while she was in trance. While that would be the most difficult possibility to verify, one cannot dismiss it as irrelevant, since she was a woman of importance *because of the Spirit* she was channeling. Understanding the meanings of the singular and plural—as elaborated below—allows us to look beyond the physical people present around her when she was with Kunyaira to the spirit entities that gave her the politico-religious title of Nehanda in the first place. In any event, whatever Charwe meant in the first part of her statement, it is the part that seems to hold the least (obvious) ambiguity.

The second part of her statement makes reverse translation important because it is the most cryptic part of her testimony, and it is very
difficult to understand or envision what went wrong with the translation, as the pronoun shifts from singular to plural. The latter part of her
statement—"so we ran away we did not go close to him at all that's all I
have to say they did not bring him up to the [homestead]"—succeeding "I
heard" and "they brought him to me," is at once fascinating and peculiar.
In chiShona she probably said "nezvo takatiza hatina kuswedera pedyo
naye zvachese, ndizvo zvandingataura, havana kumuunza pamusha." In
the first part of the statement, the translation tells us that she utilized the
singular pronoun twice—"I heard" and "brought him to *me*"—yet in the
latter part of the statement she utilized the plural pronoun *we* twice—
"*we* ran away *we* did not get close to him." How that statement—without
breaking—changed from the singular to the plural in one breath is itself
breathtaking because it invites the question, Was the singular for Charwe
the medium alone with the physical people around her; and the plural
for Charwe the medium, the physical people around her, as well as Nehanda the spirit, altogether? One also wonders whether the native commissioner deliberately mistranslated her testimony. Did her testimony
contain information that implicated Pollard or other BSAC officials and
prospectors in the Mazoe or something unacceptable to the court as evidence, for example, in recourse to her religion and/or spirituality?

Another possibility is that her testimony was produced under torture or harsh interrogation that the colonials did not record, leaving
us with fragmented testimony.[37] As noted in an oral-history interview
highlighted in chapter 5, Nehanda-Charwe was kept in solitary confinement, "in a hole."[38] That confinement and possible harsh treatment could
explain her confusing testimony. I raise this possibility because I find
Nehanda-Charwe's testimonies at the preliminary and the actual trial
(discussed in detail below) the most contradictory and cryptic of all the
prisoners' statements that I read in my research. The cryptic nature of
those testimonies raises important historical questions about the making
and/or destruction of evidence of a key figure in a significant event. It
also raises the question whether the testimony was fudged by the translator and the judge who transcribed the trial. The important point here
is that Nehanda-Charwe's statement sheds little light on the issues from
her perspective, while casting a long shadow on the events of 1896–97
and her role in them. It makes one wonder why the prosecution never

asked her (or any of the significant prisoners) anything about the wars proper, focusing instead on the death of a low-level colonial bureaucrat, Pollard. On the other hand, the mangling of Nehanda-Charwe's testimony speaks volumes about the contrived nature of colonial archives, where the colonized had very little or nothing that they self-produced to offer as counterhistorical perspectives.[39]

Colonial (In)justice in the Courts, Part I

In the late summer of 1898 Judge Watermeyer in Salisbury began the trials of those convicted of leading or participating in the insurrections in central Mashonaland. The general indictments included direct or indirect murder of European settlers and African friendlies.[40] According to the trial records, Kaguvi-Gumboreshumba and his companions (Marimo, M'bobo, Chigonga, and Makatsini) were tried first, followed by Nehanda-Charwe and her codefendants (Hwata, Zindoga, and Gutsa, all men). What is key to note here is that both trials had, for the most part, the same judge, the same set of assessors, and the same defense lawyer. Also important to note in this section is that unlike Beach, who argued that Charwe was convicted because of her gender, as she was surrounded by African and European men who wanted her dead, I show here that that it was more complicated than that, especially the fact that three out of four witnesses who testified against Kaguvi-Gumboreshumba were (memorable) women. The female witnesses against Kaguvi-Gumboreshumba had been captured women (war loot), mostly widows of former (African) policemen-cum-messengers. The male witnesses against Nehanda-Charwe had left their employment with private settler employers or the BSAC in what later became the Native Affairs Department.

On Wednesday, March 2, 1898, Nehanda-Charwe and Kaguvi-Gumboreshumba went up for trial—Kaguvi first, then Nehanda.[41] Since these cases have been the subjects of much historical writing and debate, I will not wade into the same waters. Rather, I will focus on women and gender dynamics, which have not been fully addressed in the historiography of the 1896–97 wars. This, I hope, will also illuminate the fact that Nehanda-Charwe, despite her prominence in the historiography and in popular memory, was not the sole female in those courts.[42] If gender was manipulated to "frame" her, as Beach argued, it could be counterargued that gender was also manipulated to "frame" Kaguvi-Gumboreshumba through the use of female witnesses. Though one cannot, and should not, easily equate these forms of discrimination, considering that patriarchy has historically favored men over women, it is particularly telling that in the major trials of Nehanda-Charwe and Kaguvi-Gumboreshumba the numbers of witnesses were gender-skewed; that is, there were more male witness against her and more female witnesses against him.

The real issue that divided these two key African figures, in my assessment, was how to handle the war, as Kaguvi's testimony suggests. Three of the four witnesses in the trial of Kaguvi-Gumboreshumba (and his codefendants) were women—Siodzi, Majeki, and Shisutumwe; the fourth was the new NC for Mazoe, Edward Kenny.[43] Kaguvi's crime was the murder of an African policeman-cum-messenger named Charlie, who was seen as a *bafu,* a sellout, pandering to the needs of European settlers. The crime that men like the late Charlie committed was taking advantage of new opportunities within the colonial bureaucracy, defying the power of older privileged men, who often controlled not only women's sexuality but that of younger men as well. Women who married men such as Charlie—like those witnesses against Kaguvi—were also defying arranged marriages, usually with older men, a practice that had become prevalent by that time.

Justice Watermeyer presided over the court, with Messrs Aria, Wylie, van Praagh, and Eustace serving as assessors. The native commissioner for Salisbury, A. C. Campbell, was the translator. Significantly, Mr. Mick J. Murphy, an Irishman, served as advocate for most of the African defendants in the Salisbury trials—an irony not lost on most, considering his native Ireland's history with British, or rather English, imperialism. Shortly after the prosecution stated its case on behalf of the "Queen against Kakubi," Siodzi, a "Mashona woman," took the witness stand. Siodzi and her co-witnesses were some of the women referred to as Kaguvi-Gumboreshumba's "wives or followers" in the intelligence reports by Kenny when Kaguvi was still on the run. Siodzi, by her own account, was the widow of one of the African policemen-cum-messengers, Jack, who had been killed during the insurrections—an important detail in a trial of men accused of murdering Charlie, also an African policeman-cum-messenger. No other biographical details are given to tell us more about who Siodzi was and what she had done before she found herself in that predicament during the war. She was a witness in the case against Kagubi because, as she testified, she had been "taken prisoner to Kagubi's homestead, Marimo and Zhanta took me." Siodzi and the other two women said that they were out collecting firewood when they witnessed the killing. Siodzi emphatically told the court: "Kagubi ordered [the other prisoners] to do it. I heard Kagubi give the order. I heard it with my ears. Kagubi's words were 'Take Charlie and kill him. He is *Bafu*—not on our side.'" She said that "they took Charlie towards the river," killed him, and came back to report to Kaguvi-Gumboreshumba that they had "finished him off." Siodzi testified that because they had witnessed that gruesome event, she and her companions were always guarded by the men, who warned her that if she "ran away they would finish me off at the same place."

On cross-examination, Siodzi emphasized: "I was not a wife of Kagubi, I was given to Kagubi's brother [Chigonga]," a man who broke out of jail with forty-five other men but had the misfortune of being one of only three recaptured.[44] This "marriage" detail was one that had been discussed in the magistrate's court during Kaguvi-Gumboreshumba's preliminary examination. It was in that lower court that Kaguvi-Gumboreshumba had first accused Nehanda-Charwe, VaMponga, and Goronga of "starting the rebellion." What is particularly interesting about Siodzi's testimony is that the details she gave were similar to the details given by the male witnesses in Nehanda-Charwe's trial; that is, the war leader told others to take the victim near the river and kill him there. The killing at the river was a common motif in Shona cosmology in the case of "unnatural" deaths. This was done to "cool" the spirits of the murdered—regardless of age, gender, race, or ethnicity—so that they would not turn into avenging spirits, *ngozi*.[45]

Majeki was the second witness, and she too entered the record as "a Mashona woman" and the widow of a "native police killed" during the war. For the most part, Majeki corroborated Siodzi's testimony, with the difference that she had known Charlie while she lived at Kaguvi-Gumboreshumba's and was standing a few feet off from where the incident happened—along with her female comrades. Her testimony emphasized the visual as well as the auditory, since she had heard Kaguvi-Gumboreshumba order the death of Charlie "down at the water." The third witness was Shisutumwe (Chisitumwe), who was also "a Mashona woman, formerly wife of a native policeman." Her story of how she got to Kaguvi-Gumboreshumba's was the same as Siodzi's: she had been captured by Marimo and Zhanda, probably on the same day or within a few days of Siodzi's capture. She had known Charlie from "long ago [when] he was Mr. Taberer's police."[46] Much of her testimony corroborated the other two women's testimonies.

The case of Kaguvi-Gumboreshumba is less ambiguous (compared with Nehanda-Charwe's) in terms of what transpired in the courthouse about the alleged crime and the defendant's responses. The witnesses said they had heard and/or seen the crime take place, and there was little discussion about Kaguvi-Gumboreshumba. This "tangible" firsthand evidence was important for those administering justice, guaranteeing that nothing would backfire when the information hit the desk of those higher up in the colonial bureaucracy. Kaguvi-Gumboreshumba, like Nehanda-Charwe, was charged with murder, and not with instigating the rebellion—which would have been much harder to prove if those so charged had not been caught with weapons on their person. In response to the charges and witness testimonies against him, Kaguvi-Gumboreshumba said: *I have heard what these women say but it is not true. I only want a place where I can live. If the government wants me to pay for their things I will pay with a young girl. I want Nyanda [Nehanda], Goronga, and Wamponga [VaMponga] brought in they started the rebellion.* Kaguvi-Gumboreshumba was dismissive of the women's testimonies. He did not even address the issue of Charlie's murder; instead, he told his "truth," which included a veiled apology to the BSAC-cum-government for the crimes he was accused of, stating that he was willing to make amends and pay with the life of a little girl.

Kaguvi-Gumboreshumba's offer of the life of a little girl in exchange for his freedom does tell us that women and girls from poor households were used as warfare currency or pawns to settle debts and other scores.[47] Kaguvi-Gumboreshumba tried to extricate himself by telling the court that he was not responsible for his actions against the BSAC, that instead the women Nehanda-Charwe and VaMponga and another man, Goronga, were responsible for his actions against "the government" and for the murder of Charlie. The defendants' lawyer, Murphy, challenged the women's evidence by asking why they had not reported the events "at once." That question, while valid, did not take into consideration that those women were prisoners of war, loot that was distributed among the men, as Majeki's testimony explained: "I was not Kakubi's wife . . . , I was given to his brother." The women were under surveillance, as African leaders saw them as both a liability (if they escaped, they could report

them) and an asset (they could be exchanged for other valuable commodities, including their freedom). Considering that the women were
widows of former employees of the BSAC and had been captured against
their will, one can understand their emphatic testimonies against Kaguvi-
Gumboreshumba and his codefendants. For those women, the opportunity to testify against their captors was an opportunity to free themselves
of forced marriage and abode, colonial consequences notwithstanding.

Colonial (In)justice in the Courts, Part II

After Kaguvi-Gumboreshumba's trial, Nehanda-Charwe was brought before the court with the only other defendant, Hwata—the other two,
Gutsa and Zindoga, having escaped from prison.[48] Judge Watermeyer was
still presiding, and Herbert Hayton Castens, the acting public prosecutor,
entered the plea that "Nianda, a Mashona woman . . . , Zindoga a native
kitchen boy residing at Nianda's kraal [homestead] . . . , and Wata and
Gutsa both native hunters are all and each or some or one of them guilty
of the crime of murder" of Henry H. Pollard, a native commissioner. The
witnesses against Nehanda-Charwe and her companions were working
(or had once worked) for the Native Department as messengers or providing some other service. All the witnesses were men, four Africans and
two Europeans, with an additional expert witness, a (male) medical doctor, Thomas Stewart, who came in to testify about bones that had been
found in a riverbed in Mazoe and speculated that they were Pollard's.[49]

The most elaborate testimony was given by an African man named
"Pig," and this was corroborated by two other (African) witnesses. (Pig
was also, unclearly, named "the Court" in the documents, further confusing the identity of the speaker, but not the testimony.) All these men had
known Nehanda-Charwe before the war. The fourth witness, Marimbi,
a messenger, was someone Nehanda-Charwe did not know; he entered
the scene by way of a sack of human bones he brought from Mazoe at
the command of the chief native commissioner, Taberer. The bones had
been examined by Stewart, the district surgeon, who testified that they
were male human bones and that the skull was missing. However, he
could not definitively say that they were Pollard's. Thus Stewart's statement that "they are some bones of a human male" raises the possibility
that they may have been the bones of any male. The "race" of the man
was not clear from the bones, and with the limited technology available

at the time, the whole idea of bringing the bones as evidence was rather contrived. Either way, it was important for the prosecutor and the defendant that Pollard's body was never found, as Charwe maintained her innocence right to the end. The lack of evidence leaves open the question of her innocence or guilt of the murder charges. For the colonial administrators, the missing body proved the "mythical" powers of Nehanda, which kept the Africans from telling where the body was in deference to the idea that Pollard's body could well be an *ngozi*, and who would want that on their head in the future?

The trial transcript also informs us that "the Court" spoke against Nehanda-Charwe. It is not clear whether "the Court" was the prosecutor, one of the witnesses, the codefendant, or "Pig," the man designated to provide information on who Charwe was and her place as Nehanda in the sociopolitical life of the Mazoe valley. However, the statement of "the Court" gives important clues suggesting that it was made by an African man from Nehanda-Charwe's area. Particularly striking is the statement's emphasis on the fact that Nehanda-Charwe was a woman who ruled over her brother, Chief Chitaura, who held the title Hwata and was her codefendant. The speech ("By the Court") is worth quoting in full, as it reveals some of the turning points in the "invention of tradition"[50] rather than an imagination from history.

Often in colonial encounters, as shown in this testimony, African women were portrayed as never having belonged in power circles in Shona history. *Nianda was chief of the [village/town]. Chitaura is her brother. Chitaura was the chief but Nianda had the power. Nianda was over Chitaura. I don't know how we came to be under a woman. Nianda is a mondora [royal spirit]. She gave orders. Chitaura obeyed her. All the people did what Nianda told them. This has been for a long time. I know of no other women who rule [towns]. If people didn't do what Nianda told them, I don't know what would happen. I don't know of her punishing people. I was afraid of Nianda. I was afraid to refuse to do anything she told me. I don't know why I was afraid. I don't know of Nianda punishing any member of the village.*[51] That statement was supported by Edward Kenny when he testified, as native commissioner of Mazoe, that Nehanda-Charwe had formerly lived on the west bank of the Mazoe River and had moved her homestead to the east bank during the war. He went on to say, "Natives throughout my district called it Nianda's [town]. That would mean she ruled it." Perhaps more than any other testimony about Nehanda-Charwe given at the trial, the foregoing two revealed who she was and what others thought of her, but not how she defined herself.

The statement that "Nianda had the power" is quite provocative. That the speaker did not "know how we came to be under a woman" speaks of ignorance of the history of the people concerned, or historical amnesia to please the judge and assessors in that court of (in)justice, or denial of historical reality, as the speaker was cognizant of the changing political and social order in the young colony. What is baffling is why the speaker knew of "no other women who rule[d villages]." He seems to have been suggesting that Shona women had never held political power, which would have been inaccurate, since the spirit of Nehanda that Charwe channeled was that of Nyamhita, a woman/female. Conversely, if the speaker meant that women had not been visible figureheads of power in recent Shona memory, then his assessment was to some degree accurate, as women had become increasingly less visible as power holders—even by the sixteenth century, when the Portuguese first recorded their contact with Africans of the southern African interior.

The irony, of course, is that the plaintiff in all cases was Queen Victoria of Britain, herself a female ruler and figurehead of a patriarchal imperial power largely administered and controlled by men. Most importantly, the speaker at Nehanda-Charwe's trial told the court that he had been afraid not to do her bidding, not because of anything she had ever done to anyone but because he had never known of anyone not doing what she told them to do. "If people didn't do what Nianda told them, I don't know what would happen," he said. "I don't know of her punishing people." This tells us that the power of the ancestors and the power of the spirit of Nehanda (channeled by Charwe) were articles of faith. It tells us that Charwe as a Nehanda, wielded a kind of power not talked about in the courtroom (or not recorded in the trial transcripts). That the speaker "was afraid of Nianda [and] afraid to refuse to do anything she told me" suggests that she wielded the power of the invisible, the ancestors, who had the power to bestow favors and also to withhold them from those who did not listen to what the mediums told them to do, including chiefs like Hwata. In fact, spirit mediums installed chiefs and in the event of untimely death were custodians of that position on behalf of a particular people until a new one was inaugurated, especially if there was a succession dispute. It also suggests that Charwe, as a person, perhaps did not wield malicious power against any member of her clan or ethnic group because of her high position as spirit medium. Instead, she worked through the power of persuasion that her office stood for in that society.

Incidentally, Nehanda-Charwe defended herself against the testimony that she was the ruler of that area, stating, "Wainzi musha wangu [or "Rainzi dunhu rangu"], asi raingowe zita chete" (It was called my area, but it was only in name), which was true only if we discount that she was a woman of politico-spiritual power among her people, in a long line of such women.[52] Indeed, by 1884 the British traveler Montagu Kerr, as noted earlier , had written about a "large Mashona town called Neanda." To the charge that Nehanda-Charwe had given the orders to kill Pollard, she consistently responded: "Kwete, handina kumbopa chirayiridzo" (I deny giving the order) and "Ndinoramba, kuti ndakatuma Hwata kuti awuraye Kunyaira. Kunge ndakamutuma ndaigorambireyi" (I deny that I sent Wata to kill Pollard. If I had sent him, I would own up to it).[53] At the conclusion of the trial, the assessors' verdict was that Nehanda-Charwe was guilty of ordering the murder of Pollard, but for Hwata they recommended "mercy on the ground that he acted under fear of Nianda." To that verdict, Hwata did not have anything to say, but Nehanda-Charwe contested it, saying, "Handina kumbopa chirayiridzo. Ndingago zvivanzireyi kana ndakazviita?" (I did not give the order. Why should I hide it if I did it?) Her contestation did not overturn the verdict nor prevent the issuance of a death warrant for her execution the following month (fig. 4). Sexism and patriarchy from both cultures had won the day. More crucially, her recorded testimony did not reveal what else was at stake other than Pollard's disappearance/death from Charwe's perspective. Unlike Kaguvi, who engaged the government through the court, apologizing and offering to pay in return for his freedom, Charwe centered her testimony on Pollard's death, with no sense of the bigger picture of why he died—rather than how he died, which was the focus of the court's record.

The verdict came in, and it was not good for Nehanda-Charwe. The *Rhodesia Herald* ran a report of the trial of Nehanda-Charwe (among others) on March 9, 1898. The report, a summary of the trial, included a commentary on her behavior that gives another perspective on that elusive historical figure: "Nyanda [Nehanda] is the lady who, in opposition to Kagubi, started the rival establishment in the Mazoe District. As a war goddess, she had numerous *clientele* who worshipped at her shrine."[54] The report's reference to Nyanda's rival establishment in Mazoe affirms my earlier assessment that Nehanda-Charwe and Kaguvi-Gumboreshumba

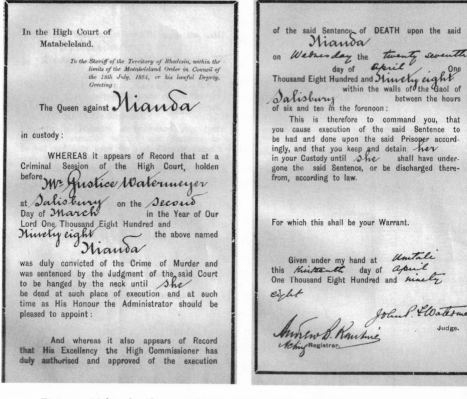

Figure 4. Nehanda-Charwe's death warrant, 1898. (NAZ/S. 2953)

had philosophical differences about the war. Those differences—along with British firepower—exacerbated the internal divisions on the African side, making it easier for imperial forces to make significant gains during the war. This assessment is also a departure from Terence Ranger's interpretation of African resistance as generally united against the British. Kaguvi surrendered, while Nehanda had to be captured; that reality, as we will see in chapter 7, was "forgotten" when the nationalist movement resuscitated those two heroes from the 1940s on.

The shrine the newspaper mentioned would have been one of the caves McMahon mentioned in his report as having been blasted in the Mazoe to show that "the white man" had no fear of her—or of African gods. The "numerous clientele" were the people Kenny had often mentioned in his reports, in colonial proprietary tone, complaining to his superior that Nehanda-Charwe was "keeping a lot of my natives from surrendering" for fear of what she might do.[55] In a way, this statement from the newspaper report undoes Nehanda-Charwe's self-defense that she did not rule or hold power in her district. The newspaper report concluded its assessment of Nehanda-Charwe's behavior in prison by noting that "the stoical effrontery and natural romancing powers she exhibited during the trial, and with which she is largely gifted were no doubt the best qualifications in the eyes of the Mashonas, for the profession she had adopted."[56] That is a description of a self-assured woman, not of a victim. If anything, the description given of Kaguvi-Gumboreshumba in the same paper (and in the court records during his own trial) is that of a man who turned on his values and principles. As the *Rhodesia Herald* reporter concluded of Kaguvi, "His appearance greatly belied the great power which it was said he held over the minds of his deluded and superstitious followers" (see fig. 5).

In figure 5—more believable as her image than figure 3 because other prisoners were photographed with the same wall as background—Charwe appears more self-possessed. By contrast, Gumboreshumba looks nervous and on edge. She appears defiant, while he seems diffident, and fearful too. Father Francis Richartz's chaplain's report of Nehanda-Charwe's last days in prison describes a woman of agency and self-possession rather than a victim. It was that report that nationalists would later treasure as evidence of Nehanda-Charwe's anti-imperialism. As Richartz reported, "Kakubi, the leader of the Mashona rebels was sentenced to death. With him were condemned Neanda, the famous 'prophetess' of the Mazoe and eleven others."[57] After the execution dates for Charwe and Gumboreshumba were changed several times, they were finally fixed for April 27 and 29, 1898, respectively. Richartz, as the prison chaplain, was charged with ministering to the prisoners, including telling them the grim news of their execution dates and "preparing" their souls for the next world—Catholic style.[58] The prisoners hoped against hope that their sentences would be commuted to life imprisonment or lesser sentences. Between March 2 and April 27, Richartz traveled between his mission base at Chishawasha, about twenty miles northeast of Salisbury, and the gaol, in the center of the township. He went to instruct prisoners in Catholic catechism and prepare them for baptism so that they could die like the prisoner who, Christian tradition says, converted at the last minute as he hung alongside Jesus of Nazareth. It was a rather bizarre way of spreading the gospel, but one seemingly effective in getting more converts from

Figure 5. Nehanda-Charwe and Kaguvi-Gumboreshumba awaiting execution. (NAZ/Image 172)

among the prisoners and especially those Africans on the outside who heard the horrendous news of their spiritual leaders, holders of important politico-religious office in the Shona religious system, made trifling by the colonial judicial system. Where were the ancestors in all this?, they must have asked.

Father Richartz's report told of visiting Nehanda-Charwe in the last days of her life. "For good reasons, I abstained from visiting Neanda till the day of execution was at hand, as she would have given much trouble to the warders by her hysterics and restlessness," Richartz wrote. However, to his surprise, when he did visit her the night before her execution, "she listened willingly and quietly." That Richartz abstained from visiting Nehanda-Charwe until the day before her execution is quite telling. Even though there is little other evidence of what transpired in those last weeks and days of her life, from Richartz's report we get a sense that she did not take her condemnation and situation without a fight. Her "hysterics and restlessness" were protests and lamentations.

When Richartz finally had to tell her news of her execution the next morning, he waited until the evening "in order to avoid a scene." Probably knowing that the delivery of such grisly news would not be easy, Richartz took someone along to help him deliver the news: Victor, an African convert and catechist. *However, when in the evening about 6 o'clock I saw her again and in the presence of Victor, who tried his best to persuade her to listen to me, told her that she had to die the next morning [April 27], she began to behave like a mad woman. She took her blankets and wished to leave the cell, and when told to remain and keep quiet, she refused and said she never would endure to be locked up. When I saw that nothing could be done with her I went away with Victor, and Neanda began to dance, to laugh and talk so that the warde[n]s were obliged to tie her hands and watch her continually, as she threatened to kill herself.*[59] The Nehanda-Charwe we encounter in Richartz's report was not psychiatrically "mad"—which I believe Richartz meant—but mad at what had happened to her, penned up in solitary confinement in a little cell and condemned to die a most inhumane and undignified death for a woman/person of her status—or for anyone, for that matter. That she could, and could not, sit and listen to Richartz proselytizing tells us that she was an engaged person, not a helpless victim mentally beaten down by men, European or African. Since Richartz did not record most of what she said to him when he spoke to her, we have to read between the lines of his descriptions to understand what was going on in that tormented woman's mind.[60]

At the beginning, Kaguvi acted much like Nehanda-Charwe each time Richartz visited him to proselytize, refusing to hear any of his Christian messages. However, that all changed once Kaguvi's daughter was brought in by Richartz. The daughter, Dziripi, was one of the Jesuits' new converts at Chishawasha Mission, and Richartz brought her as an insider who could potentially convince her own father of the "good news" of Christ Jesus that the Catholic priest was bringing to him.[61] Of her, Richartz wrote: *As Dziribi, Kakubi's daughter, one of our school-girls, wanted to see her father before his death, I asked for permission for her from the acting Magistrate, Mr. Bayley, and called her to town on the Tuesday. She arrived in the afternoon with her sister, Likande, and I went with them and our native Christian boy, Victor, to the gaol and had a conversation with Kakubi, who had given me in the morning some hope of changing his mind, when he should see his child. The conversation with Kakubi, during which Victor and Dziribi did their best to induce him to yield and listen to my instruction and receive baptism, had the good result that Kakubi promised to do as they asked.* Once Kaguvi agreed to conversion, Richartz increased the time he devoted to Kaguvi, heaping him with praises of what a "good man" he had become before his death. Kaguvi did get baptized just before his execution and was given the name Dismas. We do not know what Nehanda-Charwe told Richartz each time he tried to convert her, other than that each time, including the morning of her execution, when he "tried to bring her to a better frame of mind, she refused, called for her people and wanted to go back to her own country—the Mazoe—and die there."[62] Nehanda-Charwe was certainly a self-possessed woman in control of her mind and body, but she also seems not to have been the fiery anti-imperialist nationalist imagination turned her into two generations later.

Executing Nehanda, Resurrecting Nyamhita: Ancestral Revivals and Colonial Complicities

Charwe wokwa Hwata, medium of Nehanda in the Mazoe valley, was executed by hanging in the Salisbury jail, the site of today's Central Police Station in Harare. Her body was secretly buried by the colonial government on the grounds of the jail—which extended past today's busy intersection of Kenneth Kaunda and Samora Machel Avenues—so as to quell any shrine buildup. On April 27, 1898, a woman and a history were buried; but a memory seed was sown, the seed of a mythical legend that was to fuel compliant and fierce nationalisms from the 1940s on. After the war and execution of the African leaders, the colonial government instructed its native commissioners to document all the clans and ethnic groups ("tribes") in the Mazoe District and throughout the colony. That process gave NCs unprecedented power and control over African lives, and that power applied to all sectors of society, including the appointment of chiefs, which historically had been the jurisdiction of spirit mediums. That corrupting patron-client relationship between colonizer and colonized would define African politics in the colonial period and beyond.

In his April 1898 Yearly Report, E. T. Kenny, the NC for Mazoe District, wrote that his district was quieter after the war. He told the chief native commissioner that he had been out and about in the district collecting guns; he had already collected three thousand guns and anticipated collecting upwards of ten thousand by the time the exercise was completed.[63] The fact that he was able to collect that many guns gives credence to the memories of the men who remembered surrendering their weapons, the lynchings, and the general brutality of the frontier war (see chapters 5 and 6). Along with collecting guns, Kenny was busy restructuring the political and social landscape for Africans, keeping an eye out for someone who would make a good chief. It did not matter whether that person had the right to inherit the title or had the leadership qualities; what mattered was that the appointed chief do the NC's bidding to suit the colonial machinery. The Hwata people (of Charwe) was one of those whose chief had "died in the Salisbury Gaol," while others had died during the war. Interestingly, Kenny's whole nineteen-page handwritten report does not mention Charwe by name, not even once. It is as though Kenny, the British (South Africa Company's) boot on the ground, wanted to erase Charwe's and Nehanda's names from history and from memory in the Mazoe valley.

Things might have remained that way but for a crisis that occurred in the Mazoe District in 1906 with the appearance of a woman claiming to be the new Nehanda medium. Her given name was Mativirira. But unlike other mediums before her, including the recently executed Charwe, who had chosen Nehanda as their name and office title, Mativirira chose the name Nyamhita, the name of the original Nehanda (see chapter 1). Her appearance immediately came to the attention of the CNC and the local NC, as she allegedly incited people to slaughter or destroy their pigs so that the government could not collect any taxes on Africans' livestock. The CNC traveled from Salisbury to the district on a fact-finding mission at the end of 1906 but was unable to establish any facts on the matter. He then instructed Kenny, the local NC, to conduct an investigation on Mativirira, the events leading to the destruction of the pigs, the people involved, and African attitudes toward this new Nehanda/Nyamhita. Failing to intervene when another "Nehanda" emerged eight years after Charwe was hanged was a chance the CNC was not willing to take. Kenny was happy to oblige his boss.

"Sir," Kenny's letter to the CNC began. "In reference to your visit in regard to the destroying of pigs by the Natives. I have since made full enquiry into the matter, and although no proof can be obtained, I am

firmly of the belief at present that the woman Nyamita has been instru-
mental in the destruction of those pigs."[64] He went on to detail how at
some homesteads he had found a wholesale slaughter of pigs, evidenced
by high piles of dried pork. The worst of it was that the "kill-the-pigs
rumor" not only had affected the southern part of the district but had
spread to the northern part, which was serious, as it evoked scenes from
the war less than a decade earlier. It was not only that the Africans had
heeded the call to slaughter their pigs to subvert the colonial government's tax-collection efforts but also the specter of a Nehanda who had
the ear and support of the "influential natives in this district" that rattled
the CNC and the NC. By Kenny's judgment, based on the "amount of
grass stamped down, and the tracks made by that gathering," the crowd
at Mativirira's must have been very large. The people of Mazoe (north
and south) had gathered around Mativirira as the new medium of the
spirit of Nehanda/Nyamhita, the spirit of land fertility and rain.

The Africans who had gathered there obviously cherished the memory
of Charwe, and this new medium of Nehanda offered an opportunity to
hold a public *bira* (ceremony) for rain and perhaps covertly invoke the
spirits of those executed at the end of the war. The people may have believed that the spirits of the recent dead had turned into *ngozi* and were
wandering around causing the drought that was plaguing the area at the
time (1906–7). They spent three days at her homestead, dancing and
praying for rain, but the new medium was not satisfied and said that "the
spirit [of Nehanda] would not respond to their pleas owing to insufficient
offerings being made [to her, Mativirira]. Therefore, until the same offerings as were usually made to the late Nyanda [Charwe] were made to her,
and . . . unless Bazingwa, wife of the current Chief Chidamba, and lately
the principal attendant of the late Nyanda, joined her [as aide and atten-
dant], she [Mativirira] could not assist them" in any way.[65] The idea that
the new Nehanda medium was demanding the same homage, privileges,
and service accorded her predecessor, Charwe, is provocative. It suggests
that Nehandaship had become a powerful political tool coveted by ambitious women, who sought it for themselves in what had clearly become a
male-dominated African political structure. It also shows mediumship as
a human influenced institution claiming divine origin.

It did not help that the colonial government reinforced African patriarchy with its own version of European patriarchal rule, taking over the
appointments of chiefs, one of the mediums' major erstwhile duties and

raisons d'être. Sure, there were male mediums; dynastic founders were generally remembered as male, but the few female mediums of ordinary and royal spirits (*mhondoro*) held powerful positions in private families and among the larger public. Mativirira's demand of the same treatment as that accorded her predecessor, Charwe, suggests the power of the office of the Nehanda medium. More importantly, she wanted to perpetuate that office as it had been when Charwe was alive, demanding that she be assisted by the same woman who had been Charwe's principal aide. By incorporating Charwe's entourage, Mativirira wanted to legitimize her own claim to the power of the office of Nehanda mediumship and perhaps covertly keep the memory of Charwe alive, even though she preferred the name of the original Nehanda, Nyamhita. The fact that the colonial government was still nervous about the emergence of yet another Nehanda medium in the Mazowe affirms the power of the ethnic memory of the spirit among the Shona and its most recent medium at the turn of the century, Charwe. Kenny, as the resident NC, was well aware of the power not only of the memory of Charwe but also of the spirit of Nehanda over the people of Mazowe and central Mashonaland, living life as a conquered people in a historical script that had gone horribly wrong.

As should be evident by now, Charwe's lived and remembered life presented, and presents, a historical paradox: on the one hand, she was an elite woman who did business with the Europeans, including Pollard, before they permanently settled; on the other, she was a spirit medium ambivalent about African chances of winning the war against European firepower. Even with that knowledge, she seems to have fully immersed herself in the war, casting her lot with those keen on driving the (white) settlers off their land. After the war, the Hwata people, Charwe's dynasty, were without leaders, as many had been executed in 1898. The combination of the shock and awe of British frontier war plus the execution of significant religious, political, and social leaders in the community left a terrible power vacuum. Many young people who were orphaned by the war, including some of Charwe's own children, turned to the nearby Catholic mission of Chishawasha. However, going to the mission station did not mean forgetting one's history—or parents. For example, Charwe's eldest daughter, Makandipeyi, while at Chishawasha Mission used to have "people come and visit her [and] they would sit in a circle while she talked to them; she tried to keep the memory of her mother and her mission alive, because she would often cry. The second of Charwe's daughters, however, refused to come to the Mission because she was anti-Catholic."[66] The memory of Charwe was feared by the colonial bureaucracy, while it was variously guarded and rejected by Africans in Mazowe and surrounding areas. Remembrances of the 1896–97 war meant different things to the colonizer and the colonized, so that the Mazowe valley remained a site of contested memory, as each side remembered its own version.[67]

Kenny's fact-finding mission about the new woman medium and the incident of the slaughtered pigs signified undercurrents of resistance. His meeting of chiefs at Chiweshe's homestead turned out to be a hearing that included Mativirira herself. At that meeting, Kenny wrote to the CNC, "I explained to those present that I had been instructed by you to meet them and to ascertain from them as to why they had killed their pigs, as the crime of spreading such rumors could be a very serious one."[68] As it turned out, Kenny "could not get no information from the natives"; in fact, they told him that they had killed the pigs because they were "infected with mange." Unconvinced, he threatened them with the authority of his office, telling the African leaders that "it was for their own good that I was endeavoring to get at the truth of the affair." Even that did not yield any information, leading him to wonder if it was "the woman, Nyamita's" presence that produced what he perceived as denial of the guilt of that woman—and their own participation. Even though there was no evidence and no witnesses willing to testify against her at the meeting, Kenny was "more than ever of the opinion that her influence—especially among the elder people—is very considerable, and in time the matter at present before us will be traced to her."

Unwilling to accept silences, evasions, and outright denials, Kenny decided on a divide-and-rule strategy of meeting a smaller circle of about six men, including, "Mutumba, Bushu, Kamtaku, Masarirambi, as well as the Paramounts Chiweshe and Hwata," in whose jurisdictions the largest numbers of pigs had been slaughtered. Kenny wrote down their statements in what reads like a little kangaroo court, as each person said that he had heard from Such-and-Such, a native from the Salisbury district, who had told him that his pigs were going to be taxed. It was obvious that most people preferred to literally have their pork rather than give it to the government in the form of livestock tax, as they did for their other animals, like cattle and dogs. None of the statements even remotely gestured toward the new Nehanda medium; in fact, the only statements that made full reference to her were those made by two men closest to the history of Charwe: Hwata and Chiweshe.

In his testimony, Chiweshe said: *I am Paramount Chief of the tribe known as Chiweshwi [sic], and about a month ago, I was sent for by Nyamita, a native named Mandonzo of Wata's came to call me. He came saying that Wata was complaining of the dry weather. Wata said when we arrived there. We shall go to the Mondoro (Nyamita) and find out why we have had no rain. On arrival at Nyamita's we stated our case, but got no satisfaction from her, the Mondoro. The headmen Gamanya, Munyawiri, Chipunga, his brother Wata, Shutu, and the representatives of Kamteku, Masarirambi, and Chiriseri were present at this meeting as well as a very large gathering of younger people. Before leaving after a three day stay, Nyamita said: "Why do you allow the Mazweti [Madzviti, "invaders" or "foreigners"] to take all the riches that belong to Nyanda." Nyamita has inherited the spirit, when the spirit enters her she is Nyanda. We do not like using the name because Nyamita asked us not to do so, this woman's real name is Matibirira, and she is daughter of the late Shutu.* That sideshow, especially Chiweshe's testimony, confirmed all of Kenny's suspicions about the "lying native," leading him to conclude in his dispatch to the CNC that special attention should be paid to Chiweshe's testimony, for "we must ask who the Madzviti are, certainly not their old enemy the Matabele. Undoubtedly, this, if said, was meant for the government." Kenny was alarmed at the emergence of a new Nehanda.

For Kenny, it was important that the CNC (and the government) not ignore the fact that Chiweshe had evaded or been instructed not to use the name Nehanda. In Kenny's view, "this evasion is on account of Nyanda's connection with the late rebellion. In a great many cases no doubt the so called 'Mondoros' confine themselves to rain-making, but in this case when so prominent a name as 'Nyanda,' or Nyanda's Spirit is inherited by one, it is quite wrong, in my opinion, to assume that it may not become a power, not to be too lightly dealt with." Kenny may have been the quintessential proprietary colonial, talking of "my natives" and claiming to know their minds. Yet one cannot ignore the voices of the African men who testified to Kenny, especially Chiweshe and Hwata, who were family and historically closest to the memory of Charwe but supplied the most information. Confronted by a new Nehanda, Mativirira, and the history of Charwe's central role as a Nehanda in the 1896–97 war in their own district, the men chose to lean on history as water under the bridge rather than on the new memory that had bloomed in their midst in the person of Mativirira. Kenny's letter to the CNC in which he quoted Chiweshe at length did not include a quotation from Hwata's testimony. Instead, Kenny used it to draw conclusions that confirmed his own suspicions and prejudices about the spirit of Nehanda, which he thought had died or disappeared among the people of the Mazoe valley with the death of Charwe.

Hwata, whose testimony to Kenny confirmed Chiweshe's testimony, spoke with the authority of one who had the expertise and bloodline to ascertain whether Mativirira was a genuine Nehanda medium or a charlatan. As he told it, *I am a paramount chief in the Mazoe district. I know the woman Nyamita. I have visited her on different occasions for the purposes of praying for rain. She is supposed, to us, to have inherited the name of Nyanda or Nyanda's power of making rain. I visited her one or two months ago, she was not successful in producing rain. I presented her at the last meeting with a piece of limbo [cloth], as an offering for her spirit. I do not believe in her powers. I sent for Chiweshwi [sic] to come to the last meeting as I had got a message from Nyamita through Shutu to attend. They asked me to send for Chiweshwi, and said as many people as possible were to appear. A very large gathering, did eventually arrive. We stayed at her huts, dancing for three days. She gave us no satisfaction. The spirit did not enter her. I saw Nyamita go into a trance, but she did not tell us anything.*[69] The vigorous exercise of memory with which the new Nehanda came onto the scene, or at least to the NCs' attention, is quite telling of how the people of the Mazowe valley saw their district as a site of memory.

The fact that Mativirira chose Nyamhita, rather than Nehanda (Nyanda), for her official name reminds one of the names Catholic popes choose for their papacy, now with a Benedict XVI after John Paul II. They disrupt history and yet remember an important continuity in the history of the Catholic Church. Mativirira (as we saw earlier) wanted to be accorded the same rights and privileges that went with the office of the Nehanda, including the entourage. She wanted people, including the Hwata (chief and people), to recognize her as a "true" Nehanda, though she chose Nyamita rather than Nehanda. Invoking the name of the "original" Nehanda, Nyamhita, meant that Mativirira could claim legitimacy of autochthony that reached beyond her immediate predecessor, Charwe. Invoking a deeper past—and continuity with that past—was Mativirira's (and perhaps the Mazowe people's) way of signifying to the colonial government that although it might have conquered and executed Charwe, it had not conquered the female spirit of the land, Nehanda, now manifest through another woman.

As we saw in chapter 1, the "original" Nehanda was what was called a *pinga nyika* or *binga pasi*, a ritualized virgin who participated in a founding act that occurred once in a people's history and dynasty, an incestuous act with her brother, in order to lay claim to the new land they had inherited from their father, who had died before they had reached the "promised land," as it were. That the original Nyamhita was an active political personality, commanded authority, and had her own territory illustrates how Mativirira was recasting the place of a Nehanda medium in a colonial space whose overlords were no longer other Africans but people deemed so alien that she had to reach far back, to before Portuguese or Arab contact, to claim deeper autochthony in the colony—a history that the white settlers could not certainly claim. Thus, Mativirira's presence rubbed salt into the wounds of people like Hwata and Chiweshe, for rather than standing by her, they—Hwata especially—cast her as a kind of charlatan out to extort wealth from the local people in the name of Nehanda. It could also be that Hwata was trying to break with the tradition of appeasing the Nehanda and her medium with gifts, such as the cloth, which was a historical throwback to the time of the Mutapas, when fine cloth brought in by the Portuguese from the sixteenth century on was reserved for royals and, after their death, for their mediums. After all, the mediums offered the dead their bodies so that the dead could relive a life they could no longer live. When the medium was in a trance, she or he became the dead ancestor, who could demand royal treatment and respect for the body that she or he came through to meet the living. On the other hand, the men could have been jealous of those women mediums, who commanded not only Africans' attention but now that of the colonial rulers as well.

Ironically, Hwata's testimony against Mativirira invoked Kaguvi's betrayal of Charwe at the trial, as we saw in the previous section. Kaguvi hoped for a more lenient sentence and testified that it was "Nehanda who had started the rebellion." The way Mativirira's story was handled also mirrored how Charwe's arrest and trial had (once) been handled by the colonial judicial system. Both women said little in their own defense (or it was not recorded). Instead, colonial authority and the African male authority generally adjudicated African women's voices and place in society. Emasculated African men reported what they thought of the women, and the European men recorded it; the African women have a looming silent presence.

Tellingly, the office of the CNC in Salisbury responded to Kenny's dispatch and testimonies with great satisfaction at a job well done. It instructed Kenny to warn Nyamhita Mativirira that she was courting danger and to relocate her to a place where she could be under constant surveillance. Kenny was also to tell the chiefs, again, that the "people are foolish to be led to destroy their animals by such stories, and that when the government wishes to make a tax, they are always told of it a long time before they are required to pay."[70] It seems not to have occurred to the colonial administration that the people deeply resented what they considered unfair taxation without fair representation and that they had fought a bitter war in 1896–97 to register their dissatisfaction with things colonial, including taxation. Instead of adopting a win-them-with-honey postwar policy toward the Africans, the colonial administration seems to have drawn a line in the sands of history to demarcate the losers and winners. The losers were to do as the winners said; the memory that mattered in building a new colony or nation was that of the winners; and crossing those invented lines in the sand could and did have serious consequences for the Africans.

Concomitant with the new Nehanda-Mativirira saga were other land deals negotiated and struck in the Mazoe between Africans and Europeans, complicating the "them and us" versions of history. William Johnston, on behalf of the Salvation Army Mission, entered into a lease agreement with the headman Chiripanyanga for the establishment of a mission at Chiripanyanga's village in the Mazowe District.[71] That the Salvation Army was able to secure a long-term lease to build a mission in the Mazoe in 1907 was significant as a contestation of postwar memory in that district and in the colony in general. In 1891 the Salvation Army had secured land in the Mazoe valley to set up a mission run by one Edward Cass and his family. Cass had been killed during the war in the Mazoe in 1896 and was remembered (at first mostly by the settler community) as a man who had given his life not only for the good word but for the British Empire as well. News of his death even made the major newspapers in London, which carried the stories of casualties in the war in Matabeleland and Mashonaland, including the notation "Mazoe

District—Edward Cass, Salvation Army Farm; James Dickinson, mining commissioner; William Faull, bricklayer. Missing in Mazoe—Pollard, Thomas, Salthouse, Hodges, Boks, and Flanasan."[72] That the Salvation Army's presence increased right along with the memory of its slain missionary, Cass, just as the memory of Charwe, medium of Nehanda, was receding shows how much parallel memory was exercised, even by the missionaries. We also see how some Africans cast their lot with the new world order of colonial rule and Christianity.[73]

Significant for the triumph of British colonial history over African war histories and memories in the Mazoe in 1907 was that by year's end the CNC was satisfied that he had quelled any dissent in the district through verbal intimidation and the power of the state to arrest anyone who disturbed the peace. Most of the African chiefs, for their part, had shown their loyalty to the new world order by cooperating with Kenny and doing as he told them. Satisfied with most of the Mazoe chiefs' performance, the CNC wrote to Kenny about the Badges for Native Chiefs, a kind of loyalty program for chiefs who had proved themselves since the 1896–97 war, and especially during the Mativirira crisis. The chiefs had shown themselves to be committed and loyal subjects of the British colonial government. For that loyalty, the CNC instructed Kenny to immediately issue or return badges to "Chiweshe, Wata, Bushu, Mutumba, Makope, and Chipadzi, and retain in your Office for Negomo until he proves himself deserving of a badge. Inform him of this and the reason thereof."[74] The men the CNC afforded badges were not unlike the men on Carrington's list of famous men deserving imperial medals during and after the 1896–97 wars.

The CNC in Salisbury and the local Mazoe NC had, with the stroke of a pen, used the memory of the war to reconfigure African power and the chain of command in the colony's "Native Reserves." The Africans, it was made clear, could only act as the CNC and the NC dictated, with little deviation. The people had to be told that the government, and not their old chiefs or spirit mediums, was the new powerbroker. He who issued the badge called the shots, as it were; one was a citizen, the others subjects. Ironically, the chiefs who were later remembered as African "traditional" authority were those appointed by the colonial government rather than the ones with the historical title and claim to land, the ones who had a longer memory of belonging to a particular place than those handpicked by the colonial bureaucracy. In that patriarchal and colonial scenario, assertive women—and female spirit mediums, no less—did not belong; they were to be broken in like young farm animals. Settler history and memory had triumphed as the history of Charwe, medium of Nehanda was driven out of the public eye. As Mativirira was put under NC surveillance with the leading African men's approval, it seemed that Charwe's memory had been stamped out. But for how long?

As this chapter demonstrates, the frontier wars of 1896–97 laid the foundation for the settler memory in the making of Rhodesia, with the key figure, Nehanda-Charwe, slowly fading from view owing to colonial surveillance and the nature of the surviving evidence. The history charted in this chapter and the previous one provides a historical context for understanding the past from which cultural and political nationalists cherry-picked historical memories they liked, memories that became foundational material for nation building. Lastly, this chapter in particular shows the deeply gendered nature of colonial (in)justice, which not only disrupted African societies but also created racialized parallel memories of colonial triumph and victimhood. It also shows how African men colluded with the colonial state at women's expense. That gendered response to colonialism by Africans and the racial binary of memory was to define much of the colony's history, separating citizens' ideas of the past from their belonging together in the present.

3 Remembering Rhodes, Commemorating Occupation, and Selling Memories Abroad

As the sun set on life as it had been known by most Africans up to that point, European settlers made way for their own ancestors and their "mediums" in the new colony. In addition to the ancestors that had made the British Empire mighty, the settlers focused on new ancestors who had made occupation and settlement in Southern Rhodesia possible. Of those, none was greater than Cecil John Rhodes in South Africa and the two colonies that came to bear his name, Northern and Southern Rhodesia (today's Zambia and Zimbabwe). It was Southern Rhodesia, however, that captured Rhodes's heart, and it was there that he chose his final resting place, in the Matobo Hills (sometimes spelled Matopo or Matoppos). Matobo, a beautiful landscape of solid granite hills, balancing rocks, and valleys, was a long-settled and long-contested ordinary and sacred space for successive African societies that had made it their home and/or place of worship in the long and recent past. Each society left material and nonmaterial markers of presence and ownership, as evidenced by the rock art, the marked springs, the shrines of talking rocks, royal burial caves, hunting grounds, agricultural lands, and leisure space.[1]

Unlike in the previous two chapters, each of which provides some historical background and both African and settler perspectives, beginning in this chapter I discuss African and settler memories in separate chapters, though issues relating to the other inevitably emerge and merge in all the chapters. In this chapter, then, I focus on settler experiences at home (in Southern Rhodesia) and abroad (in the United States and the United Kingdom). I use three examples to showcase the uses of history to remember and forget the colony's European settlement, wars, and conquest—especially the men who made it possible. The chapter poignantly shows that the history and memory of Rhodesia had investors beyond (what I call) entitled colonials—the British. The making and memory of Rhodesia was an investment made by (most) people of European descent in many parts of the world. For though it was a British colony, with many British settlers, other Europeans (or people of European descent from elsewhere) settled there too, shaping its color-coded history and memory.[2]

The first case focuses on "national" holidays in the colony, especially "Occupation Day." Apart from Christian holidays, Southern Rhodesia's high holy days on the calendar were Rhodes Day (the first Monday in July), Founders Day (first Tuesday in July), and Occupation Day (September 12). These holy days were commemorated from the late nineteenth century in very small ceremonies that became elaborate over time.[3] Thus, Occupation Day is especially illustrative of the gradual development of white nationalism in Rhodesia from the early days of British settlement in the colony.

The second case is about the emergence of a foreign archive devoted to the British conquest of Southern Africa. It was a collection by an American testimony seeker turned collector-archivist, Howell Wright. His search for settler testimony started as a hobby and slowly became a large-scale operation, fortuitously coinciding with the first official celebration of Occupation Day in 1930. This second case study is also important theoretically because it contests Ricoeur's analysis of history and epistemology, especially its three stages—"documentary phase, explanation/understanding, and the historian's representation."[4] Ricoeur theorized those stages with a focus on history as made by the socially visible, the "big men," and not necessarily by the "little people." In other words, Ricoeur's model of the "operationalization of history," which later serves the making of memory, works better if it is applied to our understanding of history as made by and of big men (like the colonial founders Rhodes, Beit, and Jameson). The operationalization of history also assumed that the collection and preservation of the archive happened immediately after the historical events, yet as we see in the case of the American archive illustrated here, the three phases were turned around or sideways, especially when applied to the "little men" of empire. Many of the ordinary participants of imperial conquest in Southern Rhodesia gave testimony to their experiences only forty to fifty years after the fact, a reality often seen as the province of "preliterate" cultures. In Wright's collection, we see how oral testimony turned into written narratives as settlers documented invented identities of belonging to Rhodesia—as Rhodesian.

The chapter closes with a different kind of memory contestation, a forgetful memory that simultaneously sought to preserve by selling inherited memories of empire. It was one woman's attempt to sell her deceased husband's collection of Rhodesiana to Howell Wright, the American collector, in what may or may not have been a case of trying to keep body and soul together as German bombs shelled London in the early 1940s. The collection was that of Lieutenant Colonel Hugh Marshall Hole, the author (and editor) of the influential, if biased, *Reports of the Native Disturbances in Rhodesia, 1896–97*, discussed in chapter 2, reports that shaped colonial policy long after the war. Marshall Hole (hereafter Hole) also published two influential histories of Rhodesia, some of whose primary sources were in his own private collection. It was that collection that his widow wanted to sell, and it brought great anxiety to the Government Archives of Rhodesia (GAR), which felt entitled to the collection for free or for a token fee. The tension around Hole's archive is illustrative of the fickleness of memory keeping, especially by those who inherit, rather than live through, the historical experience (being) preserved in the archives. It also shows the gendered tensions of colonial memory and archiving a past not representative of the (female) self. If the narrative in the second and third case studies seems to shift its focus to Wright, the American, and Mary Marshall-Hole, in London, rather than staying focused on settler Rhodesians in the colony, that is my intention. The stories of Wright and Marshall-Hole show that being Rhodesian was more than a national identity for settlers. It was also an ideological identity for those who believed in Rhodes's imperial ideology as laid out in his spoken and written ideas; after all, not all Marxists were (or are) Prussian/German.

Remembering Rhodes, Celebrating Empire

Rhodes's choice of Matobo Hills as his burial space and as a future "national" burial ground for all (settler/white) Rhodesians, who would have served their country with honor, was a final act of inscribing new ancestors onto a long-inhabited landscape as though it had been an empty space all along. "The tomb of Cecil Rhodes in the Matoppos," remembered one of his "pioneers" in 1937, "is hewn out of solid rock. Visitors from all parts of the world travel thither to spend a reverent hour beside the tomb and to gaze in awed wonder at the indescribable beauty." Most of those visitors included Rhodes scholars from around the world. On the same hill was a monument to the memory of the Wilson Patrol, wiped out in Shangani.[5] Atop the hill was an inscription that served as a reminder to all: "This is consecrated ground and is reserved as a burial place for all time for those deserving well of their country."[6] By setting the standard for the suppression and/or erasure of African societies' real, imagined, and invented founding histories, Rhodes's choice of final resting place and settler national shrine legitimized "the heritage of founding violence."[7] More importantly, his burial in the Matobo Hills meant the obscuring of the landscape as a sacred African space and royal burial ground, with the most recent royal person buried there being the Ndebele kingdom/nation founder, Mzilikazi.

Rhodes's choice of the Matobo Hills as his burial site and the absurd idea that solid granite be carved for his remains—by cheap African labor—set a new standard for founding rights and memories. His associates' acquiescence to the idea meant that in most colonial circles in that period in Southern Africa, Rhodes had become a kind of deity in the British Empire (even before his death). "The influence of Rhodes upon the minds of Rhodesians is very remarkable, and real," stated H. Wilson Fox, also a former "pioneer," whose own connection to Rhodesia dated from 1894—after the key dates of 1890 and 1893.[8] Fox was memorializing Rhodes as an invited guest speaker at a dinner hosted by the Royal African Society in London in June 1915—with no Africans present. He was asked to shed light on why Rhodesia (meaning its white, especially male population) was not doing more for the war (World War I) effort. Fox made the case for Rhodesia, arguing that pulling more whites out of the colony for the war effort would cripple it, as the Africans would have no supervision and all colonial efforts would come to naught, as settler society was still relatively new and small. For though Rhodesia was the youngest colony in the empire, Fox said, it had pulled its weight and "won its way to a position of public estimation." For that reason, Rhodesia should not be asked to give more to the war effort than it was already giving to the empire, Fox emphasized. Still imbued by the spirit of its "great founder," Rhodesia was still giving, and it was going to give in the future, building on the foundation laid by Rhodes in 1890 that all was for God, for country, and the empire. If Rhodes had been alive, Fox intimated, he would not have spared a penny from his deep pockets for the imperial war effort, and that was the spirit Rhodesians still carried. By Fox's telling, even in 1915 one would not have known that Rhodes had died more than a decade earlier, in 1902. "He is not merely a national hero, but a legendary hero. His memory is a great possession." Invoking the sacred, Fox emphasized "that his spirit pervades the land, and that influence radiating from his lonely grave in the Matopos tends to keep the country which bears his name in the paths of courage and patriotism."[9] He could not have been more hagiographic.

To most Rhodesians—such as ideological adherents of Rhodes's imperial ideology, as well as white settlers, for whom it was a national identity—Rhodes's memory was up there with the sacred. It was a memory that infused everyday colonial life and thought, including discussions, heated or otherwise, as each asked herself or himself, what would Rhodes have done or said? Not only did Rhodes's memory live in their minds and on their lips, but visits to his grave in the Matobo were "of the nature of pilgrimages."[10] Fox, as many other characters in this book attest, was not only talking about Rhodes the "great man"; he was also being nostalgic about a world that Rhodes and his (imagined) pioneers had made, often oblivious to a world they had destroyed.[11] Rhodes's men, or "my Boys," as he liked to call them, were defined as *(a) the pioneer and police forces organized to occupy and settle Mashonaland in 1890 commonly known as the 1890 Column that consisted of—(i) the Pioneer Corps commanded by Major Frank Johnson . . . ; and (ii) the British South Africa Police commanded by Colonel E. G. Pennefather . . . ; and (b) the military forces of the British South Africa Company commonly known as the 1893 Columns which in 1893 overthrew the Matabele and took part in the occupation of Matabeleland. Provided that any European persons, if any, who were members of any one or more of the said Columns but whose names do not appear in any of the lists, shall nevertheless for purposes of this Act be considered pioneers.*[12] For those men, the need to reminisce and wax nostalgic often meant that they were eager to share how they had "made" a colony, even as they lamented that no one seemed to appreciate the sacrifices they had made in doing so. Any opportunity to remind the greater British Empire—or the world, for that matter—that Rhodes was a great man, almost Jesus-like, and that the Pioneers were disciple-like men, gave the whole Rhodesian project not only a great aura of legitimacy but also a sense that to be Rhodesian was to belong to a great idea brought forth by a great man. The religious symbolism cannot be overstated. Rhodes often told his friends that he wanted to be, and would be, remembered for at least four thousand years.[13] Remembering Rhodes at the start of those "four thousand years" in Rhodesia meant that the myth of founding justified, if it did not transcend, the violence perpetrated during that founding.

Commemorating Occupation Day: The Early Years

Rhodes Day, Founders Day, and Occupation Day became sacred on the Southern Rhodesian calendar. However, over time Occupation Day came to hold a particular resonance, as it celebrated the pioneers who had settled in the colony and worked with the Chartered Company to build an industrial economy exploiting African land and labor. The first public sign of the importance of Occupation Day to settlers in Salisbury was a short notice published in the *Rhodesia Herald* on August 25, 1893: "A meeting of all Members of the Column will be held at Hatfield Hall, at five o'clock this Friday afternoon, to form a Committee for the purpose of arranging for the celebration of Occupation Day."[14] That first meeting seems to have been a success, for in the following year Occupation Day was "declared a Rhodesian public holiday," and it attracted more people each year.[15] The interesting aspect of the celebrations of that Rhodesian holiday in the early years—at least in its public (newspaper) reports—was the focus on the old country, on sports, and on entertainment rather than on any substantive discussion (or speeches) about what the day meant.

For example, the 1895 Occupation Day invitation advertised it as the "Gymkhana Club Meeting." On the day of the celebrations, the dignitaries included the former administrator and Rhodes confidant Leander S. Jameson, Colonel H. Rhodes (CJR's brother), and Judge Vintcent. Vintcent addressed the gathering as a guest and a representative of the Chartered Company administration. The settlers present were overjoyed by the presence of these dignitaries, and the *Rhodesia Herald* noted that "the event was not only the most successful of the series of O.D. dinners, but of dinners given in Salisbury, one of the best and happiest on record."[16] What is striking about the report of the "best and happiest" event on record is that it was printed in the section titled "Sports and Pastime." Obviously, those celebrating Occupation Day at the time were still, in the main, the same people who had participated in the expedition directly (in the columns) or as administrators. And this was before the 1896–97 war. To the celebrants, who had participated in the occupation mission in 1890, it was still present reality and not yet sacred memory, as it would become decades later when there were fewer survivors and their descendants turned history into a sacred memory. Such celebrations were slowly turning Europeans into Africans, even as they denied the presence of African autochthons through silence and derisively referring to them as "natives"—similar to flora and fauna, not humans with agency to migrate in search of better opportunities as the British had done.

By 1896 the tone of the advertisement for Occupation Day had subtly changed, as more people began to value a commemorative day focused on the "pioneers," many of whom had become large landowners and were pushing for a larger political voice in the colony administered by the Chartered Company, rather than the Colonial Office in London, as was the case with most colonies. The change in tone was significant, because 1896 was the year the war began, and Occupation Day paid tribute to a number of ordinary members of settler society instead of only to Rhodes and his close circle. Occupation Day thus legitimized the settlers' belonging—if only by "right of conquest," to borrow from Ricoeur. The 1896 invitation notice requested "all Members of the Pioneer Corps to attend a meeting to be held at the Commercial Hotel this (Wednesday) evening at 8:30, *for the purpose of considering the best means of celebrating the Sixth Anniversary of Occupation Day.*"[17] The subtle change in tone from previous years—and on the heels of the 1895 meeting, dubbed the best yet—forebode a change in mood in the colony. The most important change was the attention paid to the issue of "natives," a source of anxiety and tension between the Company and settlers. At that meeting, one of the most prominent settlers—William Harvey Brown, an American—spoke forcefully on the issue, stating that the Company practiced monopoly labor laws, which put the ordinary settler at a disadvantage. "If Mr. Brown does not consider himself a profound politician," the newspaper report about the meeting read, "it can at least be said for him, as the Spanish have it, that an ounce of mother's wit is worth a pound of clergy."[18] Brown expressed the sense of frustration most settlers felt toward the Company's administration of the colony, and especially its allocation of cheap labor in its (own) favor.

During that 1896 celebration other forms of difference also came to the fore. For example, the report about the event praised Brown's passionate speech, which was well received, but regretted that Brown was an American, "not an Englishman. Nevertheless, he is a good South African."[19] The muted tension over ethnic and national differences among the settlers is provocative and tells of the less-told gray history of white memory. As we will see, ethnic and national differences among settlers were often buried under the thin soil of whiteness common to settlers, but the differences sprouted thorns as class and regional differences threatened to rend that cohesion, such as it was. The construction of African life and history as "uncivilized," then, allowed settlers to take comfort in the thin veneer of racial superiority that justified colonial conquest. Celebrating conquest, while nurturing an emerging settler identity, was a way of maintaining a constant silence on "native" presence and subjugation at most of those celebrations. Sometimes, as we will see, Africans were acknowledged, but often their presence was largely excluded from the narratives of a young colony and a nation in the making.

The celebration of Occupation Day continued as a Gymkhana Club event, with sports, dances, and dinners, into the early twentieth century. It might have continued that way if not for some discontented voices that saw the marking of "sacred national" memory with sports and dances as a desecration of an important holiday—a violation of the spirit of patriotism. That discontent was captured exquisitely in a letter to the editor of the *Rhodesia Herald* on September 8, 1904. "Sir, allow me to draw your attention to the fact that the Anniversary of the Principal Day in the history of Rhodesia has been omitted from the list of Public Holidays," the letter began. "I refer to Occupation day, and to those of us, who have the true interests of the country at heart, I cannot but express it would be a reflection on our patriotism if we allowed the day to pass unnoticed." The author of the letter, who signed his name in capital letters as the LOYALIST, was affronted by the omission of an important date in "national" history. In the Loyalist's opinion, though it was too late to "right the wrong" of the forgotten holiday, something had to be done to remember the day. Those in authority, the Loyalist emphasized, "can rise to the occasion and although sports, dances, and dinners such as we have had in the past thirteen years may have to be dispensed with, the spirit of the day can be fully entered into and a determination formed that in future years the day should be kept in such a manner worthy of the tradition of all true British subjects." What seemed to irk the Loyalist the most was the nonchalant attitude of the settlers toward a momentous day not only in the history of Rhodesia but in the history of the British Empire. As he put it, "Today, Matebeleland and Mashonaland are only known as Rhodesia and there are many amongst us who formed the column which entered this portion of Rhodesia on September 12, 1890 and added another jewel to the diadem of the British Empire." He concluded his letter by reiterating that "such an event is worth commemorating and I trust that the Chamber of Commerce and those in authority will not allow such a blot to be placed on the annals of our history." The Loyalist's letter to the editor put a finger on the pulse of settler Rhodesia, for it raised important issues of memory, including some that became contentious as claims of belonging to the Pioneer Column (of 1890) rubbed against the "secondary" columns of the police as well as that of 1893, which attacked King Lobengula's Matebeleland.

The Loyalist's letter certainly struck a nerve, for in November of the same year, at a dinner held at the Commercial Hotel in Salisbury, the idea of forming Pioneer Associations was motioned and seconded by informal associations of volunteers and members of the administration. The dinner meeting, held for the first time in a public place and with administration officials in attendance, also captured the kind of nostalgia and reminiscing that was beginning to happen among pioneer settlers as the past was receding, some of them dying of old age, while others were immigrating to other parts of the empire. Telegrams sent by those who could not attend arrived from other parts of Rhodesia and elsewhere, with the one from Bulawayo (in Matebeleland) most capturing their spirit: "Patriots, Bulawayo: Greetings and Congratulations to Comrades of '90 and '93. We shall toast you tonight and wish you long life to continue the founder's great work. May our fervent patriotism be a constant aid to the welfare of our country."[20] Over and over, the telegrams invoked the comrades who had made the creation of Rhodesia possible in the good old days and the founder's dream, which had to be kept alive, not only through commemoration but through the pioneers and other European settlers living in the colony as entitled princes who had inherited land and a dream from their wealthy monarch father to be passed on to future generations. Starting in 1905, Occupation Day exercised the minds of those in authority as well as ordinary citizens, who began to see the value of the commemoration of that day—beyond the Gymkhana Club.

However, there were also dissenting voices. The dissent was not on behalf of the excluded Africans but a contestation of settler memory by other settlers. Key among the issues being contested were the date (September 12) and the part of the colony being commemorated by Occupation Day. Some believed the date itself was wrong, for it celebrated the raising of the Union Jack rather than the arrival of the column in what became Salisbury (September 11). The empiricists wanted September 11 to be the commemoration day, while the imperialists wanted September 12, and the imperialists won the day. The empiricists registered their discontent, along with the notion that 1890—and not 1893—was the important year to remember. The touchier subject, however, was whether to celebrate 1890 or 1893 in the entire colony. As one empiricist put it in a letter to the editor of the *Rhodesia Herald* on August 3, 1906, "Sir, I was sorry to see the report appearing in The Herald that Councilor Hughes has deemed it fit to introduce a motion for the re-instatement of Occupation Day as a public holiday." His discontent was that "September 12 is strictly the date of the Occupation of Mashonaland and could not be recognized in Matebeleland with any great cordiality." As he saw it, the return to September 12 was a "matter not to be allowed to go through without the amount of controversy it deserves." It is particularly significant that he signed his letter "Pre-Pioneer near Salisbury," participating in a pattern of telling pseudonyms common among writers of letters to the editor, especially those that bucked a popular trend among settlers in the colony.

Responses to the Pre-Pioneer's letter came in the form of two reports-cum-articles in the weekend edition of the paper the following week, presumably from the editors. That the newspaper had become more substantial demonstrated that the settler society was growing more confident about the colony and its place in the British Empire. The articles in the paper responded vigorously in support of the proposed reinstatement of Occupation Day as a "national" holiday, and especially of September 12, not September 11, as the day to commemorate. The issue of whether celebrating 1890 was enough for those that participated in 1893 was argued away with the statement that many of those who had participated in the 1890 occupation had also participated in the 1893 conquest and many had settled in Matebeleland. Thus, it would not matter to them which year was celebrated—1890 or 1893. As the first report reiterated, though the Pioneer Columns were "not the first whites to arrive in the country, they were the first armed force of any dimensions to strike a blow toward the establishment of civilization in the country."[21] The emphasis on colonial violence at the time is noteworthy, as up until that point settlers had taken pride in the fact, or more the fiction, that not a single British taxpayer penny had been spent in the occupation of Mashonaland. Therefore, in the minds of many in the colony the reinstatement of Occupation Day was desirable.

A consensus seemed to emerge on eliminating other holidays from the calendar, for example, Rhodes Day or Founders Day, but not Occupation Day. The reasoning was that the other holidays would inevitably be replaced—maybe not Rhodes Day but others of less significance to the majority.[22] The contestations over which holidays to keep and which to eliminate was also addressed in the second article, which was a report of the proceedings of a growing and increasingly powerful political and economic group in the colony: the landowners and farmers. According to that report, it was better to replace Founders Day—which marked the first group of people to cross a small river into the new colony—than to tamper with the two sacred holidays, Rhodes Day and Occupation Day. The latter holiday was even more worth preserving because "not only was it an historical day in the annals of the country, but also in the annals of the British Empire."[23]

Occupation Day went on to become a singular holiday on the Rhodesian calendar, as most residents and their children attended the events on Cecil Square (now Africa Unity Square) in ever larger numbers each year in Salisbury. By 1908 the celebrations had all the trappings of rituals and traditions so well theorized in different works and from different perspectives by, among others, Halbwachs, Vansina, Ranger, and Connerton. Celebrating Occupation Day was a way to distinguish European settlers from the autochthons and for settlers to remember racialized differences between themselves as citizens of the colony and the natives as subjects, to borrow from Mamdani.[24] The report of 1908 emphasized the ritualization of Occupation Day as though it were the most normal noncontested event in the history of the colony. This was significant because the numbers of pioneers were dwindling, and so it was important to expand the pool of those who could participate in organizing the event. In that regard, the issue of passing on the baton to the children of the pioneers became pressing. Those were the children who would inherit the land from their parents and continue a tradition that had seen much transformation from a little ceremony of comradely get-togethers to Gymkhana Club sports and dances and finally to an elaborate local and later national event that included all sectors of settler society.

At that 1908 commemoration the chairman of the Pioneers Association emphasized the importance of Occupation Day, saying that it was "for the little guests to learn the significance of the events of 1890 and fit themselves to play a part when their turn comes to set an example to another generation."[25] There were large numbers of children in attendance that year, as there were of adults, and it did not escape the chairman that it was an opportunity to emphasize the point of perpetuating the commemoration of that day of conquest. By targeting the children and their parents, the Pioneers Association was hinting to the Chartered Company, which until then had not officially participated in or organized the commemoration and celebration of those events, to get involved. It would seem that the Company regarded Occupation Day as a civic event of little economic significance to its shareholders. The commemoration of 1908 was also marked by a reported African presence normalized as a spectacle and in self-congratulation of the successes of the civilizing mission. The Africans noted in that year's commemoration and celebrations were children and youths, members of the Chishawasha (Mission School) Band, which had become a fixture. The band, the reporter noted, "arrived betimes in all the glory of their quaint uniforms and brass instruments, and lined up south of the flagstaff, round which most of the children and nearly all the adults assembled." Then as the flag was being hoisted "the Chishawasha Band gave us another demonstration of the truth of Kipling's lines: 'But you can't get away; / From the tune they play; / To the bloomin' old Flag overhead.'"[26] It is quite telling that the report did not say much else about the band or even individuals within the band about their service to the empire on Occupation Day. That Africans' presence at such colonial events was acknowledged but dismissed illuminates the tending of parallel gardens of national memory, which put settler history and presence at the center of each story of how the colony/country was founded. Is it any wonder that the young would grow up with such racialized ideas of their belonging (or not) in the country of their birth?

The celebration of the twenty-fifth anniversary of Occupation Day in 1915 marked a turning point both in the history of the event itself and in public relations between the Company/administration and the municipal government in Salisbury. According to the newspaper report, "The 25th anniversary of the occupation of Mashonaland was celebrated in accordance with custom by the hoisting of the flag at the masthead on Cecil Square. There was a large attendance, and for the first time, too, the Mayor of Salisbury, Mr. W. M. Epton, was present in his official capacity attired in the robes and chain of his office."[27] The excitement about the most important day on the colony's calendar finally receiving official recognition was palpable, twinned with the longing for even more recognition. The report expressed the disappointment that though the ceremony had been conducted with the usual simplicity, which had been impressive, "Occupation Day was not made the occasion for a more eloquent ceremony in which its significance, as an Imperial event, could be more fittingly touched upon for the benefit of the younger generation." The report went on to say that "many present felt that the anniversary could be enhanced by the simple statement of facts of the great expedition, and all it meant, and still means to the Empire." The sense of the inadequacy and/or lack of imperial recognition of the significance of that holiday to the British Empire is itself a fascinating sentiment, one that stayed with most Rhodesians right through the drama of November 1965, with the Unilateral Declaration of Independence (UDI) from the same British Empire.

What was also significant at the twenty-fifth anniversary was that the mayor of Salisbury, a newcomer, was quite impressed by the ceremony and proposed that an honor roll of all the occupying columns be placed in some prominent public space in the city. That suggestion turned the tables on him as one of the pioneers suggested that "instead of the mayor being a guest of the pioneers, it should be the other way around."[28] That statement prompted the mayor to suggest what he thought was a new idea, but it was one that had been debated before with traction. It was that the administration officially recognize Occupation Day as a national holiday. The BSAC was still determinedly running the colony like a business venture for its shareholders—though it was not profitable. The mayor promised to do everything in his power to make it a reality. By 1915 Occupation Day had given an otherwise ugly colonial history some charm, invoking nostalgia for the good old days among not only settlers but also ideological Rhodesians who lived abroad and wanted that history of occupation and violence—in the name of civilization—preserved for posterity. That story of ideological Rhodesians invested in Rhodes's imperial ideals was embodied in Howell Wright, an American who had yet to set foot in Southern Africa. It is to his story that we now turn.

Preserving Memories of Rhodes and the Occupation of Southern Africa Abroad

Apart from commemorating Occupation Day at home, (settler and ideological) Rhodesians got to wax nostalgic about their experiences, ideas, and memories of Rhodes, their founder, and of occupation through correspondence with one Howell Wright, of Cleveland, Ohio, and later Newtown, Connecticut. Selah Howell Wright was born in Swansea, Massachusetts, in 1882 to a clergyman and an unmentioned mother.[29] Wright was a quintessential ideological Rhodesian, born in an old British colony that was now an independent country but fervently believing in Rhodes's idea that the "Anglo-Saxon race" should unite and keep the British Empire and the world safe forever. Wright's story is important because it reminds us that though cultural and political nationalists often wanted a "pure" nation founding uncontaminated by Others, often influential outsiders shaped a nation's idea of itself in unforeseen but welcomed ways.

A Yale alumnus, class of 1906, Howell Wright, like most North Americans of European descent, was not immune to what the anthropologist Renato Rosaldo termed "imperialist nostalgia."[30] Those people who often "enjoyed the elegance of manners governing relations of dominance and subordination between the 'races'" in the colonies as depicted in colonial literature (and much later in cinema) were keen on preserving the memory of the white man's burden in Southern Africa.[31] Thus, where others saw imperialism as the domination of some cultures by others, nostalgic imperialists like Wright perceived colonialism as "innocent and pure."[32] Wright believed that imperial innocence and purity were worth preserving for posterity, not only in physical monuments but also in ephemeral "sites of memory," such as archival collections. Reinscribing colonial conquest through reminiscences about the founder in pioneer narratives was imperative to him and other imperialists. Archival nostalgia was a way of exercising the memory of (fictive) progenitors who had bequeathed their Anglo-Saxon heirs colonies in Southern Africa.[33]

The Wright story is significant here because of the ways in which it tells us how important diasporas were (and are) in the construction of colonial and postcolonial memory in Africa and elsewhere. Often arriving out of the blue, Wright's letters were a great and pleasant surprise to those who received them. Wright not only wanted colonial pen pals but was after firsthand accounts of the occupation and colonization of Rhodesia and of nineteenth-century British South Africa from those who had directly participated in the events.[34] Many who received Wright's self-introductory letters were, in the words of one recipient, "curious to know why you should be so interested in the South African affairs."[35] Wright's initial interest in the subject of British imperialism in Southern Africa was sparked when he wrote a high-school essay on Rhodes in the year of his death, 1902. After that exercise, the idea of an archive bloomed in his young mind, and with encouragement from like-minded people, he started his collection as a hobby in the 1920s, focusing on the British Empire's expansion in Southern Africa. Wright evolved from hobbyist to collector, a memory maker and keeper.[36] He was a great admirer of the (mainly British) imperial personalities, especially Rhodes and his closest associates. He also had a particularly soft spot for the "Pioneer Corps which entered Mashonaland in 1890." In almost all of his letters of self-introduction, he told the "old pioneers" (or their surviving families) that he was keen to keep the memory of that imperial history alive because the "occupation and settlement of what is now Rhodesia is one of the outstanding events in the history of the British Empire."[37]

What Wright lacked in pioneer experience or familial connection to Southern Africa, he made up for by doing enough research to interest his intended audience, which in turn produced a lot of memories for his collection. To sweeten the deal and elicit even more donations of memorabilia for his collection, Wright emphasized that he was not keeping the material for himself but was amassing it for donation to the library at Yale University, a university named "after its generous benefactor Elihu Yale, one time English Colonial Official in India, governor of Fort St. George, Madras, and now buried in Wrexham, Wales."[38] Wright, a "far off American citizen deeply interested in the British Commonwealth and the life and work of its South African Pioneers,"[39] jogged the memories of many when he wrote them requesting material. To his mind, getting those pioneers to preserve the memory of colonialism meant that imperial history would also be preserved in that former colony the United States for future American students. American students, he contended, needed to know about Rhodes's "ideals for Anglo-American Union," as they were the future of that union. Indeed, one of the original ideas for the famed Rhodes scholarships was to make the recipients members of a secret society of "Anglo-Saxon reunion" in space and time, modeled on the Society of Jesus (the Jesuits).[40] As Wright put it, the pioneers of Rhodesia and South Africa were "citizens of that Great Democracy, the British Empire, and I am a citizen of another Democracy, the U.S. of A."[41] His description of his growing collection and his call for more pioneers was published in newspapers in the Rhodesias and South Africa, bringing out more people than he might have ever contacted by means of the snowball methodology that had served him well up until that point. Wright was evidently participating in the making of Rhodesian memory from abroad, gathering physical and ephemeral memory from an ageing population that was feeling increasingly unappreciated, as new settlers did not often feel gratitude toward individuals, but to the British Empire more broadly.

Ironically, Wright and his reminiscing pioneers in the 1930s and 1940s often gloried in imperialism, all the while forgetting that imperialism had brought about the demise and/or irrevocable hammer that transformed colonized societies. By 1938 they often remarked that Adolf Hitler was a great threat to European peace with likely global consequences, yet they did not seem to grasp the fact that millions of people were under the boot of British (and western European) colonial rule in much of Africa and elsewhere. What was more, African Americans and "non-white" peoples living in that "other great democracy, the U.S.A.," lived under the legalized terror of Jim Crow (and lynchings, especially in the South). While imperialists—and their fans—rightly saw the late 1930s as frightening because of the rise of fascism personified by Adolf Hitler and Benito Mussolini, it did not translate to an empathetic understanding of the impact of European colonialism on African and Other peoples around the world. If anything, Wright and his pioneer pals reminded one another that in the British Empire white English-speaking peoples needed to realize Rhodes's dream of Anglo-American union, as "they came from the same stock which had pioneered the whole world and upon our friendship and cooperation depends the safety of the whole world."[42] That paradox of horror—looming totalitarianism in Europe, while Europeans were the cause of horror in others' lives—was a classic case of remembering forgetfully. Many Rhodesians, settlers and others, who were happy to oblige people like Wright with memories of imperial conquest seemed oblivious to a terror that they too had unleashed on Other peoples—minus the scandal, scale, and efficiency of Hitler's Nazi Germany.

Roger W. Adcock was one of the South Africans/Rhodesians who was greatly surprised and pleased by Wright's correspondence and requests for Rhodesian and South African pioneer memories and memorabilia. Born in Bethulie, in South Africa's then Orange Free State Republic (now the Free State Province), in 1867, Adcock took pride in having been born into a pioneer family: "My grandfather was Christopher Adcock who landed with the settlers in Algoa Bay, Port Elizabeth, in 1820. My father, William Adcock, was at Kimberley [diamond] diggings in 1869."[43] Roger grew up to become an active "pioneer" himself in South Africa, Bechuanaland (Botswana), and Rhodesia (Zimbabwe). In his first letter, he waxed nostalgic, saying how pleased he "was to get your welcome letter and to find out how interested you are in our memorable march to Mashonaland in 1890." He wrote in some detail of what he remembered about that journey north into what became Mashonaland and the men involved. After the occupation mission was accomplished and the corps disbanded, Adcock and five others had joined together and formed a company they called the Excelsior Syndicate to prospect for mineral wealth. Their company, like many, however, did not get off the ground because the equivalents of the Witwatersrand gold fields or the diamond fields of Kimberley were not found in the colony at that time. The few companies that made it were controlled by the BSAC, which administered the colony until 1923. Although their company did not make them rich, for Adcock it was enough that he and his comrades had been part of a "great" historical event, which they would recall with pride and would relate to anyone willing to listen.

The occasion to exercise the memory of a colonial moment that Wright accorded men like Adcock meant that they (and their families) cherished reunions of occupation and conquests organized in Rhodesia to commemorate Occupation Day with little guilt about the violence that had accompanied the process of colonization. Reunions, for example, were opportunities for those (mostly) men—from near and far—to travel back to Southern Rhodesia and relive "those days," especially "that day" when the Union Jack was raised, guns were fired, and "God Save the Queen!" was chanted. Adcock reminisced wistfully to Wright about the 1930 reunion he had attended in Southern Rhodesia, which would "ever remain green in my memory. Just picture us, meeting again, some not having seen or heard of each other since that memorable day, 12th September, 1890."[44] As he remembered it, the BSAC "and the people of Rhodesia and Salisbury treated us with such kindness. All our expenses were paid, 1st [class] return railway tickets and 1 pound per day for expenses were allowed." The reunion was not only about great commemorative events; it also made "those of us that are left look forward to the 50th anniversary in 1940." The trouble, of course, was that as time went by, the number of pioneers "proper" shrank, and the importance of shifting from history to memory became even more pronounced.

As the numbers declined, it became obvious that the performance of history needed to be passed on to the next generation, who acted on behalf of their male progenitors. As Paul Connerton observed, "All rituals, no matter how venerable the ancestry claimed for them, have to be [re]invented at some point, [for] over the historical span in which they remain in existence they are susceptible to a change in their meaning."[45] Howell Wright, as we have seen, actively participated in the making of Rhodesia settler memory even before setting foot in the colony or the region. Wright's story reminds us that outsiders sometimes exerted tremendous influence, shaping national memory and ideas about what was important for the privileged to remember. Cherished outsiders like Wright were important to white nationalists because they affirmed their imagine-nation and reminded them of the importance of keeping British settler traditions and white supremacy so as to pass them on to future generations.

Going Native: Apportioning the Land for the "Segregation of the Races"

The 1930 Occupation Day commemorations that Adcock remembered were the first described as "Official celebrations in connection with the Fortieth Anniversary of the Occupation of Mashonaland in 1890." According to the *Rhodesia Herald* report, *Many of the 1890 Pioneers who will be the guests on this historic occasion have already arrived and the remainders are due to reach Salisbury this morning. Yesterday there were many reunions between old comrades who had not seen each other for many years, and who, indeed, did not at first recognize each other, for as a number confessed, beards and advancing years made a disguise not easy to penetrate. There is no doubt that the opportunity to attend this Fortieth Anniversary is greatly appreciated by the Pioneers, and equally, the occasion has now taken a strong hold on the popular imagination.*[46] Occupation Day commemorations transformed the imagination of the (white settler) population into an embrace of its colonial history. It was especially poignant that the fortieth anniversary happened seven years after the 1922 referendum on having a responsible government rather than joining the Union of South Africa after the BSAC liquidated its interests in the colony. The 1930 commemorations, then, were legitimizing white settlers' autochthony claims too. As owners of the new colony/nation, Rhodesians could claim to have ancestors in and of the land to venerate and remember in what was now firmly a British colony destined to become a dominion, like Canada, Australia, New Zealand, or, indeed, the Union of South Africa.[47]

The unfortunate turn, of course, was that up until then, the term *Native* or *native* was used as both an identity marker and a derogatory term for the Africans in the colony. The native did not or could not share in that new (Rhodesian) identity and, in fact, designating the older autochthons as "Natives" and settlers as "Rhodesians" threw a monkey wrench into the whole colonial memory project of autochthony. The definition of a *Native* or *native* in Southern Rhodesia was "any person not of European descent who is a native of South Africa or Central." It did not seem to occur to those settlers to ask what would happen in the future to people of European descent born in southern and central Africa, people whose only "native" home would be Africa.[48] A. C. Jennings, the assistant director of native lands in Southern Rhodesia, reinforced that definition of *native* in 1935 when he wrote that "a Native is any member of the aboriginal tribes or races of Africa, or any person having the blood of such tribes or races, living among and after the manner of Natives. This means that colored people and Asiatics, etc., do not fall into this category."[49] The mix and confusion of biology, ethnicity, nationality, and culture is telling of the attempts to exclusively define the colony as belonging to settlers, whose recent ancestors' arrival was being marked by the fortieth-anniversary celebrations. The problem with such definitions of "the Native," of course, was that a generation or so later, as settlers became "native," as born there over several generations, it became more difficult to claim autochthony while denying being a "native of Rhodesia." Were settlers Europeans or Africans? When, if at all, did they cease to be European? When, if at all, did they become African? Those questions did not seem to permeate the consciousness of many as the first official commemorative events of Occupation Day in 1930 revived the mostly imagined history of those who had founded the colony.[50]

The first official public commemorative events of colonialism and occupation in 1930, I would argue, were no mere coincidence. Though couched in the language that all "races" belonged to Southern Rhodesia, the first official public commemoration celebrated white settlers in a colony they believed their ancestors had bequeathed to them. I base this claim on important legislation passed in the Rhodesian parliament that same year: the Land Apportionment Act. The legislation, based on a report by the Land Commission, chaired by Sir William Morris Carter, in 1925, was designed for the "segregation of the races," following a precedent set by South Africa's Native Land Act of 1913. In its articulation, the legislation was to apportion land according to each "race's historical ability" to utilize it. As the then member of Parliament for Salisbury North, and later prime minister of Southern Rhodesia from 1933 to 1953, Godfrey Huggins, was to recall, "The passing of the Land Apportionment Act, 1930, was a definitive milestone in the history of Southern Rhodesia. It marked the first attempt in Southern Rhodesia to affect a measure of segregation as between the Europeans and Africans."[51] The "land issue" was to be one of the issues, if not *the* issue, at the heart of Zimbabwe's political, economic, and cultural crisis. The memory of the land issue is still ripe with emotion as it continues to press that country's people, its politics, and its economy. The Land Apportionment Act of 1930 also smoothed tensions among settlers, especially along class, ethnic, and nationality lines, that often came to the fore in the jockeying for power and position in the new colony.

The Land Apportionment Act and its implications, however, were not important to Adcock as he reminisced to Wright about the 1930 Rhodesian occupation commemorations. Rather, his great regret was that though the reunions and commemorations had been wonderful, there were "very few of us left of the original 200 of the Pioneer Corps under the direct command of Colonel Frank Johnson." Many had died in the ensuing decades. It saddened him, too, that with each passing year there were fewer and fewer men to reminisce with about the occupation and the colonization of the British Empire's youngest colony. What is more, his memory of those historical events still bore the class distinctions usually suppressed among settlers. That is, as we saw in the last section, the

Pioneers belonged to different groups, and there had been arguments over which column was being celebrated—the Pioneer Corps, the British South Africa Company Police Corps (BSACP), or the 1893 Matabele Column—before Occupation Day became a "national" holiday. How men had been organized in those corps was the dirty (public) secret among those commemorating Occupation Day. Basically, there was more equality among the members of the Pioneer Corps than there was among the members of the other columns, including the BSACP. That class distinction and hierarchy was important in the making of Rhodesia and unmasks the foundational myth of united imperialists that the settlers projected. While the participants in the historical events were still alive, the class distinctions continued to be a part of the commemoration of the events.

Members of the Pioneer Corps were the new nobility; all pioneers were the new landed gentry; and all whites were the "natural" rulers, the upper middle class of Rhodesian society that settler memory affirmed. It was therefore important that the Land Apportionment Act allow for that class system to take root, served by cheap African labor penned up in the now legal Native Reservations, also known as Native Reserves or Native Areas. The history and memory of the colony's founder and his pioneers triumphed at the expense of those whose sweat and undervalued labor had also built the colony that was being celebrated in 1930.[52] In most of the contemporary newspaper articles, few colonials referred to the radical change that had taken place in African societies.

Fractures in the Founding Narrative: Social Class in Occupation

For those who commemorated Occupation Day in 1930, the events brought a new energy to the colony; the commemorative events were an occasion for pomp and circumstance. As a news reporter put it, "There were many great hearty greetings between old friends and comrades, some of whom had not seen each other since the Column first marched into Rhodesia and occupied Mashonaland." The main ceremony was to be held on September 12, 1930, at 9:00 a.m. at Rhodes Statue (fig. 6), with the governor, Cecil Hunter Rodwell, "inspecting the parade of pioneers, the flag unfurled . . . , and 'Land of Hope and Glory' sung."[53] The pioneers, as honored guests, as well as members of the public, participated in many receptions and events, including the laying of wreaths

Figure 6. "12th September Occupation Day, 40th Anniversary, 1930" (HWC MS 565, Series II, box 32, "Photographs, 1892–1900, 1890 Expedition to Mashonaland")

Figure 7. "1890–1893 Pioneer Group. Presented by Major L. H. Symons, Rhodesian Pioneer, Member, British South Africa Company Police." Symons is seated third from left in the front row. Note the sole unnamed young girl or boy in the foreground. (HWC MS 565, Series I, box 22, folder 425)

at the graves of those who had not lived to see Salisbury and Rhodesia forty years after occupation.[54] One of those, mentioned by name, was Sister Mary Patrick Cosgrave, a Dominican nun who had led her band of (religious) sisters in nursing the sick pioneers as they marched north to what became Rhodesia.[55] The organizers also made sure that the public were informed that they would be "able to distinguish the members of the Pioneer Column by the rosettes all members will wear." The distinction between the Pioneer Corps and the police, the same one Adcock had emphasized to Wright, was also reiterated: "Both groups will wear red, white and blue rosettes, but those worn by the members of the Pioneer Corps will have blue streamers, and those of the Police will have red streamers." The other class marker was the type and number of war medals the Pioneers wore on that day, as shown in figure 7.

The differentiation between Pioneer Corps and police in 1930 exemplified how Rhodes originally designed the occupation groups, enlisting in the corps not only those from well-to-do families but also regular young men of no name or blue blood, to give his whole project legitimacy and support from the well connected.[56] Those who had been issued what turned out to be second-class tickets on the occupation train took their chances, buoyed by the prospect of land and gold north of the Limpopo River. However, some members of the police objected that distinctions were made between the two columns, as Howard Arnold, another of Wright's pioneer correspondents, remembered decades later. The class system, he wrote, had been set up by Rhodes and the BSAC right at the start. All those who registered in Rhodes's Pioneer Corps and police were, upon fulfillment of their duty to occupy Mashonaland (and later, all of Rhodesia), allowed to peg *a farm of 3,000 acres given unconditionally, as well as a right to peg out as many gold claims. A farm of 3,000 acres was also given to the Pioneer Police (and the right to peg gold claims) with the restriction that they should occupy the said farms within three years (a condition I consider most unfair) as they should also have been given unconditionally in the same way as the first contingent.*[57] Yet, despite that painful unequal history and his resentful memory thereof, Arnold delighted in being able to participate in the fortieth anniversary of Rhodesia's occupation. It was as if the commemorations had all but erased his resentment for being treated unfairly or unequally by those considered members of the Pioneer Corps "proper."

Arnold told Wright that at the commemorations, *I had the privilege*

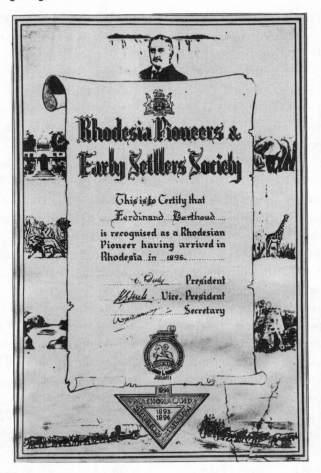

Figure 8. Pioneer membership certificate of Ferdinand Berthoud. Note the overlay of African and imperial symbols. At bottom left, for example, is Rhodes's grave, and at bottom right is the Great Zimbabwe. (HWC MS 565, Series I, box 1, folder 16)

with 90 other men belonging to the Pioneers, of attending the 40th anniversary of the occupation of Rhodesia. We received nothing but kindness from the Governor General down to the humblest citizen. They gave us a right royal time. I had the honor of leading our section (the Police) on the parade ground, and now I hear the government of Rhodesia intends conferring upon us the Freedom of the City of Salisbury.[58] The commemoration of the colony's founding reaffirmed the status of those who had taken the risk to go to Rhodesia and now belonged. They had formed exclusive Rhodesia

Pioneer and Early Settlers Societies, celebrating those occupation days before the BSAC made it its business to remember. Those societies issued certificates to members, certificates that came complete with imperial and native history imagined on one platform, as though it were the most natural thing to do, or an uncomplicated and uncontested part of the colony's history and heritage (fig. 8).

Imperialist Nostalgia Rubs against the White Man's Burden

Sometimes, though rarely, a different memory of what colonialism had done to the African autochthons came through in the whirlwind of celebrating things imperial, including Occupation Day. Some of the few settlers who had a different kind of memory of colonialism—of everyday life as well as of commemorative events—registered their sentiments in the same 1930 commemorative issue of the *Rhodesia Herald*. One such story was by a settler who identified himself only as an "Old Timer." The Old Timer's great regret about the forty years since formal colonialism was a different kind of nostalgia, the white-man's-burden kind, one that mourned the demise of *much of the native legendary history—of most absorbing interest to early Pioneers—[that was] sinking into the past and becoming lost. [It] is a thousand pities. Throughout the country there is a tendency to replace the old musical native-named places with modern names—"Barrapate" (the unclimb-able) is now Hillside, while Zenda (the roamer) has become Rhodesville. Salisbury district teems with interest for those who would learn the history of native life before the white man's invasion. Trees and rocks, hills and valleys carry names pregnant with meaning or relative to action of one tribe or another. The stream from the Cleveland Dam received the name of "Makonwe" (a rocky place); the Makubuzi River which runs between lower Hillside and Salisbury should be called M'kuwisi, meaning either the river which causes the rain to cease or the river from which water can be drawn.*[59] Accuracy of African names and their meanings aside, for now, what the Old Timer was actually wishing for was what he and his kind had destroyed in the name of civilization. That he chose the pseudonym Old Timer is itself telling, if not of his pioneer status, then perhaps of how unpopular the counternarrative to the memory of colonialism was among the white settler communities glorifying things imperial. Ironically, in his own writing the Old Timer demonstrated another classic case of "imperialist nostalgia that occurs alongside a peculiar sense of mission, the white man's burden, where civilized nations stand duty-bound to uplift so-called savage ones."[60] That kind of nostalgia had ruptured another's history, culture, and self, and yet the Old Timer longed for things to remain the same, especially "native life." It was a dagger to the heart of a very few to realize that in their bravado to occupy and colonize they had trampled on all, including the precious that was now gone or irrevocably changed.

For the Old Timer and people who thought like him, the downside of the advancement of Rhodesia was what would become of African histories, now overlaid with colonial history and culture. For the Old Timer, who had traveled and worked among Africans in the colony, it was disturbing to realize that colonials were busy dis-membering African history by naming the landscape after their own (European) ancestors and landscapes in the mother country or for the colony's founders and pioneers.[61] For example, the Old Timer was troubled that Salisbury had replaced the African name Harari: *The meaning of Harari as Salisbury Hill was called in days gone by, after a man who lived there, is buried in the past. From all accounts Harari was an outcast from his tribe, living alone with his family until the arrival of Mbani, who came with his people from the direction of Seke. His first act was to kill Harari. . . . Later came Chiweshe and his brother, Wata [of Nehanda-Charwe], with their families. They were related to the powerful Chief Nyashanu, of Charter district, who drove them from home because of Chiweshe's bad temper. History has it that he was a quarrelsome fellow, always fighting with his neighbors. On arrival at Harari they approached Mbani requesting permission to occupy a piece of his country, and they were allotted a site on the hill near "Dziwa-[ra]-sekwa" or the Laughing Pool, some ten miles from Salisbury on the present Gatooma Road. . . . Chiweshe and Wata were iron workers, smelters, smelting the ore dug from the hill near the pool and exchanging with their neighbors the implements manufactured for grain and produce. Every chief had the right to summon the entire tribe to assist at such time as his crops required attention. The right was called Zunde Washe [zunde ra She]. At this particular Zunde, everyone was summoned, including Chiweshe [who after getting drunk was chopping down crops instead of weeds, at which the chief Mbani got upset and attacked Chiweshe who in turn—with his own people—attacked Mbani who fled. The next day the fight continued and Mbani was routed].*[62] This rendition of African history is quite the example of imperial nostalgia, as it both tells a history that the pioneer celebrations were not telling and also plays into the kinds of stereotypes that made those commemorating Occupation Day thump their chests in self-congratulation. The Old Timer's focus on retelling mostly histories of conflict between and among Harare, Hwata, Chiweshe, and others reinforced stereotypes about Africans as savages, always at one another's throats and/or killing one another. It gave naysayers reason to argue that it was their duty to civilize the uncivilized.

The revelers shared the civilization sentiment through pictures of the fortieth anniversary and of Rhodesia's "progress." To the settlers, it was incumbent upon them to preserve the founder's memory and that of the pioneers who were fast disappearing with age. That revival of founding myths was also important for socializing new European immigrants and educating them about the history of the colony—its race hierarchies and relations—so that everyone would know their "proper" place in society.[63] The fortieth-anniversary commemoration affirmed that only the settlers had the place of honor as heirs of Rhodes, whose statue stood as the holy shrine around which the settlers gathered to commemorate occupation.

Selling Memories of Empire and Occupation Abroad

If the celebration of Occupation Day gave the impression that empire—though contested—was sacred to all, then this last case study gives us pause. It shows the complications of preserving the past when individual memory trumps collective memory. The story of Mary "Molly" Marshall Hole, the widow of Lieutenant Colonel Hugh Marshall Hole (whose credentials in Rhodesian history are illustrated in figure 9), is an example of less-told stories of individual ambivalence in participating in the social and collective practices of memory.[64] Hugh Marshall Hole was the quintessential imperialist and settler, and his archival collection is a precious relic from the colony's founding days. Molly's story, therefore, is a counterpoint to the male (settler) stories recounted here, stories of men assertively celebrating their participation in an imperial project.[65] Rather than writing herself as an individual into a social and collective memory that included her late husband, Molly was asserting her individual right to do what she wanted with a gift from the past that others perceived as a collective gift and right. Molly's case study gives us a female perspective on a predominantly male narrative that was commemorating and celebrating empire and colony. Her story reminds us that forgetting is the other side of the coin of memory. Molly's story is an example of the

Lt.-Colonel Hugh Marshall Hole, C.M.G., B.A.,
Member of the 1890 Pioneer Corps, B.S.A.Co.,
Private Secretary to the Administrator of Mashonaland,
Dr. L.S. Jameson,
One-time Secretary of the British South Africa Company,
Civil Commissioner at Bulawayo,
Author of "The Jameson Raid",
"The Making of Rhodesia", etc.
Presented to Yale University
April, 1938.

Figure 9. Hugh Marshall Hole's colonial resume and the Wright Collection's logo appear on the back of an autographed photograph that Hole gifted to the collection in 1938. The logo features Yale University's main library bordered by symbols of British colonization in Africa. (HWC MS 565, Series II, box 32)

rupture in national memory, when nationalists would have preferred one triumphant narrative supported by history's relics. Molly was forgetting Rhodesia while remembering her husband, even as everyone was anxious to remember the Rhodesia the pioneers brought—including Hugh Marshall Hole. She was the nationalists' nightmare, refusing the memory police's right to tell her how to preserve the past's remnants, which was her personal inheritance.

Lastly, Molly was by no means the most destitute of Rhodesian widows living on a government pension in the United Kingdom or in Rhodesia. By her telling, it was need, rather than greed, that drove her to sell her husband's precious material to a library or archive. Howell Wright and the Government Archives of Rhodesia were drawn into a bidding war between 1942 and 1946, when the collection was finally sold, only to have a final twist that fits a woman like Molly Marshall-Hole. She wanted not only to retain ownership of Hugh's collection of historical papers but also to control his legacy and memory, as Hugh had left Rhodesia on less than good terms with those in charge. Wright returns to the stage as an active Rhodesian, if only an ideological one, but his choices show us, again, how outsiders helped shape memory making in the colony. It was Wright's correspondence with Hugh Marshall Hole before he died in May 1941 that opened the door of contested individual and collective memory, and it was Molly who crossed the threshold, only to find that the business of memory was a complicated one. After Hugh died, and the respectful mourning period had passed, Molly lost no time in contacting Wright. Her correspondence with Wright demonstrates that she had been quite involved behind the scenes while Hugh was alive. If she had not written to Wright while her husband was alive, Molly had had enough access to Hugh's correspondence with Wright to know what the collector was after. More importantly, though she never explicitly stated it in her own letters to Wright, it is clear that she had had an input not only in what Hugh wrote to Howell but also in Hugh's own historical writings on Rhodesian history, including the colonial favorites, *The Making of Rhodesia* and *Old Rhodesia Days*. Molly was refusing nationalists—including bureaucratic ones—the right to be the sole heirs and executors of the past.

In her very first letter to Wright, Molly got right to business, softening it as the letter progressed: *I am sending you a list of my late husband's collection of "Rhodesiana," together with other papers,* her letter began. *Knowing your interest in such historical data, it occurs to me that you may wish to make an offer for the collection, although my husband also directed that I should offer them as well to the Government of Rhodesia. You will, I am sure, have been grieved to hear of Hugh's death last spring—he always enjoyed your letter so much, and I had also begun to think of you as a friend.*[66] Not only did she write about her late husband but she invoked firsthand knowledge of Rhodes—or his closest associates. Molly knew that Rhodes was important to Wright, who idolized him. By mentioning Rhodes in her letter, she hoped to whet Wright's appetite for Hugh's Rhodesiana collection. As she told it, *I was one of the small girls in the photo you have of Mr. Rhodes playing chess on a ship-board; and I have been left Hugh's sole executor. For some time I have been meaning to write to you, but continual war-work, added to the chaos created by Hugh's death, has prevented my doing so until now. Lately, I have been studying Mr. Rhodes's dream of what our two countries might accomplish together, and the wonderful way his ideas for us are working out. For this reason, I feel it would be equally according to the Rhodes tradition for these documents to be in either country.* Aware that she might come off as someone just out to make a quick profit, especially so soon after her husband's death, Molly concluded her letter by emphasizing that *it is my great regret that I am not in a position to make any sort of presentation. I have been left very badly off, and my Widow's Pension from the Rhodesian Government is thirty-six pounds a year.* Even though she knew Wright's address from Hugh's correspondence, Molly told Wright that she had gotten his address from "Mr. Frank Worthington who I know well." This, it appears, was Molly's way of letting Wright know that she had respectable male support in her quest to find a final home for Hugh's collection and get paid for it. Frank Worthington was himself a Rhodesian pioneer, a friend of Hugh's, and a former secretary of native affairs in Northern Rhodesia (Zambia), also under BSAC rule. He had married a wealthy woman, who died and left him well off.[67]

Howell Wright, the ever-enthusiastic and sensitive Rhodesian—in the ideological sense of *Rhodesian*—was always quick to respond to mail, paying close attention to his correspondents' needs and issues, which sometimes included sending medicine, books, and whatever else people needed or were willing to exchange with him for his collection. To Molly's first letter he responded with deepest condolences at the news of Hugh's passing; indeed, such occasions made his project seem all the more important, as human "sites of memory" were dying off faster than he could get to them and preserve them for posterity. Molly responded to Wright's letter on March 8, 1942—in duplicate as always—telling him that it was important that she lay out the situation with the "Rhodesian Documents," as the GAR wanted them and deemed them their first right. Also, not wanting to come off as sly, she told Wright that *Mr. Frank Worthington advised me not to part with these records of the old days for less than two thousand pounds, and has allowed me to quote him on this opinion. However, I personally feel that this value is on the high side, especially in these grim days. I perfectly understand your not wishing to appear to "bid against the Rhodesian Government," and for these reasons, I will say frankly that I wish to receive one thousand pounds for the collection. I shall state this figure also to the Government.*[68] Molly needed to make the Rhodesian government the second bidder because Hugh had intimated, though not in any of the documents in the collection, that he would give that government first preference. But Molly wanted more for the collection, and Wright was her lever for getting it. She also wanted to make sure that her husband would be remembered properly, by people she thought would care more. By invoking the names of Worthington and other respected and respectable colonial males, Molly was countering the Rhodesian archivist V. W. Miller's slanderous characterization of her as a despicable and greedy woman willing to sacrifice the sacred relics of the collective Rhodesian past for personal gain. Molly wanted to show that she was a respectable pioneer widow with respectable connections who was only asking what was fair and due to her—even if the male management of the GAR thought otherwise. She wanted both the financial compensation and proper memorialization of her husband, as his recognition meant that she would be remembered as a pioneer's wife.

The war bombings in London made Molly fear for her life, for the collection, and for her mother, who was deathly ill, all of which took a toll on her, occurring less than a year after her husband's passing. She wrote to Wright that if the Rhodesian government was not willing to pay the price she had named for Hugh's collection, Wright could consider the collection his. In fact, she told Wright that she had instructed her lawyers that if she died in the war, they were to retrieve the documents from a bank vault and process the transaction on her estate's behalf with him.[69] Most important in all that back and forth of letters, however, is that although she never said so, Molly's investment in the collection went beyond its being Hugh's, because she may have assisted in his historical writings; and as we shall see in chapter 4, pioneer women were to be seen not heard. The only suggestion of her possible uncompensated research work is a reference she made to research she did for Sir James McDonald, a Rhodes biographer: "I did the necessary research for McDonald, and have been lately working for him on another (in addition to my War work). . . . I have also acted as his literary agent all along, and the last edition of his 'Rhodes' is still selling very well."[70] Given this revelation, it is hard to imagine that she never did any work for or with Hugh. The question is why she did not explain to Wright why she had such an investment in earning something from the sale of the collection—apart from making sure that her late husband's papers would be put to good use.

The GAR officials were upset by Molly's decision to sell this national treasure to a "stranger" rather than donate it to the national archives. Selling Hugh's collection was akin to the desecration of an important, if ephemeral, site of memory. Hugh Marshall Hole had been a key figure in the colony's early administration (its history); now its existence and survival (its memory) depended on collections like his to validate the stories pioneers told. Selling such history was betraying its memory, the GAR officials reasoned. After the GAR wrote Molly rejecting her price for the collection as too high, she quickly wrote to Wright, saying that she would take his offer and would arrange to have the papers delivered to him through the American Embassy in London. As that letter went off to the United States, Wright received another from the national archivist in Salisbury, a Mr. V. W. Hiller, registering his disappointment that Yale would have the collection, instead of Rhodesia, as Hugh Marshall Hole would have wanted. "I saw a lot of the late Colonel Marshall Hole, and was well acquainted with his wishes regarding his MS collection, which I not only examined, but listed carefully in order that we should know precisely what would accrue to the Colony after his death," Hiller wrote. "I know that it was not his intention to bequeath the collection to the Colony, but we were to have first consideration. We could not compete when Yale outbid us by offering a thousand pounds." If Hiller had left it at that, the whole tale might not have gone against Molly later on. Instead, he concluded the letter by saying that in his opinion the collection was not worth a thousand pounds, "which far exceeded the value of the documents." As if feeling the sting of his own assessment, Hiller quickly said that his assessment did not mean that the collection had no value, nor would he refuse to accept copies for the GAR. He reminded Wright that as a collector himself, he knew that copies were not the same as the original.[71] Hiller was disappointed that an ephemeral but important site of memory had been lost to an "outsider" collector and repository. Hugh's collection told a unique history of the colony from its founding by one who had been present and witnessed the events that shaped the initial years of the colony, especially the war of 1896–97, producing a widely read report.[72] Hole's collection, therefore, caused an unspoken anxiety in the colony that was expressed by its archivist.

The twists and turns of that ephemeral site of memory would not have happened had Hugh left a written record of the value of the collection. On the other hand, even if he had, the value would have changed over time, and Molly would have had the right to a revaluation. The collection, then, became a site of contestation of the ownership of the history—and memory—of a colony. It also meant also that Wright began to lean more on a fellow male collector's assessment and expertise than on Molly's own assessment of the value of those records and her own assessors. When Wright did not respond to her letter of August 6, 1942, Molly wrote to him again on February 10, 1943. She obviously suspected that Wright, who wrote often and promptly unless when he was traveling or too pressed for time, was turning against her. Collecting the memories of Rhodesia was, after all, a hobby for Wright, and not his day job—and he was not a settler in Rhodesia. Molly's February letter was a reiteration of her August letter, in which she said she would give Wright the collection as soon as he could send the money and complete the transaction. Ever conscious of appearing like a woman too greedy, Molly tried to maintain a delicate balance: *I do not wish to appear to be in a rush, I realize you would probably like to have the Collection placed in American hands without great delay, and I should naturally not like to feel that I was no longer responsible for their safe keeping. If I should live until after this war, I should like, if possible, to come to your Country and see my Husband's papers safely housed in your Rhodes Museum.*[73]

Later that year, as Wright put pressure on her by intimating that the archivist had said the collection was overvalued, Molly clearly articulated why she thought the United States would be a better place for the collection: *I would like to make it very clear to you that I would far rather my husband's collection went to Yale where his documents would be safe for all time, and, which is most important, would be available to the students, rather than be hidden in a private collection, the ultimate fate of which no one can foresee.*[74] The irony, of course, is that Wright's collection was, in fact, the private collection that Molly feared so much. If the GAR had housed the collection, her husband's memory would have remained in the public domain, unlike at Yale, where it would be part of a private collection, in a private university, albeit accessible to the general public and American students, of course.[75]

Molly Marshall-Hole had rightly suspected that Wright was turning against her, as his letters suggested he wanted to withdraw from the deal altogether in deference to the GAR. In a male-gendered manner and showing his (ideological) Rhodesianness, Wright shared some of his Molly correspondence with Hiller, "in confidence, of course," yet he did not share with her what Hiller wrote. Upon reading her correspondence to Wright, Hiller wrote to Wright that he did not think Molly was "kindly disposed to the Archives! I am inclined to think that the story of the private collector is wishful thinking, and intended as bait."[76] When she wrote to ask Wright whether he was still interested in the collection, he responded that he was but said that he would not bid against the GAR. If the collection did not have any takers, he would acquire it. Molly wrote back, telling him that if he was still interested, she would refuse the offer she had received from an interested person in London and let Wright have the collection as originally agreed.[77]

By March 1944 the matter was nowhere near resolution, and Molly had clearly been outmaneuvered, as Wright—ever the diplomat—and Hiller were in cahoots, greatly reducing what she would have gotten for the collection. Both were men of means, with day jobs that paid well, and yet their behind-the-scenes conversation did not include what it meant for a woman of Molly's social class to find herself reduced to peddling her late husband's papers to make ends meet in expensive London. To Hiller's mind, he and Wright were of "the opinion that the lady had behaved shabbily; apparently has little regard for her late husband's wishes, and is obviously out to make all she can out of the collection." According to Hiller, Hugh had set the price at two hundred fifty pounds, though there was no written record of it. Hiller thought that if Molly had been so pressed for money, she should have "stated her position, the Government would have treated her generously in that matter, especially in view of her late husband's service to this country. As it is, she simply played one party off against the other, and it would now seem she has fallen between two stools."[78] Obviously Molly, in the manner of her gender, asked no more than she thought was fair, unlike Frank Worthington when he corresponded with Wright over the collection. Why women had to stoop to begging, while men were given a "right royal time," is itself telling of the making of colonial histories and their subsequent memories.[79] Molly was a colonial woman, and no angel, to be sure; however, that she had to resort to leaning on one of Rhodes's "Boys," Frank Worthington, is itself evocative of a world skewed toward men, in history and in memory. Molly was beginning to understand that Wright, though an American citizen, was an avid Rhodesian who would protect the colony's interests in its imperial history and memory rather than hers.

Molly would have lost her bid completely had she not turned to her "private collector," Frank Worthington. Wright had contacted Worthington with his usual Rhodesia pioneer memorabilia requests. Frank was the right sort of man for remembering Rhodesia, as Wright's letter had arrived just as he was getting ready to sail to South Africa on the *Drakensburg Castle.* He was going to "revisit all the places between Cape Town and the Zambezi which I used to know in the past," including "Johannesburg where I took part in the abortive Rising against the Dutch at the time of the Jameson Raid; the Matoppo Hills, where I found in the Matabeleland Rebelling and where CJR was buried; the Victoria Falls, which I was within the first 50 white men to see after Dr. Livingstone; the Barotse Valley, where I abolished slavery—and so on."[80] Glorying in and exaggerating the memory of the pioneer civilizing mission, Worthington did not let on that he and Molly were also in cahoots about Hugh's Rhodesiana collection. Instead, he informed Wright that he had "bought it from [Hugh's] widow" hoping that eventually the collection would make it to Yale, as "Southern Rhodesia shall never have them for I cannot forgive them the mean way in which the authorities treated the Colonel and, after his death, his widow."[81] As we saw earlier, Molly had been much more diplomatic, and had Wright read between the lines, he would have figured out that Worthington was acting on Molly's behalf, but it took a couple more exchanges to get to that point, prompting Hiller to remark in an August 1946 letter that "between Mrs. Hole and Worthington, they seem determined to keep us on tenterhooks, all the time using Yale as a kind of lever." "I often wonder," he concluded, "what will be the fate of these papers. The late Col. Marshall-Hole would not, I am sure, have approved of his widow's action."[82] What Hiller neglected to mention was that Hugh had had a run-in with the BSAC, for which he had once worked, suing the company over land claims, and so at his death he had had a rather frayed relationship with Southern Rhodesia.[83] Hiller had become the fundamentalist gatekeeper of history, and its memory's police.

Worthington had heard about the twists and turns from Molly. He understood the situation to be that of two men playing a woman who was trying to get a fair deal on what was obviously precious historical material—otherwise why would the men want it? The material documented not only the life of the late colonel but also the famed early days that the 1930 celebrations had opened up, so that the archivist saw it as his personal and national duty to repatriate any and every piece of paper that documented the founding of a colony of which he was so obviously proud to be a part. On the other hand, Worthington, the distant colonial who also felt it his right to make demands of and from the colony's history—and its memory—did not relent in his letters to Wright. In each letter he repeated his now fully imagined colonial history, a history that did exist, but of which only snapshot images remained. To Wright's offer to pay only three hundred pounds for Molly's (Hugh's) collection, Worthington expressed disappointment, arguing that it was a unique collection and that, most importantly, "whatever I ultimately get for [the papers] will be passed on to Mrs. Marshall-Hole. I do not aim to make a penny for myself. I bought them from her as she was left poorly off. Marshall-Hole was a great friend of mine. Anything I can do to help his widow, I must do, even to selling the collection item by item in the open market."[84] Worthington did not say how much he had paid for the collection, and there is no written record of it, leaving us to wonder whether he made more or less money for Molly after all. He concluded his letter by asking Wright to raise his offer to at least five hundred pounds, arguing that Wright would recover the costs when he made copies for the GAR.

Wright finally contracted a Mr. J. A. Gray, the editor of the weekly newspaper *South Africa*, to be his agent and to act on his behalf in obtaining, paying for, and delivering the collection to the American Embassy in London.[85] The embassy, in turn, was to hand over the collection to the Southern Rhodesian High Commission in London, which would then send the collection to Southern Rhodesia. Wright had covertly bought the collection on behalf of Southern Rhodesia, all the while leading Worthington (and Molly) to believe he was buying it for Yale University. Wright was reimbursed by Southern Rhodesia, which also sent him microfilms and photocopies of the Hole Collection. Wright and Worthington settled on four hundred seventy-five pounds, down from the original two thousand pounds that Worthington had originally suggested to Molly. According to Worthington, he immediately passed the money on to Molly, though there is no letter of acknowledgment from Molly. In fact, her name might have faded completely from the lively correspondence and pioneer reminiscing, especially from Worthington, who had just returned from Southern Africa, where "the Old Man" (Rhodes) was sorely missed, but life was good for the settler. What brought Molly—or her name, at least—back into the conversation was a letter Hiller wrote to Wright informing him that "in comparing the list of material which we took over from Worthington with the list I secured from Marshall Hole in 1937, items 14 to 22 are missing. Could you tell me who has them?

If they are in Worthington's possession perhaps you would endeavor to secure them for us. If they are with you, could you let us have photostats, please?"[86]

The missing documents became a bone of contention, as all involved claimed they did not have them. What is more, Molly had died in the meantime. As her solicitors told Worthington, "Every possible avenue of enquiry about the missing papers has been exhausted. Neither we nor the residuary legatee has destroyed any papers, except purely personal unimportant correspondence which came into our possession on Mrs. Marshall-Hole's death." The solicitors told Worthington that they had re-examined the papers and that the missing documents had not been in Molly's possession at the time of her (undated) death. They asked him to let Yale University know that the missing documents were not among the now late Mrs. Marshall-Hole's papers.[87] Worthington forwarded the solicitor's letter to Wright, informing him that the whereabouts of the missing documents was a mystery to him.[88] The missing documents highlight the fact that Molly or someone had withheld key relics that validated the colonial making of Rhodesia. The documents' absence was like an invalidation of the settlers' occupation narratives and their reason for being in Rhodesia.

The archives in Southern Rhodesia conceded that the documents were gone and suggested that they might one day appear on the market or in some other collection. More importantly, the Rhodesians regretted that Wright's "kindness in helping this Department obtain the collection should have resulted in the necessity for those embarrassing enquiries, and we appreciate the difficulty of the situation in which you were placed."[89] Wright, the stealth go-between, was caught in a rather unpleasant place, and any attempt to put pressure on Worthington did not yield anything else, for by December 1948 he was living in Northern Rhodesia and said he was in no rush to return "in view of the condition of things in England." He ended on a note that suggested his transaction with Wright was based on the list he had given to Gray, not on Molly's or even Hugh's list, so that he could not say what had happened to the collection. As he wrote to Wright, "To the best of my knowledge and belief, Mrs. Marshall-Hole left many friends but no relatives; at any rate, I know of no relatives nor were any of her friends my friends. Of one thing I can assure you, that all the papers she handed to me I, in turn, handed to Mr. Gray."[90] So there it was: Olive Mary Marshall-Hole, wife of

Hugh Marshall Hole, one of the most involved colonialists in the making of Southern Rhodesia and an avid colonial historian, died, not celebrating her husband's Rhodesian life, but selling off whatever history—and memory thereof—there was to make ends meet and/or to spite the Rhodesian settlers who had mistreated herself and her husband. Settler Rhodesians wanted to turn Hugh Marshall Hole's experiences of making a colony (history) into a viable, if intangible, commodity (memory) that future generations of white children would look to for validation of their autochthony. Be that as it may, settler society did continue to celebrate Pioneer Day, Occupation Day, and other colonial holidays that boosted the self-confidence of the settlers.

This chapter highlights the slow but steady importance of the past to settlers, especially (white) nationalists, who felt duty bound by history to remember the founder of Rhodesia—Rhodes—and its new aristocracy—the Pioneers—even as they tried to smooth over the differences threatening the creation of a "solid" Rhodesian identity. The importance of white supremacy in a black country was finally affirmed by the 1930 Land Apportionment Act, which served as a basis for plugging the fissures that threatened to undo settler memory and, therefore, the colony's unity. This chapter also highlights the deliberate cultivation of a Rhodesian identity through the celebration of Occupation Day, a historical event that would have faded from view but for the activism of at first cultural nationalists, who celebrated it as a "pastime" activity, only to have it grow in stature such that by 1930 it had turned into a full-fledged settler national holiday.

This chapter also shows that celebrating things imperial did not require permanent residency—or even citizenship—in Rhodesia. Howell Wright's story reminds us of Ricoeur's observation that memory is a verb; it is exercised by the living as a way to validate their reason for living. Wright's story also reminds us that even though nationalists often liked narratives that showed only them or their forefathers as the main actors in the history of the nation, they were often willing to bend the rules for outsiders who did not threaten their mythmaking. Lastly, Molly's story reminds us that not everyone was willing to remember the past the way nationalists wanted them to. Molly, by refusing to donate or even sell her late husband's archival collection for a small fee to the GAR, was contesting nationalists' right to dictate how the past was preserved and where.

Molly's (or someone else's) withdrawing the relics of the past that legitimated nationalists' memories reminds us that the process of national
memory making is always fraught with unexpected needs that throw the
avid nationalists off. On the other hand, where people like Molly had
even some historical relics to sell, African history was scattered to the
wind, some of it collected by interested colonials—like the Old Timer—
who published their findings in the *Native Affairs Department Annual*
(*NADA*), itself an artifact of history and memory waiting to be studied.
The making of the colony into a nation, then, was based on uneven remembrances of founding moments and uneven endowments of history's
artifacts—an unevenness that still haunts the country.

4 A Country Fit for White People
The Power of the Dead
in Mazoe Settler Memory

One of the major impacts of the official celebrations of Occupation Day in 1930 was that they turned settlers in smaller towns and rural areas into avid, if amateur, historians eager to preserve a past they had not cared about collectively before then. Once the official commemorations of 1930 captured the imaginations of recent and more settled (colonial) immigrants, communities that had not done so already turned to finding their local pioneer histories for heroes to commemorate. Thus, the 1930 commemorations turned a once very small local event in Salisbury into a national event for settlers; the commemorations, in turn, reinforced the notion that the pioneers and settlers had been "courageous men and women, inspired by the spirit of their great leader [Rhodes, to extend] the British Empire, establishing more and still more homes" in the colonies.[1] The settler community of the Mazoe was one such community that turned a national event into a local one; the settlers turned generalized white nationalism into a particularized sentiment as they dug up long-neglected local heroes of the pioneer days. Mazowe is highlighted again in this book on the history and memory of making Rhodesia because it was Nehanda-Charwe's district; it was also the district that earned Colonel Alderson, Captain McMahon, and Native Commissioner Nesbitt war medals.[2] However, local remembering in the Mazoe was not about those imperial officers (who had returned to Britain) but about local unsung heroes.

Much like the story of the men and women in Wright's collection encountered in the previous chapter, the story of local heroes in Mazoe analyzed in this chapter was mostly told (by the survivors) as oral history, a politicized oral memory—and only later written down for posterity. In all its incarnations, the history of the Mazoe Relief, or the

Mazoe Incident, as it was later called, went from history to memory to invention, with those processes sometimes happening simultaneously, especially the farther away in time the story was told or written. Here, the historian-anthropologist Jan Vansina's methodology of testing oral traditions for meaning and accuracy vis-à-vis other primary sources is very useful as narratives like those of how the Mazoe settler community escaped annihilation bring to light the pioneer clichés that the Mazoe story acquired.[3] I highlight the contested nature of testimony, especially when the dead are glorified, even as the living's testimony entangles the imagined (dead) heroes. After all, as we saw in chapter 2, only some men made Carrington's list and were awarded imperial and local medals for their valor in the same 1896–97 wars; others were knocked off the list, or dis-remembered altogether. In the Mazoe of the colonists, we see how societies often selectively choose from history convenient clichés and "safe" icons, those that do not provoke too much controversy about the sacredness of the past and its (untarnished) dead, who could be held up as symbols of the highest levels of self-sacrifice in a settler society craving heroes to legitimize its autochthony.[4]

Competing Memories about Three White Women, Two Telegraphists, and a Bitter Survivor

The celebrated feats of valor by settler men and women of Mazoe were highlighted whenever romantic pioneer adventure stories were told about the making of colonial Rhodesia. The Mazoe story made it into just about any memoir or retelling of the making of Rhodesia, including the *Pioneer Number*, a supplement to the *Rhodesia Herald* about the official Occupation Day celebrations in 1930.[5] One W. S. Honey wrote an article remembering the two telegraphists, John Lionel Blakiston and Thomas George Routledge, and the Mazoe Incident in a way that embellished the historical facts, inviting letters to the editor that pointedly or not so pointedly said his version was "wrong." Blakiston and Routledge were employees of the Transcontinental Telegraph Company in the colony when they met their fate. They had attempted to send a telegram to nearby Salisbury for rescue support for a band of settlers trapped in a laager in Mazoe and fearing annihilation; the two were ambushed by the Africans and killed. The trapped settlers that the two telegraphists and others most wanted saved were three white women; male settlers feared the worst if they were captured by the Africans. Both during the historical event and in memory, the three white women were generally remembered as wives, rather than in their own right as pioneer women whose husbands had met an unfortunate fate in the frontier war.[6] There was (and still is) less history about those women's individual biographies in the larger colonial narrative, as emphasis tended to be on the men who died rather than on the living—women or men.[7]

The story of the rescue of three white women in a black country was told with drama and historical amnesia by W. S. Honey, who wrote that *the women were placed in a light wagon. [They] were splendid, handing out ammunition to the men, and one, Mrs. Cass, it is said, joined in potting the rebels. It was a great privilege to be with such brave and noble women facing calmly and courageously the risk of death or disablement. [Someone] was mortally shot, and I remember taking hurriedly from his body the bandolier with cartridges lest they should fall into the hand of the rebels.*[8] Honey's recollection of those women's heroic acts was a qualified, almost forgetful one. He wrote as an eyewitness remembering an event; yet, when it came to remembering the women's participation, he qualified his remembrance with the words "it is said," and in the next sentence he continued as though he had been a firsthand witness to the women's courage and participation in their own defense, as well as that of a white settler community under siege.

Honey's memory of those women's heroics also did not include the white community's fears of miscegenation, which pervaded the colony at the time and was part of the reason why Nesbitt's patrol was always the most celebrated of all the war patrols—except for Wilson's patrol at Shangani, memorialized at Matobo, near Rhodes's grave. The fear of white women falling into black (male) hands was uppermost in many settlers' minds.[9] As one settler remembered, during that fateful night "a Basuto native took up a position on the kopje above us, and kept firing at us, and shouting out in English what he intended to do to the women when we were killed."[10] That detail about a "Basuto native" shouting at the settlers in English, rather than a local language, also tells us about (South) African immigrants in the making of Rhodesia—immigrants who took sides, such as that Mosotho, who was an obvious asset to the African side of the war. His language abilities helped his side send real or empty threats to the laagered settlers in their own language—English—heightening the tension even more. On the settler side, Victorian sensibilities and gender roles were accommodated and challenged as the women's protection was couched in the language of defending the defenseless, yet the women were not passive victims. The lens was rarely reversed, however, when it came to thinking of black women captured in larger numbers, and very few records exist of their treatment in white hands during the war. All we know is that many were captured, but the sexual or other violence they may have suffered is still unrecorded in the historiography.

The most important and most actively resuscitated pioneer memory of the 1896–97 war in the Mazoe, however, was that of Blakiston and Routledge, two men cast as ardent imperialists. That remembrance, as will become clear, reflected more the passion of memory in the 1930s than the actual historical figures of 1896. The memory of those two men is a quintessential example of history as imagination in the sense that the events recounted had, indeed, happened but the protagonists were not what was portrayed in the memorializations, at least not in the documentation about one of them, Blakiston. John Lionel Blakiston was the younger son of the Reverend Douglas G. Blakiston, of Trinity College, Oxford, who was later the vicar at Saint Margaret's in East Grinstead, England. John Lionel's brother Herbert, with whom he corresponded frequently, was also a clergyman at Trinity College. The senior Blakiston had called on his network of people to find someone who could afford his son employment and perhaps an opportunity to find his place in the world, as he was not interested in the religious life.

John Lionel Blakiston went to Buenos Aires, Argentina, and eventually made it to South Africa (which then included Southern Rhodesia). He did not initially like the place and its (white) people. He told his father, "I neither like the country nor its supporters, and the former is either too wet or too dry, devoid of any particular interest except to the mining engineer and the trader neither of whom fascinate me."[11] He found the colony full of (white) people who were seeking a fortune but whose worldview was limited. As the young Blakiston saw it, "You scarcely ever meet a man of any education or refinement, or if you do find one, the very fact of possessing such unremarkable qualifications (for refinement is distinctly a drawback in this country) has driven him in desperation to drink. I have no intention of staying here, so I can afford to indulge my prejudice against both place and the people."[12] He found Salisbury to be pleasing, however, because it "represented an English settlement in Rhodesia. There are many quite respectable buildings and the place is clean and English."[13]

After the wars began in Matebeleland (to the southwest) in March 1896, Blakiston assured his family that since he was located in the north of the colony, he was safe, perpetuating a colonial myth that the people of the north were passive, wretched victims of southerners, who saw the settlers as their saviors and so would not molest them. In a letter of July 17, Blakiston told his mother not to worry about "some alarming reports which have familiar currency hereabouts recently and I want you to thoroughly understand that there is not and never can be any danger to Salisbury. If the whole country were to rise, we should not be in any danger for we are impregnable."[14] He concluded by assuring her that he had received news of a better job with the Transcontinental Telegraph Company, which would allow him to move up the socioeconomic ladder once things had settled. That letter to his mother would be his last, as he died two days later. Blakiston and Routledge died because Routledge could not ride a horse well and Blakiston could not work the telegraph machine well on his own, highlighting class differences among settlers. Blakiston volunteered to ride out to the telegraph office with Routledge, and neither man made it back to the laager, being ambushed and killed. Their half-finished message got through to Salisbury, and the rescue patrol made it through and accompanied the beleaguered settlers to Salisbury on June 20, 1896. Two ordinary men had died in the Mazoe; they later became heroes in the colony's local and national histories.

In November 1935 an article by Harold D. Rawson titled "The Mazoe Patrol Recalled by One who Took Part in It: Heroic Telegraphists: Proposed Memorial" appeared in the Rhodesia Herald.[15] The article was preceded by a short editor's note highlighting the fact that the article was related to a "movement originating in the Mazoe district [with] a proposal to erect a suitable memorial to the two telegraphists." Those involved in organizing the event hoped the memorial would be "unveiled next June on the 40th anniversary of the deed of heroism which it will perpetuate." Settlers in and around Salisbury, or the colony for that matter, interested in attending were to go to the Meikles Hotel the following Wednesday, where a meeting would be held and action plans discussed.[16] The remembrance that Rawson most wanted to share in his article, however, was not the celebratory note that everyone was buzzing about, that is, the two dead men and the memorial plaque in their honor. Rather, Rawson's memory was a bitter one, about the forgotten survivors he deemed unsung heroes, not honored by plaque, medal, or otherwise. "It must be remembered," he wrote, "that all these patrols [around the colony during the war] were undertaken by volunteers, practically the same men stepped forward every time when the call was made for volunteers."[17] The failure to acknowledge volunteers as heroes who had saved the day for many an isolated settler community outside large town centers like Salisbury or Bulawayo meant that praise and awards were shifted from the first volunteer responders to salaried officers, who hogged the limelight and the benefits thereof. More importantly, Rawson's bitter remembrance put a finger on the pulse of why it was some forty-odd years before a monument to the Mazoe Incident was erected in the valley.

The fact that only one of the volunteers, Edward Cass, a Salvation Army missionary, had a stone monument erected in his memory by his family and/or church in the Mazoe speaks volumes about the contested memory among settlers about who the "real heroes" of 1896–97 were. Rawson himself had gone out to the Mazoe as a volunteer, along with another now dead volunteer, Routledge. It was Routledge who was being remembered and not Rawson himself or the other survivor volunteers not in BSAC employ. Rawson's complaint did nothing to dampen the enthusiasm of what the political scientist Benedict Anderson called the "imagined community," which had found a common history and a common "ancestry" to invoke in the Mazoe to make the settler community believe in its viability.[18] By choosing the memory of the two dead men, Blakiston and Routledge, over the living, the settler community decided that its imagined (dead) ancestors were better role models for the living, and especially the young who were to inherit and live up to that memory—the known living were flawed.

Cooking for the Blakiston-Routledge Memorial Committee

Mr. E. Seymour White, of Glendale (about twelve miles northeast of Mazoe), and his wife, along with interested settlers in that district as well as in and around Salisbury, took it upon themselves to form the Blakiston-Routledge Memorial Committee. The committee's mission was to collect funds toward the erection of a monument to the memory of the two telegraphists. After E. S. White's advertisement of the effort to memorialize Blakiston and Routledge was published in the *Rhodesia Herald* in late 1935, people wrote to him with donations and their thoughts on the prospective monument in the Mazoe and the importance of memorializing such men across the colony. Among those who wrote was H. M. Moffat, a descendant of the hallowed London missionaries who had established mission stations in what became western Southern Rhodesia and who had been "pioneer" Protestant missionaries before Rhodes's "pioneers."[19] Moffat wrote that he was "glad to see funds being raised for a memorial" to Blakiston and Routledge at Mazoe. He told White he had "always felt that this should be erected as these men gave their lives for the relief of the men and women who were besieged and cut off at Alice Mine" in Mazoe.[20]

Another person who took an active interest in the Blakiston-Routledge Memorial Committee was James E. Nicholls, an attorney employed with the British South Africa Company in Salisbury. Nicholls was also an active member of the Associated Members of the 1890 & 1893 Columns and dubbed himself a "20th century pioneer," relishing colonial life as he involved himself in many activities. On official letterhead of the Associated Members, he responded to White's advertisement expressing his pleasure that he had been "appointed on the Committee to collect funds, as I am in very great sympathy for a monument to be erected to the memory of those two brave telegraphists." He told White that "directly I saw the notice in the paper, I started collecting funds," and he said that he was going to continue with the effort. He praised White for taking the initiative, adding that others ought to be honored along with Blakiston and Routledge. Echoing Rawson, Nicholls wrote that more men needed to be given military awards for their relief of the besieged, not only in the famous Mazoe but in other patrols around the colony that had saved white lives. Nicholls intimated that he was "approaching the Government to see whether they are sympathetic with [the] suggestion" of memorializing more men. Nicholls had done some groundwork and told White, "I might inform you confidentially that I have had an interview with His Excellency [the governor] who is very much in sympathy and will do all he can to get the War Office to grant these clasps."[21] There was no talk of Africans needing any remembrance, even those like Hendricks who had been pivotal to the survival of the besieged Mazoe settler community.[22]

Once elected to the Memorial Committee, Nicholls took to writing White quite often with suggestions on how to proceed with the whole endeavor. In addition to suggesting that more than the Mazoe Patrol needed to be recognized for their efforts, Nicholls also made a radical suggestion that heightened tensions on the committee, particularly with White. Nicholls suggested that "instead of putting up an isolated column or tablet at Mazoe where comparatively few visitors would see it, the money raised should be devoted to placing a permanent Memorial in a new section of the Salisbury [Anglican] Cathedral."[23] The location of the monument to the Mazoe men was very important to Nicholls. He wanted them to be memorialized in the manner of other (mostly military) pioneers whose names were already carved on stones or columns in Salisbury Cathedral—following the model of memorials in European churches. When White said that he did not think the monument should be moved from the scene of the historical event, Nicholls replied that the problem with the Mazoe was that people would whizz past in their cars and never stop to take a look at the monument. In fact, he had heard from one such person who, when sending his donation of one pound and one shilling, had told Nicholls that he was one of those who had whizzed by a one monument already there, the monument commemorating Edward Cass. For Nicholls, that gentleman gave the best support to the idea of moving the monument from Mazoe to Salisbury, where it would be most visible.[24]

When White and the committee did not take to the idea of moving the monument into the Anglican cathedral, Nicholls suggested another idea: a memorial outside the General Post Office in Salisbury. A memorial in the Mazoe, he stressed again, would be disastrous because "there are few people who will know about it and when one thinks that most people in Salisbury have never heard of the Cass Memorial, I am rather apprehensive that this memorial at Mazoe will meet the same fate."[25] To Nicholls, memorials were supposed to be convenient and visible to the living, not to the dead, so the living would care about their (colonial) history and memories thereof. He thought it was foolhardy to insist on sites of memory in obscure and less trafficked places, even when those memorials honored the dead in the places where they had died. When White insisted that since the event had taken place in the Mazoe, the monument ought to be there, Nicholls saw his point. Knowing that he could not win the argument, Nicholls took a different tack, emphasizing the company the two men had worked for when they met their fateful end. He argued that "we must not lose sight of the fact that they were telegraph clerks, and therefore a memorial outside the place that they worked would seem a very fitting place."[26] It did not seem to occur to Nicholls that the General Post Office had not even been built at the time of the 1896–97 war. All he wanted was to cut a shoot of history from its native context and graft it onto a visible platform—a larger oak, as it were—so that those who did not know, or even care, about that history would do a double-take every time they entered the General Post Office in Salisbury. What Nicholls had not calculated, of course, was the emotional investment the local settler (farming and mining) communities in the Mazoe had in the history of their newly found imagined heroes and the tourist potential that history could bring to their district. White became testy and reminded Nicholls of the importance of the local heroes to local communities: "If you will excuse my saying so, I don't think there are any grounds for apprehension and you should not lose sight of the fact that the incident which we propose to commemorate took place at Mazoe."[27]

The tensions might have escalated and delayed, if not derailed, the whole project had White not invited Nicholls to his house, perhaps at the suggestion of his wife. There, Nicholls had the opportunity to experience Mrs. White's culinary expertise and her grace as hostess. The fact that Mrs. White—also a member of the committee—was not brought into the discussion (at least on the record) and was relegated to the stereotypical gender role of charming hostess reminds us that nationalists tended toward a masculine memory of history. Nicholls later remembered that lunch meeting fondly, asking White in a letter after that meeting to "please give my kindest regards to your wife and tell her I am still thinking over that most enjoyable lunch we had." That lunch meeting—no doubt prepared and served by African servants—turned out to be about not only smoothing ruffled feathers over differences of opinion but also strategizing how to get permission from a Mrs. Priscilla Singer, the wealthy settler widow who owned the land on which the monument was to be sited.[28]

In response to the committee's request, Mrs. Singer responded that she had "no fixed objection to such a step. However, before giving you my unqualified permission to put up the memorial, I would like to have some idea of the nature and the size of the monument."[29] White took up that correspondence and explained to her the importance of having the monument in the Mazoe, writing, "I can assure you that there was a very strong movement to have it erected in Salisbury which would have been a tremendous pity because after all these two young men were murdered just close to where we propose to erect the memorial, and had this been done, the district would have sustained the loss of a great attraction."[30] White assured Mrs. Singer that the "Public Works Department will undertake to keep it in order," which meant that her property's value would either go up or never decline, because it would hold an important site of memory that would be well maintained in perpetuity in the colony.

Nicholls, it turned out, was actually Mrs. Singer's solicitor, but he had not told White this at the lunch meeting before the issue of her land came up. Once it did, he pointed out that the next time White wrote to Mrs. Singer, he should ask whether she was willing to make a free land grant or sell it to the committee. More importantly, "you should make it quite clear that not only is her consent to the erection of the Memorial requested, but also the title to the land." He wanted that point emphasized, because in his working with her he "had always found her not quite easy to deal with."[31] Mrs. Singer, whose address at the time was the Hotel Metropole in London, responded to White's letter of February 25, 1936, giving her consent after seeing a drawing of the monument and saying that she was glad it would be a public-works project, cared for by the National Monuments Office.[32] Once White had Mrs. Singer's consent, he went ahead and got a quote for the cost and installation of the stone from Geo. M. Gillespie, a Salisbury granite and marble works company, of one hundred fifty pounds sterling.[33] Once the kinks were straightened out, the committee turned to the completion of the project, for which more than two hundred pounds had been collected by March 1936.[34] At that point the committee realized, to its chagrin, that it did not have much biographical information on the two men.

Mr. E. C. Alderson, treasurer and secretary of the committee, did some research on the two men and discovered that Routledge had "two sisters and an elder brother still living in England," though not well off. He also located Routledge's widow, who had remarried but was again widowed and living with her daughter in the Cape, South Africa. He intimated to White that "if funds will go so far, it would be a graceful act to invite [Mrs. Routledge] to come to the unveiling at the Committee's expense," as she was elderly and not well off.[35] There was a little more information on Blakiston than on Routledge; a family member sent a copy of Blakiston's family history, which was useful but did not trace the family tree all the way down to the deceased John Lionel Blakiston. That family tree showed a history of an English landed gentry whose title had been inherited by males over many generations, some of whom had no male heirs, so that the title went to agnatic males when the nucleus line died off—which was the case with the current Blakiston title holders, to whom John Lionel had been born.[36] Because of his family history, and his family's ability to pay, Blakiston's memory lived longer in Rhodesia than did Routledge's, as a school and a street in Salisbury were named in Blakiston's honor.[37] With most pressing matters taken care of, the committee prepared to commemorate the Mazoe Incident and its two dead heroes. It got settlers in the district, its surroundings, those in Salisbury, and the colony at large excited about commemorating pioneer days and heroes. Most important, perhaps, White and Nicholls ended up with a win-win situation when the governor and the postmaster agreed to have memorials in both places: a plaque in Salisbury and a stone monument in the Mazoe.

Black Backdrop and White Memory in the Public Domains of Salisbury and Mazoe

On the morning of Saturday, June 20, 1936, two ceremonies were held to remember Blakiston and Routledge. The first was in Salisbury, where *the ceremony of unveiling a plaque to the memory of the Mazoe heroes J.L. Blakiston and T.G. Routledge was performed at the entrance of the General Post Office by his Excellency, the Governor. The Governor said they had met to do honor to the memory of two of the most notable heroes in the Rhodesian Valhalla. As long as the romantic story of the Mazoe Patrol was remembered, the names Blakiston and Routledge would be held in honor. The Acting Postmaster General, Mr. C.J. Swift, said on behalf of the Department of Post and Telegraphs, he had the pleasure of accepting that beautiful memorial tablet and the Department would take over its custody. [The plaque] would serve to remind the officers of the Department of the gallant deed performed by two of their colleagues in the early days of the history of Southern Rhodesia. The cost was borne by residents throughout the colony and it would be truly regarded as a national appreciation of those two officers. The memorial would meet the eyes of every person entering the Post Office by the door as they read the inscription and would realize the noble sacrifice that would be remembered from generation to generation.*[38]

Three key issues emerge from the foregoing: First, invoking the Val-halla of Norse mythology at the plaque's unveiling ceremony was a provoc-ative idea, a means of ancestor making and ancestor veneration. It was a signifier of the power of heroic mythology in a colony plagued by a high rate of attrition rate among white immigrants, who often did not stay long, preferring to settle in South Africa or elsewhere in the empire.[39] Of those who stayed, many did not seem curious about settler "romantic" mythology or even to care about it, partly because the colony's narrative of how it had come to be—save regarding Rhodes and his Pioneers—was so fractured. The irony that did not seem to strike those unveiling the plaque was that unlike the souls in Norse mythology, who had died in battle, Blakiston and Routledge, although they had died during a war, had not died in a pitched battle, nor had they been warriors wielding weapons. Rather, they had been civilians caught in the crossfire of an empire's cannons pointed at a resistant autochthonous society keen to restore the world order as it "used to be." Honoring those two men along-side the heroes of old (Europe) was a great signifier of how paradoxically confident and anxious the settlers were to claim their new autochthony through their dead, whose blood had made their existence and (oppres-sive) freedoms possible.

Second, whether or not employees and customers of the Department of Post and Telegraphs believed in the now "national" narrative of the two heroes of Mazoe, they could not escape it, as it had now been brought into the Postal Department's walls and care. Customers could only avert their eyes so long from the memory of the two men now plastered where the "memorial would meet the eyes of every person entering the Post Office." Apparently, it did not occur to the Memorial Committee that other people had ideas, let alone their own heroes of the Mazoe; if it did, those ideas and those heroes did not make it into the heroic narrative. The plaque made obvious that the General Post Office was not a space where Africans and "Others" were expected to enter, at least not through the front door.

Third, the "romantic story" of the Mazoe did not include any (white) survivors, male or female. The invocation of the dead at the expense of the living was an integral part of the exercise of memory in the making of national myths—forgetting in order to remember, forgetting in order to construct a narrative of "one nation under God," as it were. This forget-ting while remembering is an important aspect of national mythmaking and parallel memory making, as it simultaneously defines who belongs to the nation, who is a citizen and who is not. It upholds one memory at the expense of others, exclusions that become fertile ground for resentments stored in the collective archive of the excluded.

In the afternoon of that same Saturday, June 20, 1936, a large crowd gathered in the Mazoe valley. It included *"the children who should remember, reverently and gratefully, the splendid deeds which the pioneer did in the days before they were born,"* said the Governor when unveiling the Blakiston-Routledge memorial at the junction of the Mt. Hampden and Golden Stairs Roads in the Mazoe Valley on Saturday afternoon. *The monument is half-way between the mine and the spot on which the telegraph hut stood forty years ago, and intersects the route taken by the two men on their heroic dash for help. Prime Minister Huggins attended, so did Mrs. Edith Gates, daughter of Routledge and her daughter, large numbers of people from Salisbury, Mazoe, and girls and boys high school pupils.*[40] The master of ceremonies, Nicholls, recounted how White had learned of the dead men's heroics in 1909. White, on his way to somewhere else in the colony, had pitched his tent not far from the spot where Blakiston and Routledge supposedly had died. While there, he had happened upon "a prospector who was working close by and at about the same time a Zulu native in his employ told how he and his contingent of 'Cape boys' had combed the Iron Mask Mountain Range to drive out the rebels."[41] It was that memory that had stirred in White as the fortieth anniversary of the event approached—never mind that the memory had been kept and told by an African. That it appeared that the event would not be acknowledged had led him and others to form the Blakiston-Routledge Memorial Committee, which had brought them all to the Mazoe that day.

The influence of the 1930 "national" celebration of Occupation Day was unmistakable. Unlike the "national" memorial discussed in the previous chapter, which emphasized surviving "pioneers," the (local) Mazoe memorial put an emphasis on the dead, the children, and the gratitude of the living. This was made very clear in White's speech, as reported in the *Rhodesia Herald*. He emphasized that the blood of the dead had made Rhodesia a white country. *"I want to welcome the children who will have to carry on the country when the older generation have passed away,"* said Mr. White. *"I want this monument to be a reminder to you that although Mashonaland was taken without bloodshed, the cost of lives of holding it was considerable among the early settlers, both men and women who made the country fit for us to live in. While commemorating the dead, we must not forget the living; one would especially like to mention Mr. R.D. Rawson who volunteered to come out with Blakiston." The memorial stone unveiled was to serve two purposes: a) the top portion of the panel on the stone was occupied by the plaque to Blakiston and Routledge, but a large space was left below so that at some future date, the names of the members of the Mazoe Patrol could be inscribed on a separate plaque and inserted in the panel. The Governor was happy to see the children and said "it would fall on them to carry on the traditions which they had inherited from the Pioneers who had made the country fit for white people to live in." It would be for the children to make it more glorious: "They gave their lives that others might live and their memory will be held sacred," the Governor said.*[42] That this sort of memorializing stoked the fires of parallel memory goes without saying.

What is remarkable is the recruitment and education of the young into the traditions of those who had made the "country fit for white people to live in." Not only that, those children were tasked with the (historical) burden of making sure Southern Rhodesia would be "more glorious" in the future, upholding its white heritage. Given such a speech, it is no surprise that in 1965 the Rhodesia Front, led by Ian Douglas Smith, made the illegal Unilateral Declaration of Independence from the British Empire when Britain called for universal suffrage and decolonization in Southern Rhodesia, as was happening in much of the empire by 1960.[43]

Mr. J. Arnold Edmonds, chairman of the Pioneer Corps, who also spoke at the unveiling ceremony, changed the tenor of the memorializing, accurately noting that Blakiston and Routledge had not been aiming for gallantry when they died, because their deaths had not occurred in the heat of engagement. They had been killed while doing the right thing for "their people," huddled in the laager. Edmonds "also paid tribute to the heroism of the women; Mrs. Salthouse, Mrs. Cass, and Mrs. Dickinson who were in the Alice Mine laager. He asked the children particularly to respect this memorial as the people of London did the Cenotaph and when they pass it, to acknowledge the heroism of the men it commemorated."[44] The irony, of course, was that the majority of those in attendance were women, and yet the stories of the three widows were muted by the memory of their dead husbands, also not remembered on the plaque at the ceremony even though all three had died during that same fateful June in 1896. Neither the women's first names nor their own individual biographies were noted in the memorial ceremonies. What remains of them in the public narrative is their courage in helping the men fight their way to Salisbury.

Last, and perhaps least important to those gathered but also acknowledged as present at the Mazowe unveiling that June afternoon, were the Africans, and what an acknowledgement: *"We have with us today not only survivors of the Europeans of those days, but also survivors of the natives, who were then our enemies but are now our loyal subjects. The descendants of the people who were attacked and the descendants of the people who attacked them are now loyal subjects of the same King [George VI]. I hope you will remember this day as sacred to the memory of the two fine fellows,"* the Governor said. The ceremony concluded with a brief speech to the natives present by Major F.J. Wane, NC at Mazoe: *"I want you to realize what this monument stands for,"* he said. *"It stands for two men who laid down their lives for others. You commemorate brave people of your race by passing their names on to succeeding generations. This monument is our method of remembering men who have done good work for their people. You were then our enemies, but now you are our friends. Today, speaking as your Native Commissioner, I know that you are."*[45]

To argue that at least the Africans were acknowledged, and for the time period it was a magnanimous gesture, would be plausible but indefensible. The fact that the Africans were addressed by the native commissioner and not the governor says a lot about the parallel existence of life and memory in the colony. Some were citizens, while others were mere natives. Though the NC's address to the Africans was couched in the language of friendship, it was also a master-servant language, and the address was an instruction rather than an address to fellow citizens. The servant-master, aggressor-victim, and pseudo-subjects-of-the-same-king language that the native commissioner used to address the Africans is breathtaking in its irony, self-consciousness, and sense of triumph, even as it affected humility. The lecturing to "friends" about how they or their ancestors had killed the two men fleeing flying bullets hardly made for reconciliatory dialogue.[46] If anything, the Africans were made to feel guilty for having slain innocent men but were not given the opportunity to respond to the allegations of memory.

Nothing, of course, was said about how and why there had come to be a war in Southern Rhodesia in the first place. The reporter recorded no conversations with any of the Africans present, showing how the memory of the Mazowe became an us-and-them memory, contested in private by the Africans, who were the backdrop, while proudly and pub-

Figure 10. Constructing native servants and settler masters. This photo was originally captioned by hand, "Lunch on the Verandah; waiter 'native' Sarmie 7 years." (HWC MS 565, Series II, box 32)

licly displayed by whites. If the "Address to the Natives by the NC at Mazoe" does not say parallel national memory, then nothing else can, for by 1936 Southern Rhodesia's settlers were becoming increasingly comfortable and assertive in the reproduction of rhetoric about "our country" that often rubbed dirt into the wounds of the conquered. To be black in Southern Rhodesia at that time was to be a servant, not a citizen. African history—and the memory thereof—was left to those Africans who still cared about it, clandestinely keeping it alive in their native reserves and townships or in white spaces. As figure 10 shows, young Africans were raised to be servants, while the settlers' children were taught that Southern Rhodesia was their inheritance from Cecil John Rhodes, the Pioneers, and men like Blakiston and Routledge, who had made it possible for children like the seven-year-old "waiter 'native' Sarmie" to grow up knowing their place, while young white people were entitled to Africans' obedience, service, and loyalty.

Almost a week after the unveiling of the memorial to Blakiston and Routledge in the Mazoe, the *Rhodesia Herald* carried a surprising retroactive article in its Round and About the Town section. Titled "Legacy Left by Pioneer Women: Heroines of the Mazoe Patrol," it was about the madams (or memsahibs) of empire, who were not quite full members of the patriarchal colonial establishment in terms of political and economic power but were powerful agents in their gendered roles of reproducing the sociocultural milieu of colonial memory.[47] The article, in words both contradictory and stirring, spoke of the need to acknowledge the role of pioneer women in the history and development of the colony: *It has been said that we do not appreciate the efforts of the Pioneer women. In that critical time (the Mazoe Patrol episode) the calmness, bravery, and pluck of the three women faced with instant death at any moment was marvelous, and their heroism was equal to that of any man. We must change our ideas with regard to the weaker sex. It was high time these words were said. They were used by Mr. J. Arnold Edmonds one of the survivors of the Mazoe Patrol, at the unveiling of the memorial to Blakiston and Routledge in the Mazoe Valley on Saturday afternoon. They will meet with the entire approval of everyone who has sufficient imagination to realize the terrible ordeal experienced by the three women to whom he referred—Mrs. Salthouse, Mrs. Cass, and Mrs. Dickinson—before and during their rescue from the Alice Mine in the Mashona rebellion. . . . The women of Mazoe deserve a memorial, too. Their courage was typical of the Pioneer women of this country, and they left a rich legacy of heroism in the face of the most disheartening odds that must inspire succeeding generations of Rhodesian women in their efforts to make Rhodesia what it deserves to be.*[48] Those Rhodesian women, like their male counterparts, did not make it easy to write about them, for like most Rhodesian settlers, they seemed to tend toward an intellectually landlocked mentality that was a metaphor for the landlocked colony bequeath them by Rhodes and his Pioneers.

Written memorials of pioneer women were first cobbled together as a history of Rhodesia's pioneer women by Jeannie M. Boogie, an ardent imperialist and settler herself.[49] Boogie's history was not a feminist manifesto of female liberation in the colony. Rather, it was a conservative wife-of-the-empire book that showed white women enjoying the freedoms colonial life afforded most of them, freedoms that would not have been possible for most people of their social class back in Europe. It did not help that many of the white women in the early days of the colony were not well educated. For much like the memory of the "two fine fellows of Mazoe," the memory of colonial women took a long time to be recognized, and when it was, its proponents were more keen on perpetuating a colonial image than they were on perpetuating a feminist history.

Speak, Bones: Reburying Memory When "European" and "Native" Graves Mingled

As though fate were mocking the 1936 hype about the Blakiston-Routledge Memorial, a local constable in the Mazoe wrote the head office
in Salisbury to say that while on his beat, he had stumbled upon old
unmarked graves. That was in 1953, seventeen years after the memorial
plaque was unveiled. A. S. Hickman, deputy commissioner of the British
South Africa Police General Headquarters, went down to Mazoe on a
fact-finding mission. He filed a report titled "Isolated Graves at Mazoe:
1896 Rebellion," a fascinating record of how the politics of memory did
sometimes trump historical fact—what I earlier referred to as nationalists passing memory as history. The commissioner's report is fascinating also because it added complexity to the colony's idea of itself and
its (honored) heroes, especially in outposts like the Mazoe, which had
developed into a key mining and farming area.

By 1953 the Mazoe valley was producing a famous citrus drink, Spa
Mazoe Crush, now (Schweppes) Mazoe Orange Crush concentrate juice
(fig. 11). Mazoe, as the drink is popularly called, became and still is a
staple in many Zimbabwean households, even those in the diaspora experiencing nostalgia for "home" across the color line. That turning of a
colonial luxury commodity into a necessity was captured well by the historian Timothy Burke, who, writing about the history of a different commodity, soap, asked, "How do people acquire deeply felt and expressed
desires for things they never had or wanted before?"[50] Mazoe had turned
itself from a mere farming and mining district in the colony into a metaphor for pioneer grit and success at building a colony from scratch—with
"no help" from anyone. The "Mazoe Drink" had done what capitalism
(marketing) is good at—it had made it easy not only to drink but to swal-
low with pleasure and/or ambivalence the bitter historical truth of the
parallel history and memory that the Mazoe District represented in colonial Rhodesia.

It turned out that Blakiston's and Routledge's graves had been unrec-
ognized and unmarked since they died in 1896, so that by 1953 (fifty-
seven years later) no one actually knew where they were buried, and
there seemed to be no record of their burial place. As Hickman's report
made clear, it was best to do more research into the matter before name
plaques could be commissioned for the two graves to distinguish them

The *One* good thing they missed

To the Pioneers, the men who founded the Rhodesias . . . how regrettable that in their fleeting moments of relaxation SPA MAZOE CRUSH was not available to sustain, refresh and fortify them in their heroic efforts.

Figure 11. Pioneer advertisement for Spa Mazoe Crush. (*Southern Rhodesia, 1890–1950: A Record of Sixty Years of Progress* [Salisbury: Pictorial Publication Syndicate, 1950], Wright Collection, BBk 22, Yale University Library)

from all those around them. The graves made it all the more confusing, as Africans also had their own burial spaces in the vicinity, complicating the memory of dead; the bones did not say whether they were those of a native or a settler. Would reburying or marking unknown bones likely scuttle assumptions of "us" and "them"? The commissioner did not say, but his long report reveals the nervosa of constructed memory on the bones and memory of the dead. Here, in part, is what he wrote: *On the afternoon of 25th October I went to Mazoe Police Camp where I met Constable Edwards who expressed his willingness to show me the graves which he had found recently on the hillside above the camp. These two graves are situated within a few yards of each other and the larger of the two has been laid out with some attention to detail and could well be that of a European or Europeans.*

The second grave I was not so happy about. The outline of the grave was not squared off in the usual European manner and was not of the normal length. However, if it were a question of burying bones sometime after the death of those interred that could account for it. I inspected the whole hillside with Constable Edwards and particularly in the direction of the Alice Mine, which lies about a mile distant from the brow of this hill with open land between. It is not exactly certain where the old Mazoe telegraph office was situated. From my reading it appears that the only survivor of the Alice Mine laager who was present when Blakiston and Routledge were killed is H.D. Rawson and the best solution would be to get him to go to the Alice Mine and to give an indication of the direction from which he saw Blakiston and Routledge coming when they were attacked and killed by the rebels. If the position is in the valley then it is most unlikely that their burial took place on the hillside as there would be no point in removing the remains to that position. The sketches of the graves which were copied from Archives in "The Rhodesia Herald" of Saturday, 24th October, indicated that the burials took place on the kopje just below the Alice Mine but it is not known who made the sketches whether from nature or from information received. Certainly the graves portrayed in no way resemble the graves found by Constable Edwards. If the burials took place in the position indicated, near the Alice Mine, then it looks as if more recent mine dumps will have covered them, but a close survey is necessary. Those recorded as having been buried in this position were killed at different places around Mazoe and it would well be that the remains were brought to a central place like the Alice Mine, which apart from the Telegraph Office and a few other properties was one of the few places occupied at that time by Europeans.[51]

Hickman's report shows the complication of, among other issues, fully trusting archival material to tell all about the past. For although the National Archives had images or drawings of what were supposedly Blakiston's and Routledge's graves in the Mazoe, the graves Hickman found clearly did not resemble the images in the archives, raising doubts about the primary source and the unknown depositor of that source. Hickman's report showed that while the memory of the dead was sacred, it did not stop the living from going on with the business of living. The mine continued its mining work, implicating the Chartered Company as it reburied the dead by dumping mine debris over those graves. The debris suggested a complication for settlers keen to remember their few dead, as it meant either conducting an expensive excavation or just letting the dead be reburied, with their memory preserved on the 1936 plaques in

Salisbury and the Mazoe. Most importantly, questions about the "Euro-peanness" of the graves reflect the ephemeral nature of constructed identities, especially racial differences. As in the trial of Nehanda-Charwe, in which the supposed bones of Pollard were brought in from the Mazoe, the dead bones of the 1950s also did not reveal their identity. Hickman went to great lengths to pose several scenarios to certify that the graves he had found belonged to Europeans and not Africans. But as he noted in his report, there were complications: *I have been informed by Father Victor of the Anglican Cathedral that the Reverend Douglas Pelly buried the remains in August 1896, two months after the deaths took place, so it is likely that little will have remained but bones and clothing. Adjacent to the graves found by Constable Edwards are definitely recent African graves and he informed me that this area had been used for the last several years by African employees of the Mazoe Hotel as their burial ground. I instructed him to find out why they chose this particular area. It could, of course, be that they found what appeared to be a European grave and thought that it would be appropriate to make their own graveyard nearby. In that case, Africans could have been responsible for placing the enamel plate, billycan and drinking cup on the largest of the European-style graves as propitiation to the spirits within. On the other hand, the grave could originally have been African and these symbols could have been placed there when the burial took place. During our wanderings on the hillside I found a third grave about 150 yards downhill from the two found by Constable Edwards. This grave had a native pot made fast to it and a flowered enamel plate with a hole knocked in it. It was European in outline and rather sunken in the middle, but it could well be an African grave. There was a more recent African grave beside it. It is obvious that a good deal more research will have to take place before any authoritative statement can be made.*[52]

Hickman's entire report shows that by 1953, sixty-three years after "permanent" European settlement, the settlers were comfortable and more confident in what they considered their country. At the same time, settlers were unsettled by the slightest hint that sacred national memories were not what they seemed. Hickman's report makes clear that it was important to distinguish Africans from Europeans through their burial customs, to preserve "Europeanness"—nurturing parallel history and memory. Colonial society wanted the graves to tell the stories of the dead within them, but that was complicated, as the living could, and did, "tamper" with the graves, including "appropriating the spirits" within—European or otherwise. It is telling that rather than going with Constable Edwards to talk to the Africans about those graves and find out what they knew (or did not know) about them, Hickman outsourced that task to the local guy. That act was reminiscent of the governor's decision at the 1936 memorial unveiling in the Mazoe to let the NC speak to the Africans rather than addressing them fully himself. True, in the colonies the local (colonial) bureaucrats often spoke African languages better than the higher-ups, but the decision was also indicative of the divorced nature of colonial life, which sanctioned parallel worlds to coexist, if uncomfortably. Africans had access to European life as servants and cheap labor, while Europeans had very little access to or interest in Africans other than as cheap labor and servants. The dead were gone, their bones seemingly all mixed up, defying the racial codes of history and memory. Yet the living continued to maintain a parallel existence and remembrance.[53]

This chapter shows settlers' gendered investment in localized memory, beyond the generalized national version. Unlike in the previous chapter, where national commemoration put a premium on the living heroes, in this chapter we have seen that where memory was precarious, it was safer to stick with the dead (who were also all men). Settler women were an afterthought, yet, ironically, when they did their own remembering, they were just as invested in empire, rather than in female solidarity across the color line. Lastly, this chapter highlights Ricoeur's notion of "founding state of right" through the Mazoe memorialization, an idea we will return to in the next chapter.

5 Re-Membering African Masculine Founding Myths in the Time of Colonialism

The fact that the settlers controlled the limelight and the public narrative of how Southern Rhodesia was made did not mean that the Africans lost their sense of history or that they did not tell their children, especially their sons, of their exploits and defeats and the reasons for them. The counternarratives in this chapter are from oral-history interviews conducted by the then Government Archives of Rhodesia (GAR)—now the National Archives of Zimbabwe (NAZ)—in the 1970s and 1980s in an effort to correct a glaring historical record that had collected more "pioneer" stories than African histories. The National Archives oral historian and archivist Dawson Munjeri conducted the interviews, and while he was an African civil servant doing his professional duty, he also had a keen interest in the history he was researching.[1] The individual and collective memories of the six men portrayed in this chapter show an exercise of memory through what the oral historian Alessandro Portelli called "history-telling," simultaneously "institutional, collective, and personal."[2] I interpret these six oral narratives in this way because, instead of seeing them merely as invention, I am interested in the context in which the stories were told—the 1970s and early 1980s—which allows us to see the cycles through which people re-membered their dis-membered histories and what they did when amnesia cracked wide open. By *re-membering* I mean attempts to put back together what had been ruptured by colonialism, reassembling the dismembered past.

The six men—we meet mostly men in this chapter—remembered their people's founding myths elided by colonial history.[3] They remembered the different waves of European entry into their ancestors' lands from the time of the *wazungu/vazungu*, the Portuguese in the sixteenth century, to that of the more recent *warungu/varungu*, the British, who had come before Rhodes's 1890 Pioneer Columns. Other storytellers in this chapter narrated histories of participation in the columns or described seeing the columns and their African-led wagons creak their way north to what would become Fort Salisbury. Many of those men remembered the wars of 1896 as participants and/or retellers of tales told to them by their own fathers and grandfathers, who had shared founding myths and legends of nations before there was a Southern Rhodesian colony/ nation. The men's gendered oral histories and traditions were an act of re-membering their people's dis-membered real and imagined histories and the invented traditions derived from those histories. Unfortunately, very few stories in those African founding myths and traditions illuminate women's lives.

I read the interviews as sources for understanding how (mostly privileged) African men re-membered African history, long shunned and marginalized by successive colonial governments. Colonial history textbooks suppressed any real and perceived African heroes of the 1896–97 wars (and any African heroism before European imperialism), whose stories might have ruptured the neat triumphalism of colonial history.[4] My reading departs from the historian David N. Beach's interpretation in his *A Zimbabwean Past: Shona Dynastic Histories and Oral Traditions*.[5] In that book, along with telling Shona history, Beach was keen to show how "wrong" or "fictitious" most Shona oral traditions and oral histories were. I recommend Beach's book to all who will read my rendition of Shona history in this chapter with incredulity at what might read like tall tales of history. In this chapter, though I use interviews from the same collection, the African Oral History Collection, I do not do so in order to register disbelief at the "fabrication" of history. Rather, I do it with an ear and an eye for the ways in which history was re-membered to suit founding myths in a newly independent African country after various forms of colonial and settler rule for ninety years. These men's stories of colonialism are the few fragments we have of Africans' experiences of colonialism. This does not mean that they should not be critiqued, nor does it mean that they should be dismissed as fiction. My analysis of these oral narratives leans on the Nobel laureate Toni Morrison's reflections on the importance of understanding the self-representation of the dispossessed—in Morrison's case, the incomparable slave narratives in American history. According to Morrison, while slave narratives buoyed an abolitionist movement eager to show the evils of that unspeakable institution, they did not often get a "fair appraisal from literary critics. The writings of church martyrs and confessors are and were read for the eloquence of their message . . . , but the American slaves' autobiographical narratives were frequently scorned as 'biased,' 'inflammatory' and 'improbable.'"[6]

Here, then, are some of the histories the men re-membered from pre-1890 African histories, the 1896–97 war in Southern Rhodesia, the stories of Nehanda-Charwe, and life at the margins of their country of birth. The men are, in the order that they appear below—with the initial *Va* meaning "Mr."—VaIsaac Chiremba, VaNyamadzawo Maruma, VaMunot-yei Mashayamombe, VaRakafa, VaMarufu Chikwaka, and VaChidama-hiya Chimatira. The histories those men told share a tenor of nationalist histories that predate 1890, a tenor that speaks to a masculinized history of nation founding and nation building.[7]

For the Love of Guns: Unwitting Colonial Collaborators

My name is Isaac Chiremba.[8] I was born in 1921 here in Epworth, and I am the fourth of six children—five boys and one girl. Even my mother was born here before the whites came here. She was called Manditanda, and was Christianized [Leah]. My father was Muzambu, a Tonga who came from Siyatsale in the Zambezi Valley. While at his home on the opposite side of the Zambesi in a place called Kandindu, my father saw Selous, the great hunter. He [my father] wanted a gun. He saw the white man who was passing by, and the white man wanted porters to carry his goods. They were promised to be given guns in return. But, they did not know how to use the gun. The white man used it to shoot wild animals. [My father's people] thought the gun just made noise, poo-poo-ooo, and the animal would fall down. They did not know that a bullet came from the gun and then killed the animal. They would be surprised to see the bullet when they cut the animal. They wouldn't know where it came from, and Selous said if they carried the goods for him up to Lewanika he would give them the guns and show them. There were thirty-two young people. Selous was going down to Lewanika[, then] down to South Africa, but when they came back they did not have the guns as Selous had not given them the guns. Some of them, including my father, decided to follow him so they would be given the guns. The young men marched back to follow Selous.

My father was the son of a Chief (Siyatsale), and on following Selous, he left his younger brother, since they were only two boys in his family. He told

*his young brother to remain with the goats, and that they would be back very
soon. They arrived at Lewanika and rounded the Zambezi so they could get a
good crossing. They went through Botswana, and arrived at Moffat Mission,
I should think. There, they rested since they no longer had any food. At that
point, some of the young men returned home, saying they had travelled a long
distance. Only six were left.⁹ My father remained, and that is when they heard
of Johannesburg. They were told that in Johannesburg there was money and
the guns they were looking for. They met some white men who were going to
Johannesburg on foot, and who wanted some porters to carry their goods. They
arrived at the outskirts of the city. They still wanted guns. That is when they
met the Pioneer Column coming to Zimbabwe. The Column had assembled
outside the city so they could start moving. [My father and his friends] arrived
there and saw a wagon full of guns. They stayed for one month only. It was the
wagons coming here so they thought they could come back with the wagons
and they would be given the guns as payment and go back to their homes. But
the white men of the pioneer column also wanted people who would clear the
track and keep the cattle and other miscellaneous jobs. [Six] of them joined
the group of these pioneers and they started moving up here. They returned
without even working in Johannesburg. They worked for the people of the Pioneer Column. They were clearly told that those were the guns they were looking for. They were told that they [the pioneers] were going where the young
men had come from, and they would be given the guns and then go to their
homes.¹⁰ Since among my father's group, they did not know any geography,
they did not ask any questions, and traveled there with the wagons. He said
they left in May. By that time, the rivers would have little water to make it easier for them to cross. They arrived at Harare (Fort Salisbury) with the white
men, and they had never branched off on their own as they were traveling with
the whites who gave them worn out soldiers' tunics, and shirts and shorts. As
for the shoes, they did not bother about sizes they were just given as long as
they could walk in them. That is where they also first saw sugar, they thought
it was some kind of salt that was sweet. They arrived in Salisbury with the
white men and stayed with them until the rebellions when he finally came to
this place [Epworth]. That is the story of how my father arrived in Salisbury.
Before he met my mother, the daughter of Chiremba. Our maternal grandfather Chiremba comes from Chihota, they came from Mutasa.¹¹*

Isaac Chiremba's narrative about the history of the founding of Zimbabwe is fascinating in its affirmation and disruption of founding myths,
both African and European. Unlike the other narratives in this chapter,

Chiremba's does not claim a long patriarchal autochthony in "MaShona-land"; rather, it claims a Tonga paternity. Tonga traditions and customs were and are matrilineal and matrifocal. Because of those traditions, he was named after his maternal grandfather, Chiremba, rather than after his father, Muzambu, or after his paternal grandfather, Chief Siyatsale; most men discussed in this chapter were named after their fathers and paternal grandfathers. Chiremba's narrative also disrupts solely European founding pioneer myths by inserting the story of his father's travels and adventures into that of the self-constructed "great hunter," Frederick Courtney Selous, one of Rhodes's few valuable lieutenants, who scouted land for the empire, and for Rhodes, before leading the Pioneer Column in the colonization of Southern Rhodesia in 1890, later celebrated as Occupation Day.[12] Chiremba's narrative refuses to let Selous refer to his porters as mere "kaffirs" and cheap labor to be exploited for the white man's colonization. Rather, Chiremba lets it be known that his father and his companions were so determined to acquire the latest military and hunting technologies that they were willing to risk life and limb following a traveler who had traversed their own country several times. They trusted Selous enough to think they could make their way back home, as did those who backed out and returned home when Selous did not keep his promise of giving them any guns.[13]

Chiremba's narrative also demonstrates inconsistencies inherent not only in oral history but also in re-membering a conquered history in the time of colonialism and on the cusp of Zimbabwe's decolonization. His narration of his father's story is tinged with his own value judgments about his father and his participation in the colonial process. Chiremba's status as a convert to Christianity seems to have smoothed the edges of colonialism, in contrast to other narratives in this chapter that leave them as sharp-edged reminders of the humiliations Africans lived with when they lost their lands to European conquest. More importantly, the narrative of the acquisition of guns speaks to the masculinized narrative of the power of the gun not only for hunting but in the (then raging) war of independence in Rhodesia. Neither the teller nor the interviewer showed why, of all the stories Chiremba's father had told him about the founding of the country, the story he chose to tell was one in which guns were prominent as a symbol of a powerful history in which his father had been actively involved. Yet, even given that admirable history, the son, telling the father's story, talks about what decades of colonialism had done to those who kept their individual and collective wounds in their own archives of colonial memory, telling and retelling stories of participation and exclusion that reinforced "our" (black) history and "their" (white) history. Since colonial history did not allow for the telling and contestation of black and white histories in public, the colony's children grew up with their own version of history as told, retold, and burnished with each retelling. In the case study of Chiremba, as in others below, we see clear examples of the *individual memory* of the storyteller, the *social memory* of the teller's "people's history," and the *collective memory* of the "native" status of Africans in the colony's history.

Naming the Land, Understanding Difference

The next narrative, by Nyamadzawo Maruma, is striking in its exercise of memory that simultaneously distinguishes Portuguese and British history in the history of his people. The story contests European colonialism embedded in Selous's renaming of his society, giving it a strange and meaningless name like Masvina. More importantly, Maruma's story includes the history of the proliferation of guns in Southern Africa as Europeans competed not only for animal skins and horns but also for territory and mineral wealth. The guns Africans traded with Europeans and other Africans who had traveled to the coast in South Africa and the Portuguese territory of Mozambique made Africans of the interior think they could drive out the settlers, who had settled in their land since 1890 and were coercing them to build their cities, towns, mines, and large plantations. Here is his history:

My name is Nyamadzawo Maruma.[14] *I cannot know the precise date I was born since there was no formal education. When the Europeans arrived in this country, I had just been born. The first European to come was Gouveia (Antonio Manuel de Souza) a Portuguese who had guns.*[15] *This Gouveia distributed guns to Africans and one of those given was Matibvu. Matibvu was our grandfather and he distributed the guns among his own people. Afterwards, came a true European whose name was Selous. He is the one who introduced the name "Matasvina." Before that we were known as the Karanga but Selous introduced the name Svina. He introduced this name because he had killed an eland on the banks of the Hunyani River. Now, the Nyamwedas were asked to go and skin the eland. Selous told them, "I only want the horns and the skin." He then asked them in faningalo/silapalapa [a kind of pidgin], "do you*

take the intestines?" They replied, "Yes, Baas, tino svina (we'll clean them)."
It was this European who [after hearing them often say yes, we'll clean them
(kusvina)] told them, "so you are Masvina." That is how the name Masvina
started; it never denoted a particular tribe. We were known as either the Ka-
ranga or the Zezuru.[16]

I was born in this area, an area that belongs to us. I was born at Kapori.
This place was known as Chemapfupa. Even when the [1896–97] battles were
fought, we were at Chemapfupa. This was the war between us and the Eu-
ropeans. Chikoore's father whose (Chief) name has been given [by colonial
appointment] to Makomanichi died in this war, and so did his brother. They
were gunned down while they were fleeing and both died on the spot. [It hap-
pened] up there where today there are farms. That used to be our settlement
site, now it is part of alienated land known as Mutibvu's land. There are Eu-
ropean farms, the Kapori Farms. It was where we used to live. From there we
settled in the Marirangwe area. After a time we were told to go back to your
own area because this area belongs to Nyamwenda. Before that we had been
expelled from the land of our birth by a European called Kuwe[, whose] real
name was Mr. Hallas. After the fighting between our people and the Europe-
ans, we went back to settle in our traditional lands as friends [with the Euro-
peans]. It was then that our guns and spears were taken away from us. [In this
area], the war was started by the sjambok [whip]. Policemen, in fact, our own
African children joined the police force and they used to whip us. Now people
got fed up and asked "why should we be oppressed when we are the owners of
the country?" Oppression is why the war broke out. I think [the war] started
in the Mazowe area and then spread to this end. However, those in Zvimba
Reserve never fought. Mashayamombe fought, he was a Mtoko man.[17]

Land dispossession by any European claiming to have bought the land
and the British South Africa Company–cum-government's support of that
claim meant that the Africans were turned into squatters on land once
theirs. The point Maruma seemed to emphasize was that the land had
been theirs by marriage, negotiation, or conquest or, as some claimed,
had been allocated to them by other autochthons they had found living
there when they migrated into an area. European colonialism had disrupted that social ecosystem by instituting rigid, top-down structures for
land access and ownership. More importantly, Maruma, like most men
discussed in this chapter, insisted on naming the landscape for what it
had been before it took on European names—echoing the sentiments
of the "Old Timer" expressed in chapter 3. Maruma was (unwittingly?)

reminding his audience that if history is preserved through sites of social and collective memory, then it ought to be known that "white farms" were infused with a history that would not disappear as long as those who knew it named it. In fact, Maruma's (and others') insistence on naming the landscape does raise the question of how much African history "disappeared" with European settlement on "white farms" that marked and remembered the settlers.

Maruma continued his narrative of autochthony, saying: *Chivero, son of Ngwenayasvuura, was the first one to carry the dynastic line he was born in Guruuswa from where he emigrated to this area. Because he was the first, he distributed land to later immigrants. First were the Rozvi, proper Rozvi. [Maruma asked the interviewer, Munjeri:] From where did you, Hera, come? You came from Guruuswa. Don't you know that our totem is the same as yours but then we differ in praise name. Hwata belongs to the Shava totem, so does Chiweshe and Chivero. We are all Shava, we differ in our praise names. We are Mwendamberi, and you are Museyamwa. We came to be known as Mwendamberi because Chivero went ahead of all the others like Nyashanu, Hwata, and Chiweshe. They are one and the same people, only their praise names differ. When Chivero came the Rozvi had already gone, they left a number of ruins. He died at Manama (Hunyani) River Valley that is where his grave is, and our original place. We settled here because the Europeans placed us here. My grandfather died in Gazing or Norton, we were later moved to the area belonging to Pearson.* The emphasis on the "proper" Rozvi is interesting, as it tries to build a buffer between the Johnny-come-latelies claiming land ownership (the British) and the "undisputed" autochthons, the Rozvi, who parceled out land to new immigrants in bygone eras. Maruma, as noted above, continued to contest European ownership of the land—through names and fences—calling out African names right along with the colonial ones that had replaced them.

In his re-membrance, Maruma reorganized history as though that reorganization alone would right the world of his people, who had been upended by the violence of European colonialism. He continued: *When we left Norton we went to Marirangwe, because we had been forced to move away by a European who bought this area. That is the year I resigned from my job as a waiter for the Native Commissioner. It was Kuwe who made us move, we told our elders, "go to Hartley and report that a certain mad European had approached us." When they got to Hartley, they were told, "if that is Mr. Hallas, better expedite your departure, otherwise all your property will be burned down." That is the year we transferred to Marirangwe. There were no farms. It was while there that I got married. The only farm that was there belonged to Chindoora, or Mr. Bester. He was our good friend and he did not expel us. We later left of our own will, but to this day, some are still there.[18] When the 1896–97 war broke out, I was tending goats. Oh, yes, I was grown, do you think what I've been telling you is retold history? No, I was herding goats at the time, and we used to flee carrying with me my mother's reed mat and driving the goats away. We were still [at our original place] when we fled to Zvimba area across the Hwanga (Angwa) River. We were as far as that when we were taken back. We had with us my uncle for my father had remained behind and surrendered. His gun was taken away and he paid tax. When the war was over we were approached by some policeman who said [to my uncle] "return to your home because your younger brother has surrendered." We were by now heading for Korekore country. In those days, the policemen were taken as lords. [For example], if a girl was attractive to a policeman, the latter would merely ask, "old man, whose daughter is that?" If he said "she is mine," then the policeman would say "she should be cooking for policemen." She was taken just as easy as all that. The one whose daughter was taken would be satisfied knowing that no one would harass him.[19]*

The difference between "bad" and "good" European settlers that Maruma recalls relates to how Africans accommodated the new settlers, who had become the overlords, with no end to their rule in sight. Some European settlers treated Africans like lepers to be driven off "their" land (Hallas), while others treated them as "friends" and neighbors (Bester) and did not find it difficult to let Africans live on marked (now European) land. That history speaks to the complexity of human interaction after the wars of 1896–97, which irrevocably reshaped Afro-European relations in the colony of Southern Rhodesia. Maruma's narrative also shows how human relations changed not only between the "races" but also among and between the Africans themselves, especially those who acquired new power, as representatives of the colonial bureaucracy: the African police (see fig. 12).

The African police became the face of colonial brutality, corruption, and abuse of power as the old order of the hereditary chieftainship, among other structures, was replaced by colonially appointed chiefs. Most of those so appointed had supported the colonial side during the 1896–97 war or were compliant with the new order, as we saw in the case of men testifying against the new Nehanda, Mativirira, as the mem-

Figure 12. "Native Police," Umtali, ca. 1920s. (HWC MS 585, Series II, box 32)

ory of Charwe's execution reared its head, in chapter 2. The women in Maruma's narrative, like Mativirira and Charwe before them, were harassed by men, but in this case the harassment was sexual. The women in this narrative bore sexual harassment from the police, their fathers seeming to consent as long as they (the fathers) were left alone. This, again, demonstrates African patriarchy's willingness to use women as commodities, and it corresponds with Kaguvi's willingness to "pay the Government with a little girl" as long as he was allowed to live in peace.

The African fathers in Maruma's narrative sought to be elevated to *tezvara* (father-in-law) status by the police and so accrue power in an obvious move of selectively remembering a past that had given men more power over women's lives, without the checks and balances that "tradition" afforded women. The unfortunate aspect of the *tezvara* status the African men sought under British colonial rule was that marrying a daughter to rivals to guarantee peace was no longer an option; that world was gone. In fact, if it had existed, Selous would not have led an occupying army (the pioneer columns) into MaShonaland, since he himself had an eye for African women; he had married one by African custom and had a son with her.[20] In the new world order of European colonialism, relations were governed by invented categories of race, "tribe," and capitalist autochthony.

"Munotyei? ... What Are You Afraid Of?"

Another story of living under colonialism, albeit with a different sensibility, was told by Munotyei Mashayamombe, born in 1923. That was the year that Southern Rhodesia became a self-governing colony, that is, no longer under BSAC rule and with minimal direct rule by the Colonial Office in London. Southern Rhodesia remained a British colony, and its settlers "loyal subjects" of the British monarchy. For the Africans, the change in political and economic leadership meant living under an oppressive government without direct recourse to the Colonial Office. That reality riled men like Mashayamombe, whose remembrance of "days gone by" started with the history of forced labor and its impact on the psyches of the colonized and the colonizer.[21] Colonialism, by Mashayamombe's recollection, was a brutal waltz in which one party knew all the steps and expected nothing but obedience from the other party, who had to follow, not knowing where he or she was going. After all, a waltz is essentially a lead-and-follow dance, with one party (usually a man) leading, while another (usually a woman) follows, dancing backwards and in high heels to make the dance possible. It may be beautiful to waltz to Strauss, but colonialism was a different kind of dance, a brutal frontier dance.

Mashayamombe remembered going into the colonial community labor service in 1940: *I went to build houses for the army camp near the road which goes to Domboshava, at the place which was called R.A.R, meaning Rhodesian African Regiment. We built those poles and dagga huts, and were making preparations for soldiers who had to be accommodated there. So they [the colonial government] looked for people in this area to go and build there, and people started running away. They feared that they would be made to fight in Hitler's war. The people started running away from their homes. The police and messengers from the District Commissioner would come, they would arrive in the evening and surround the home. Early in the morning, they would get the people and it was difficult to run away; the people feared fighting in Hitler's war. As I was the youngest son of the chief, I was chosen to lead as an example, so that if I had to face any death, I would be the first to die. That is when I was given the name Munotyei by my father. He is the one who ordered me to go and participate in the community service labor.[22] We were many because people came from Mhondoro, Rusape, and Sinoia to work in the labor camp for the Rhodesia African Regiment (RAR). All chiefs had been asked to mobilize people to come and help in the [World War II effort].*

So we'd a difficult time because we were made to work very hard. There was a certain white man whom we nicknamed, Mhurudza. He would go around with a walking stick in his hand. This Mhurudza would order people to lift these building poles, so we named him Mhurudza (kumhurudza [or kumurudza] is to lift). We had a hard time, and we reached a point where we said we no longer wanted to work. We told them so, and that the money they were paying us was too little. We had been told, when we left our homes, that we'd only work for three months, and then go back; now they wanted us to work for four months. When we voiced our concerns, the soldiers were called in by a certain white man called Major Wing. Mashayamombe's narrative tells of a young man growing up in a country of dispossessed colonized people used as cheap labor for the local and global imperial project, the worst of it being the harsh treatment and terror at the hands of colonial overlords like Mhurudza and their hired African hands. For young people who grew up hearing of their parents' and grandparents' defeat at the hands of colonial rulers in 1896–97, the bitter memory of that defeat had a variety of effects, not least among them the formation of a parallel memory and ownership of a shared country between white masters and black servants.

Among us, there was a certain man whom I regarded as my elder brother, Matiyenga, Mashayamombe continued his story. *They took him and placed a gun between his legs and then pretended to load the gun and to shoot. We were told that we had not come there to cause a headache to the whites. So we were being forced to work. Some ran away to seek refuge at the District Commissioner, others went back to Rusape and others to Sinoia. They told the district officials that they no longer wanted to work, as the work they were supposed to do was so difficult. They were told that their grievances were worthless and [they] were supposed to go back to work. I had a little knowledge about guns, and I heard that we'd be shot. I told the others that we'd not be shot as the guns had no bullets. I had remained stationary [at the pretend shooting of Matiyenga] as I was the youngest while the others ran away, and that was the same year I had taken my registration certificate on 1 July, 1940. The soldiers had looked at me and laughed, and that is when they discovered that I knew that the guns they were holding were not effective if not loaded with bullets and we were only being intimidated. So, that was the community service labor in which I participated in 1940. People were forced to go to work and they would be trapped at night while they were asleep.* The fact that Mashayamombe seemed to remember the days of colonialism with such bitterness speaks to the sense of subjection those without the means of power felt as they labored under duress—from the unloaded guns to being treated as property and part of the means of production—to make the local and international imperial project a success. It also speaks to their living as aliens, permanent residents with no rights as citizens in what was supposed to be their country of birth, under the constant surveillance of the police, who had the power to confiscate their identity papers. Having no identity papers severely limited, if it did not make impossible, life and freedom of movement in a country where to be a "native" was synonymous with being an outsider or a suspicious member of society.

The irony of colonial power was that it was keenly felt when exercised by many African policemen in the colonial bureaucracy. Mashayamombe remembered one such *policeman known as Gabarinocheka [Gaba (Tin Can) for short, a nickname reserved for a rough and uncouth person]. He was very harsh, this African, and he stuttered. He would come early in the morning when people were just about to wake up. He would take people away and seize their registration certificates. Now, without a registration certificate, one could not go anywhere. The people resisted police like Gaba, they would actually fight, asking the policeman where he was taking them to, saying: "You want me to go and join Hitler's war?!" Those were the days when Hitler's war was mad and he would shout that he would eat his dinner in Salisbury that day. "Now, you want me to go to war so that I get killed?" the people would ask. So, during the days of the community service labor, we really had a hard time. We would be paid a dollar only after laboring very hard. At about six o'clock in the morning, we'd be made to stand in line. By seven o'clock in the morning everyone was supposed to start work. This Mhurudza would come along with a stick into the rooms where we lived and chase us out.*

Mashayamombe's tale also tells of what it meant for a generation of young men—never mind the women—who grew up seeing their own fathers seemingly acquiesce to the colonial system even as it was oppressive, and there were no viable channels of reporting what we today call human-rights abuses, as the colonial system was accountable only to itself; the civilizing mission labeled Africans as "backwards," and therefore anything it did to "tame" them was acceptable. In fact, as Mashayamombe explains at the beginning of his interview, his own first name, Munotyei, was a nickname that stuck after his father, who was chief, told the African men reluctant to join the forced labor camp that there was nothing to fear, as he was sending his own son: "Saka, munotyei?" (so, what are you afraid of?).[23] The protests against fighting "Hitler's war" also indicates the reality that the Africans did not know the horrors unfolding in Hitler's Germany and of people—the Jews, Roma and Sinti, and all "non-Aryans"—going through a worse nightmare of annihilation. If anything, because of the harsh life under colonialism, the lack of education, and the censored information in the colonies, many Africans tended to think that it was a good thing that Hitler was giving the British a hell of a time, as they (the Africans) were having a hell of a time under the colonial boot. Some even named their sons Hitler. Such parallel histories, and memories thereof, were among the tragedies of the colonial experience, for they meant that Britain could rightly celebrate (along with the Allied Forces) a triumph over the evils of Nazi Germany, but British colonial subjects (along with subjects of other European empires) did not see the point, as they were still living life with the imperial boot on their necks.

Mashayamombe's long narrative also tells of this paradox of history, for it is informed by a history that stretches back to his grandparents in the 1890s. In fact, he was not the first in his family to work in colonial labor camps; his grandparents' and parents' generations had participated in the forced labor that built Southern Rhodesia's cities, towns, mines, and infrastructure, such as the railroads. It was from that forced labor and general dispossession that the Africans launched the 1896–97 wars, which saw the rise of "Mashayamombe, a famed gallant fighter, whose first name was Chinengundu, along with his brother Chifamba, both my paternal uncles. The places where those battles between the Africans and Europeans were fought are well known; they are at Njatara / Fort Martin. Even nowadays, that is where we sometimes go and hold our ritual ceremonies."[24] Munotyei Mashayamombe's narration of the 1896–97 war and its heroes was supported by a visiting neighbor, who chimed in with his own memories of colonialism and its memorial sites, which the Africans had reclaimed at independence and were using as sacred sites to the memory of 1896–97.

African Policemen, Brutes from Another Land?

The indisputable history of African dispossession by colonialism is a memory that still haunts. In other parts, it haunts all the more because of the memory of those (few) Africans who participated, if not in the direct colonization of their own lands, then in the implementation of colonial policies that disenfranchised Africans. The quintessential example of that participation was the colonial African policemen, the *askari* in East African history. Those Africans also told their own versions of colonialism as they had experienced it—used by the colonial bureaucracy on the one hand while despised by the Africans on the other. Because of their harsh exercise of power, African policemen were sometimes cast as foreigners by the local people, who did not know how else to explain the cruelty they meted out to their own people—or simply other human beings. But not all of those policemen were foreigners, and as we saw in chapter 2, native commissioners were given war medals for having used their African networks to gather intelligence on the whereabouts of war leaders on the African side. One of those former policemen recorded in the African Oral History Collection was a Mr. Rakafa of Chinyika, who lived in a place allocated to him by the local native commissioner and also appointed a local powerbroker. According to his narrative, he was very much a local person, with a traceable autochthon history, including a hereditary chieftainship, which he had abandoned, preferring what the district commissioner and "Mr. Government" had allocated to him. Rakafa's story tells of the patron-client relations between the colonizer and the colonized, relations that were also mirrored in African founding myths, in which land was allocated by patrons to clients through a variety of means, from marriage to warfare. The difference between the old African systems and the new colonial one was that in the old systems an erstwhile client could become a patron, and vice versa, while in the new system the colonial color-bar policy ensured that only Europeans would be patrons, and Africans clients.

Here is how Rakafa told his family history: *This settlement [consisting of several village clusters] is known as Rakafa, in the Chinyika Tribal Trust Land. I am the owner of this settlement, and it was given to me by the District Commissioner because I had worked for them. My younger brother, Shangwa, is the one running affairs here; for example, he collects taxes from all who live in my settlement. I am the head of this settlement, and whoever tells you something should not hide this fact from you. If a crime is committed here, it is I, and not the younger ones, who are held responsible. This is my settlement, though I am exempt from paying tax. I am exempt because all old policemen were struck from the tax register. As soon as one's time is up, he is struck off. For example, if my younger brother reaches a certain age, he will be struck off. All this area is a reserve (or Tribal Trust land) and it is under our District Commissioner. In the old days, we used to give our respects to Taylor (the first Chief Native Commissioner).*[25] The power of the colonial bureaucracy was something Rakafa admired, and because he had worked for the colonial government, he felt a sense of loyalty and responsibility to it as manifested in the person of the native or district Commissioners. His own father's had possessed a hereditary chiefly title that he could claim, but he wanted nothing to do with it because his father had murdered some relatives before running away and settling elsewhere in central MaShonaland. In fact, according to Rakafa's story, taking a job with the colonial government was his way of reinventing himself and the family history so that he would not be tainted by his father's deeds, which were well known even to the colonial government, which reminded him of that fact when they needed to keep Rakafa in check.

Rakafa went on to narrate his memory of how the colony was built through the destruction of the countryside and Africans' insurrection in 1896–97: *Chinanga hill (known as Graniteside) was excavated on one side, and it built the whole of Salisbury (meaning the rock quarried from the hill was used for the construction of major buildings). Chinanga hill was all destroyed to build Salisbury, otherwise it was land that belonged to Seke. Where the (Cleveland) dam is now, that used to be where the road to Seke used to be, passing through on to Wedza via a mountain called Gonon'ono, and on to the south were Chivero and Mashayamombe. Do you know who Mashayamombe is? He did not have any territory of his own in this area, he does not belong here, but came from the direction of Mrewa, and that is where his name is famous. He came here on a hunting expedition. All these people were hunters, and many people were made slaves through hunting. The Nyamweda people are also famous hunters. So, Nyamweda had no fixed territory, and also Mashayamombe had no fixed territory. They were moving around hunting.*[26] *All of a sudden, the Europeans found themselves victims of murder. They asked, "why do you kill us?" Indeed, they had done nothing wrong. That is why the Africans were later executed by the government. The way it happened was that the government said "all those who murdered the Europeans should assemble and let us listen to your reasons for fighting and then we can settle that." They did not know that they were being cheated, and that they were going to be killed. The people left the bush and gathered and then one by one they were asked, "You, tell us why you killed a European?" Failing to find an answer some were sent to jail. Indeed, there was no more room left in the* prison. They were told, "Now we have sentenced you for your crimes of murder, and all those who murdered Europeans are going to be killed." You were not born yet and even all these children of mine were not yet born, including one of my children now living in Hartley where he bought a farm there.[27]

Rakafa went on to remember the Africans imprisoned for participating in the 1896–97 insurrection, including his grandfather, who had been imprisoned with Charwe, whom he recalled as having been put in what seems to have been solitary confinement, "in a hole." As he told it, Of those tried and found guilty, they were set for executions. This war [of 1896] was started at Mashayamombe. Mhasvi [of the Hwata] was one of them; he was one of the leaders of the rising. He was an ex-policeman. He enabled others to escape from prison, although he did not, and for that he received (as he had anticipated) a strong recommendation for pardon and was released from prison. Many Gova people were executed by the Europeans. [But those in prison] dug their way out of prison, hiding their exploits with blankets[, and] when the policemen were far away, all of them fled, and my sekuru (grandfather) was one of those who made their way out. My grandfather was in prison with Nehanda, she was the spirit medium of all the Gova people. She was also one of those under arrest, and she was detained in a hole. She was executed since she was not there when the others planned to escape. She was always under constant armed police guard.[28] [Ironically], Nehanda had predicted that the Africans were not going to win the war because the Europeans preferred to fight out on the prairies, where they were adamant they would not be defeated by the Africans. The Europeans wanted to destroy the whole mountain called Chichuru, which is where Nehanda lived. It is in the Mazowe Valley area. I was once there, I did not have time to study that area in Mazowe country that belonged to my grandfather. When I was there, the people thought that I was a foreigner and rebuked me for being a policeman. Anyway, we deserved the insults because we were cruel to the people.[29]

In the foregoing, we see a man conscious of how destructive the colonial project was to the environment, as it had destroyed all or half of the hills and mountains to build the urban environment. On the other hand, Rakafa did not seem too conscious of how exploitative to people's lives and labor the whole process had been; in fact, his narrative tells his story from the perspective of one who did not necessarily work in forced labor camps but enforced laws that made forced labor possible—as remembered in the narrative of Gaba of Mashayamombe. Rakafa's memory of how the 1896–97 wars started and, especially, why reflects the deep

fissures in African memory of the colonial period. Because of the polariz-
ing nature of colonial rule, which pitched the haves against the have-nots
in terms of not only race but also class and constructed tribalisms, the
memory of how Zimbabwe was made, from colony to independent country, is dogged by ahistorical reckonings of what happened and why the
country continues the same pattern of cycling around messianic political
leaders, who take the people into deep black holes, leaving them trauma-
tized by the physical, economic, social, and cultural violence that ensues.

On the other hand, one could argue that Rakafa's memory of the
1896–97 wars may have been shaped by his grandfather's experience as
an escaped prisoner of war and his father's memory of what happened to
the conquered people. To his credit, Rakafa recognized that the colonial
policemen were cruel to the people. His acquiescence to the colonial
order after the 1896–97 wars demonstrates the traumas of colonialism
and war that Africans suffered, especially in places where family members were executed (usually by lynchings), sometimes in front of other
family members. As Bertha Ruth d'Almeida, a woman raised at Chishawasha mission as a "colored" child of an American "pioneer" in Rhodesia
and an African mother, noted of one of Nehanda-Charwe's children after
the 1896–97 wars, "The eldest daughter, Makandipeyi, went to the mission, and was renamed Mary-Ann. I used to wonder if she had her mother's powers, but if she did she never used them. Perhaps she was afraid of
the danger after she saw her whole family hanged."[30]

The frontier wars and the lynchings traumatized communities deeply,
and some men, like Chief Marufu Chikwaka, who narrates the next story,
told of trauma and what they had seen their parents, especially their
mothers, experience. Here is how he told that story to Munjeri: [Though
I do not remember when I was born, I know] my father fought against the
Europeans and it was during that war that my mother used to run away carrying my sister who comes after me. My mother even had another child during
the war. We ran away [but] the Europeans said, "come back and settle down,
surrender your guns," thus our guns and spears were taken and that is how we
came to settle down. Many people from our territory were hanged, including
some of my own relations. [People like] Mhasvi saved many others. He called
out to other prisoners in other cells to let them know that the others had escaped. After letting all the others escape, he held one person in his custody
before alerting the prison guards. Some were later recaptured at their homes,
but some disappeared for good. Mhasvi himself had been due for hanging [for

being a renegade policeman], but after the prison escape fiasco, the author-
ities said that he should be pardoned. Mhasvi came from Gomba/Mazowe
Valley, he belonged to the Hwata clan. Even Nehanda, the woman chief was
said to belong to the Hwata clan. We in this area, Hwata, Mashayamombe,
etc., we are the people who fought against the Europeans. Mangwende did not
fight and Mtoko did not fight. They later fought with Mapondera.[31]

Sellouts and Other Memories of the
Humiliation of Defeat in War in 1896–97

Despite the traumas of war and the military defeats, some chose not to
remember the founding of their country as peopled by cowardly Africans
who did not fight to the death. Mr. Chidamahiya Chimatira of Mhondoro
remembered the heroics of the war. His version of who participated in
the wars contradicted other versions, telling us that Africans' memory of
the war was as complicated as that of Europeans.[32] For Chimatira, *Kaguvi*
made us fight against the Europeans because he said he had found rukomani
(war medicine) which when taken, would immortalize someone.[33] *It is that*
medicine that sent us mad. He himself was captured near Mt. Darwin as he
ran away, leaving Nehanda whom he told to flee also. I was in Chiweshe then.
He instructed people to scatter away as the war had now spread out. We were
captured by Jackson. He was the Major in this area. He is the one who, aided
by the Karanga from Fort Victoria, captured people. Had it not been for the
other tribes that joined the police force, the fighting would have gone on; as a
result, we were now fewer than them.[34] Despite this narration of his location and whom he was with when the thick of the action happened, including his capture, and why they lost the war, Chimatira characterized
most others as not having put up a good fight when he said that *the Hera*
did not fight, the Korekore did not fight, those in Salisbury did not fight. Only
the Mhondoro area was left to do the fighting. I had my own gun with which
I was firing at them and yes, I was there, you cannot argue with that. I was
holding the gun when we were arrested by Jackson. We were at Mukwazi, at
the boundary of Sipolilo and Zvimba (Mukwazi is a tributary of the Hunyani
River). It was in the night that all of a sudden we heard the heavy sounds of the
missiles. If you turned to that direction you would hear it. The cry went out,
"Chimatira, Chimatira, hold your children, otherwise they will die." We hid
all our guns. Jeki, Jackson's Karanga interpreter, had told the Europeans the
various hiding places and their entrances. Through Jeki, Jackson told us "You

will not be able to use even those guns you've hidden away, so you must bring them. We [whites] are not going to leave this country."[35]

In Chimatira's rendition, blame was to be leveled at those "sellouts" who had joined the other side and collected intelligence on their behalf, leading to the Africans' defeat. What he did not seem to grasp was that people like Jeki (or Rakafa above) had perhaps read the situation better and understood that the whites were "not going to leave the country" and were willing to fight to the death. Chimatira's blaming the sellout "others" highlights what had become a problem in the time he was interviewed in the 1970s, when the war of independence had reached untenable levels as atrocities mounted and the Rhodesia Front military used its superior firepower to bomb large groups of unarmed young people in refugee camps across Rhodesia's borders in Mozambique.[36] Chimatira's othering rhetoric also ignored the fact that it was not always "foreigners" who supported the fledgling colonial bureaucracy. Some local people also saw the potential for power and privilege in the colonial structure and the possibility of moving up the socioeconomic ladder dominated by those born of dynastic founders or of important spirit medium families, who were keen to maintain the status quo in the name of the "ancestors."

For some of its contradictions, Chimatira's remembrance of the war is important because it gives another perspective to the remembering of the humiliations of the 1896–97 wars, which had been hidden from public view—save as articulated by a few works of African literature, most of which was controlled by the same colonial government. The tales of near annihilation of the Africans and the general triumphalism invoked by Carrington's list arguing for the awarding of medals to European men who had fought the "Natives" in Southern Rhodesia are tempered in Chimatira's narrative by the knowledge that the Africans did not forget their humiliations but remembered how they had survived the war and its aftermath.

Chimatira went on to tell of how he and others had survived in a mountain cave, courtesy of an "Other," an outsider. *The man who saved us was my brother-in-law, the late Majoni, he was a Mbire. Majoni knew how to render the dynamite/gelignite harmless. We used to cut off the connection; say if the gelignite was thrown, and it fell on this spot, we got hold of it, and cut it, now it was harmless. Meanwhile, we would be looking out with guns in place during Chindunduma or Chimurenga. Nyamweda fought hard on the Mhanyame River. Chivero was fighting on the Mupfure banks, along with Ma-*

shayamombe, also known as Chinengundu. This Chinengundu was really possessed and this is what he used to do: When everyone in the house was dead asleep, he would fumigate the house with medicinal smoke. He fumigated the soldiers when they were asleep. Then went around taking their bullets and guns and giving them to his people. That was Chinengundu. He suffered a lot [at the hands of the Europeans] before he died.[37]

Chimatira was also eager to tell how close he had been to the action, as his father, a chief, had been among those huddled together with some of the important personalities of central and western MaShonaland, and the Mazowe valley in particular, during the 1896–97 wars. As he told it, *while Mashayamombe banded together with people like Chivero to fight, chiefs like Nyamweda and his people fought on the Mhanyame, right there where there is a pass through which the train now passes, right there where the train makes a turn heading for Norton. We [on the other hand, were] in the company of Hwata and Chiweshe in the mountain. That one there, I forget the name of the mountain which is the site of the present Mazowe dam. That was our mountain stronghold. I was in Chiweshe at the outbreak [of the war] with the gun I'd obtained at Beatrice. I still have the gun, what could have happened to it? Hwata and everyone had guns. My God, where do you think the guns that were distributed by Nehanda had come from? The procedure was that if you killed the enemy, then you took the guns and they were surrendered to the chief who would distribute them among his councilors or leading figures. The bullets were not a problem because the Europeans killed were deprived of their bullets as well. It was then that Kaguvi told people, "Run away!" He said the pressure was too much from all sides, and so there was nowhere to look and the solution was to flee. They ran away and joined up with Nehanda who was down there, in Mt. Darwin where they were captured. We who were with Hwata had already been captured. However, when we were captured, nothing was done to us, we were merely told to go back to our homes.*[38]

Founding myths, as we have seen, were based on the exercise of memory, "doing" something about remembered history. The victors of Southern Rhodesia's 1896–97 wars controlled the narrative of what became "national" history, insisting that their right of founding was based on the humiliation of the vanquished, whose "real and symbolic wounds were stored in the archives of collective memory."[39] Those real and symbolic wounds became sources of oral traditions and oral histories that the vanquished invoked as they exercised their own memories of what they or their ancestors had done in the past, as years of colonialism turned into decades. Chimatira and all the men in this chapter told stories that remembered history "as it happened" to them as individuals, as social groups, and as a collective. The history those men told was a history similar to that of the professional historian, who, as the historian Susan Crane reminds us, practices "a form for collective memory, valid for more than any single subject/ive individual; malleable and revisable. [It] is common property rather than personal memory, national rather than personal."[40] By juxtaposing these memories, we are able to see the parallel nature of the foundational myths of how Zimbabwe (or Rhodesia) was made. It was the memories of those 1896–97 wars that laid the foundations for the deep chasms between "our" History and "their" History in Southern Rhodesia, a chasm that still haunts Zimbabwe today.

6 African Autobiography
Collective Memory and the Myths of Conquered Peoples

Unlike the stories told orally by the men in the previous chapter, here we turn to a published, self-written memoir by a man of more or less the same generation. The memoir is that of Lawrence Vambe, a man who was born into colonialism and was part of a burgeoning intelligentsia who had acquired Western education and were documenting African histories and memories during the colonial period. Vambe was born in 1917 at Chishawasha Catholic Mission, not far from Mazowe, land of the famous spirit medium Charwe, or Salisbury, the colonial administrative center. Vambe recorded his memories as "his people's" history, especially their memories of the 1896–97 war, in *An Ill-Fated People: Zimbabwe before and after Rhodes*.[1] That Vambe chose to document his memoirs as his people's history of general despair living under colonialism is provocative, as it invokes the fact and fiction of the self, the individual superimposed on the collective and vice versa. I therefore treat his memoir as more *autobiomythography*[2] than conventional autobiography. This is because some of his characterizations—for example, that of his grandmother, on whom I focus in this chapter—may signify his own conflicted attitudes toward colonialism, which he chose to attribute to his grandmother rather than claim as his own, and the same could be said of his treatment of his grandfather. For that reason, I use *memoir* and *autobiomythography* interchangeably in this chapter as acknowledgment of both the fact of his life (history) and the fiction of his memoir (memory). As Partha Chateerjee astutely observed of nationalist imaginings, "The new individual, it would seem, could represent the history of his life only by inscribing it in the narrative of the nation."[3] On the other hand, Vambe's memoir reminds us of Susan Crane's call to "write the individual back into collective memory" because it is the individual that does the actual everyday remembering and perpetuating of that memory in social and collective settings.[4] It is through individual memories, however flawed, that we can tease out social and collective memories.

As in the previous chapter, where I heeded Toni Morrison's counsel not to distrust the (few) writings of the former colonized,[5] I do not treat Vambe's memoirs as all historical truth or fiction of Shawasha memories, including memories of his own individual family. Rather, I bring the same skepticism that I have brought to all my sources thus far. If Vambe concocted a historical figure—say, his grandmother—I do not blindly read it as the whole historical "truth." Rather, I use it to illustrate the point of this book, namely, that cultural nationalists like Vambe often embellished the (imagined) past. That is, although it is true that Vambe had a grandmother, whether she was like the one portrayed in his memoir does not interest me here. What does interest me is how he represented his grandmother and "his people," the Shawasha, and what that tells us about individual memory and its consequences for social and collective memory. Vambe's memoirs also remind us of Luise White's astute assessment about the effects of violence on those who experienced it: that it "threaten[ed their] ability to think historically, with immense consequences to collective public history."[6] Vambe's distorted re-membering of "his people's" history has to be understood as an individual's recollections and imaginings shaped by the traumas of physical, sociocultural, and psychological violence of colonialism.[7]

In this chapter, three case studies help us to understand Africans' gendered individual, social, and collective memories of colonialism. In the first, the intergenerational experiences of colonialism illustrate how when Africans were born affected their lives. The second highlights the impact of the Land Apportionment Act of 1930, which fostered parallel memory, as Africans were legally required to live on "Native Reservations," which kept them racially segregated from the settlers. The third case study illustrates the impact of colonial education, which emphasized Africans' differences rather than their similarities, nurturing the "creation of tribalism," to paraphrase the late historian Leroy Vail. I juxtapose Vambe's version of Shawasha "tribal" history to that of Aaron Jacha, from the African Oral History Collection, to show contrasting African memories of the same colonial experiences. The chapter closes with an analysis of sexism and gender bias in cultural nationalist writings like Vambe's memoir. By pointing to the minds and bodies of women—whether his grandmother or the "loose" women in the village—as corrupters of African culture, Vambe reminds us that African nationalism tended to be more concerned with racism and masculine exclusion from power than with its own sexism and gender equality during the war or in the future.

Intergenerational Encounters with Colonialism

An Ill-Fated People opens with several crises at Vambe's grandparents' homestead, where he grew up. The two important crises we will focus on here are the pregnancy of an unwed aunt, Josephine, living on what had become Catholic mission land, and the arrest of his grandfather, Mizha, by the colonial police for unpaid dog taxes. Those two events led to identity crises among the three generations living at the homestead as they adjusted to the reality of having been just "vaShawasha" (the Shawasha), to being "blacks" or a "Shona tribe" reaching for a "pan-Native Rhodesian" national identity. In Chishawasha, as in other districts in central and northern Rhodesia, the legend of Nehanda and her famous medium Charwe were just as important, as vaShawasha shared a history and culture with the people of Mazowe. The character who best exemplified the older generation (though Vambe wished she were otherwise) was Vambe's grandmother, Madzidza. According to Vambe, she had the most radical views of the settlers and of Christianity in all the family. Members of the oldest generation, for the most part, had both feet in the world as they knew it before colonialism. Some members of that generation were indifferent, while others were accommodating of the new world order, which they felt powerless to change. Vambe's parents exemplified the in-between generation, those who also had to adjust their lives to fit the new order, as demanded by the colonial authorities, not by their African leadership. This in-between generation had one foot planted in the African past and one in the colonial present. The youngest generation, who grew up knowing nothing else but missionary and colonial rule, is best exemplified by the narrator/author himself. That youngest generation had both feet planted firmly in the colonial world, all the while accommodating the world of their parents and grandparents through historical memory.

Madzidza, Vambe's best literary construct, or historical imagination, in the memoir, is an important character, as she illuminates not only how African parallel cultural memory was formed but also how the execution of key politico-religious figures like Charwe impacted the attitudes of the in-between and youngest generations toward missionary education and colonial rule after the 1896–97 wars in Southern Rhodesia. Madzidza is also important because she reminds us that Charwe was not the only "heroine" who rejected things European, especially Christianity, as celebrated in state narratives and popular memory.[8] Madzidza and her generation, especially the women, tended to be vanguards of a cultural nationalism that the younger generation both despised and admired. Like Charwe, Madzidza did not entirely remove herself from the colonial system—not that one really could. Rather, she found ways to carve out spaces, if only intellectual ones, to defy colonial prescriptions for African lives. Thus, when her daughter Josephine turned up pregnant while unwed and living on Catholic mission property, most of the family were aghast, some even disgusted.

But not Madzidza, *whose prejudices against anything alien were always strongly expressed. [She] spoke as if this was the best news she had had for a long time. She said she recognized no law outside that of the tribe. She was nauseated, repeat nauseated, by the views held by Mizha, her husband, and her two sin-fearing daughters, who took too much account of the peculiar opinions of the interfering white clerics at Chishawasha Mission. This matter was African, she said, and strictly domestic. Why should a white man be permitted to thrust his red nose into it. For just this once, she emphasized, the Father Superior at the Mission might be told to mind his own business while the Africans, especially her family, minded theirs. As far as she was concerned, her daughter and husband, Martin, had done no wrong whatever. God bless them, they had shown courage and true African independence of mind, in these critical times when all sorts of white men were charging about the country, expecting and demanding blind obedience from black people who asked for nothing more than to be left alone to live their own lives and follow their God-given customs in peace.*[9]

For Madzidza, "steeped in tribal conservatism,"[10] kowtowing to the puritanical alien missionaries was the worst of crimes, and she despised her husband and two convert daughters for not questioning and rejecting the whole colonial worldview—missionaries and all. "Madzidza was rebellious by nature, and saw something of herself in Josephine, whose pregnant condition she regarded as an act of defiance against the alien religious system that she detested and felt it her duty to denounce day by day. So strong were her anti-Church views that she resisted being baptized to the very end."[11] Madzidza believed that the 1896–97 wars had to be repeated, for African defeat, lynchings notwithstanding, did not mean that people could not fight back, again. That perspective was in contrast to that of Mizha, her "practical" husband, who "chided his wife for using brave words to minimize the seriousness of the situation [saying], 'what good do brave words do? We are a subject people. Your daughter has broken the white man's law. . . . What does the white man care about our customs? He has power to punish.'"[12] Vambe could have been exaggerating the extremes of his grandparents' characters for dramatic effect. However, it is telling that he gave them such reversed gendered roles: the fierce, "outlandish" female opposite the sanguine, "reasonable" male.

By attributing such contrasting characters in his grandparents, Vambe was demonstrating the internal conflicts of the Western-educated African middle class, who despised colonialism but with equal fervor liked it, mostly because they understood it more than they did their shattered past. The household tensions colonial rule produced in Vambe's family and larger community are starkly illustrated in the contrasting world-views of Madzidza and Mizha. To the younger generations, Madzidza's "optimistic belligerence" to colonial rule, "described as 'wild' and 'impractical' by Mizha," also exemplified the gendered nature of the parallel memory making that the young imbibed.[13] The young often leaned toward Grandfather Mizha's worldview more than they did toward Madzidza's, for Madzidza only raised the unwanted specter of the defeat in war two decades earlier. Mizha's attitude toward colonialism, I would argue, was similar to that of Hwata and Chiweshe, whom we saw earlier, who chose to label Mativirira, the first post-1898 Nehanda medium in Mazowe, a charlatan out to cause trouble with the colonial administration, while they were willing to acquiesce, make peace, and accept the badges.

Madzidza's and Mizha's characters also illuminate the deep fractures that occurred in African societies once they were dispossessed of not only their lands but also their sense of personhood, as color-based policies put tremendous stress on these societies. The new European gentry—the settlers as landowners—had the power to decide who could stay on "their" land and who might be ejected for whatever reason, as in the cases of Mr. Hallas and Mr Bester. For a people like vaShawasha—an ethnic mix rather than a "tribe"—life after 1898 meant living on land that no longer belonged to them, but to the new landlords, the Jesuit missionaries. It meant abiding by the rules set out by the missionaries rather than by their own historical political and social structures. As Vambe bitterly re-called, missionaries exerted a tremendous power over his people: *Now, I knew that the Church both temporal and spiritual, held the whip-hand in all tribal affairs . . . ; it could, if it so wished, toss out of its lands any man, woman, or family at any time and for any reason at all. There was no right of appeal to anyone in case of ejection or others of a similar kind. It could there-fore be said, putting it in crude practical terms, that the Church owned the VaShawasha people; its influence over everyone was overpowering. Like the air we breathed, the Church was everywhere, as much in the loud peals of its bells which rang out continually each day and was heard for miles around, as in the authority of its dogmatic but largely mystifying teaching.*[14]

Those same missionaries were often criticized for their heavy-handed-ness with the Africans, yet in the same breath they were praised for their work with Africans when the colonial bureaucracy was only interested in cheap African labor for the mines and plantations. That fire-and-ice re-lationship between the colonial bureaucracy and the missionaries on the one hand and the Africans on the other created a schizophrenic genera-tion of African youths like Vambe who, to varying degrees, were deeply scarred by seeing their grandparents, parents, and general elders reduced to non-people by colonial racial definitions, land expropriation, and eco-nomic dispossession.[15] Many of the young saw elders like Grandfather Mizha, who acquiesced to colonial power, as "practical" and those like Grandmother Madzidza, who opposed colonialism with brave words, as "tribal conservatives" resistant to change and "progress."

The second poignant example of white ownership and black dispos-session in the new colony/nation that played out at the Vambe home-stead was the arrest of Mizha, as the head of household, for not paying dog taxes: *Nobody, man or woman, raised a finger in protest. We were all reduced to a state of sheepishness and timidity. Such was the fear the lone [white] officer, and the forces he represented, had instilled into the hearts and minds of my people. All grandmother's verbal courage and quick biting tongue had melted and vanished in thin air. Even Jakobo, Mizha's eldest son by his first wife, who normally never stopped boasting of his bravery and expressing contempt for the rest of his fellow tribesmen, suddenly seemed to have become a coward like everyone else, and merely stared into space. There was his fa-ther, being removed from our presence as if he were a dangerous criminal and Jakobo had absolutely nothing to say or do in his defense.*[16] The fear for "white people, particularly those in authority" translated into helplessness and a kind of paralysis in the face of oppression that had not been present among "Africans of my country before 1896," Vambe lamented.[17] The settlers made it clear that post-1898 Southern Rhodesia firmly belonged to the whites.

The only recourse to justice the African family seemed to have after its patriarch was arrested was to call on their ancestors. Vambe's uncle Jakobo and the whole family gathered together to invoke the ancestors both after Mizha's arrest and when he returned home about two months later. The ancestors were the only ones able to understand and explain the *ngozi*, the malevolent spirit, in their midst. As Jakobo led the family in invoking the ancestors, he asked why the ancestors had allowed "victory to go to them [the white settlers] rather than to us. You must know better than we do that we shall always need care, succor and safeguards against the machinations and knavishness of the white men who say they are our masters and come into our homes as it pleases them to make criminals of us."[18] The Africans invoking the ancestors perceived colonialism as a terror attributable only to a malevolent spirit. But unlike in times past, when life had been lived according to their old ways and they had known how to find and placate the malevolent spirit(s) so they could be left alone, in peace, colonialism was an unknown *ngozi* spirit, a frightful reality. Jakobo's supplication to the ancestors, by Vambe's assessment, had the effect of a "tranquilizer" on those present. Invoking the ancestors, it seems, made true Karl Marx's critique of his own religious Germany when he said that "religion is the sigh of the oppressed creature, the heart of a heartless world, and the soul of soulless conditions. It is the opium of the people."[19] The invocation of the ancestors by Africans despairing of colonialism, while looked down upon by the younger generation, who thought of themselves as Christians, later became appealing to the same generation as they turned toward an African nationalism that put "our culture" at the center of their discourse. Invoking the ancestors became "more African," and that connection to the African past bridged all kinds of differences that had emerged among Africans. Invoking the ancestors was a way of returning the nation to its "origins."

The Seeds of Parallel Memory
Are Sown in the Native Reserves

As we have seen, for many belonging to the older and in-between generations their faith in the power of the ancestors was shaken by the defeats of 1896–97. Yet, many still held fast to their faith, as the new Christian God seemed biased against the Africans in favor of the Europeans. Ironically, the younger generations, who straddled the world of the ancestors with that of the missionaries, who preached fire and brimstone to those who did not repent from their "pagan" ways, were more invested in Christianity than in ancestral veneration—as though exchanging African theologies and liturgies for the version preached by the Jesuit missionaries would provide stability. The mixture of love and hate that Vambe and the people of Chishawasha felt for the (mostly German) Jesuit missionaries was exemplified by the Africans' attitudes toward Francis Richartz. Some Shawasha despised the Jesuits, while others greatly admired Father Richartz, the prison chaplain who had administered to Charwe and "Other Condemned Prisoners" during the last days of their lives. As Vambe wrote, *Father Richartz and his religious community were sincerely trying to make amends for the terrible wrongs that had been committed against my people. They were attempting to give the VaShawasha a new hope, dignity and sophistication which would help them cope with the challenges of the white man's civilization [and] to confound the Europeans' deep-seated belief that Africans were permanently inferior.*[20] It would seem that the missionaries were simultaneously implicated in and exonerated from the imperial project that left vaShawasha and all Africans in the colony a subjugated people. More importantly, the Jesuit paradox also shows Vambe's generation's two minds about missionaries, who were their landlords and mentors in the European world that had radically changed African life. Richartz and the Chishawasha Mission represented the ambiguities of the civilizing mission the young generations were dealing with, and so Madzidza and Mizha serve as Vambe's perfect avatars for his own ambivalence about the benefits and trade-offs of European culture, which had simultaneously dealt an almost mortal wound to the African psyche.

The other effect of growing up in Southern Rhodesia as the African world shattered as the result of colonial engineering was the tremendous stress on young people of cultures already in flux owing to Southern African regional politics from the mid- to late nineteenth and early twentieth centuries, the *mfecane*. The missionaries participated in the colonial project by battling for young African souls against the world of the ancestors. The older generation of Vambe's childhood, on the other hand, did not forget the 1896–97 war. *As time went on during my tribal upbringing,* Vambe tells us, *I was to learn that this was easily the most popular topic of discussion at informal tribal gatherings. It cropped up at all sorts of occasions and for all kinds of reasons, particularly when people were involved in religious controversies or airing their strong views on current political issues and the burdens which were imposed on them by white rule.*[21] The old's holding on to the (painful) past and (re)telling it to the young had the effect of historical consciousness-raising among young people. Indeed, remembering the 1896–97 war was of foremost importance to the young as they listened to their elders relive their experiences. The older generation's remembering and recounting of the past fascinated the young. Vambe *never tired of hearing the exciting details, and in the process developed a compulsive urge to remember as much as I could of my tribe's contribution to the struggle for freedom as well as their interpretation of Rhodesian history.* He could use his "privilege of an education" to write down what his elders told him and his generation about their exploits and defeats during the 1896–97 war for those who disparaged that history. It was a way of re-membering their dismembered history, which was excluded from the white "national" history curriculum.[22]

The colonial authorities, rather than encouraging a shared sense of citizenship between black and white, Vambe felt, often adopted a paternalistic and antagonistic attitude toward Africans, their history, and their general way of life. This often created tensions for the younger generation, the "colonial born," whose elders, both familial and in the general society, "strove to educate and bring up their young in the—to them—not unrealistic, but vain hope that the VaShawasha concept of nationhood would be perpetuated, and our people would eventually recapture their glorious past."[23] That attitude is also captured in Solomon Mutswairo's first novel, *Feso*, which invokes a glorious past usurped by an oppressor whom the ancestors had to assist the living to defeat so that they could recapture that glory.[24] For Vambe, the tragedy was that though a shared memory of the 1896–97 war was not possible with the settlers, a shared sense of nationhood should have been, but for "the Rhodesian white society [that] spoke loudly against itself, the more so when a policeman visited our village to enforce laws which emphasized our conquered status rather than making us feel proud to be identified with white civilization."[25]

Colonial society, it seemed, rubbed sand into the wounds of the conquered. Is it any wonder that white children grew up feeling entitled, while black children grew up feeling grateful for the crumbs that fell off the white table? The net effect was that (black) young people, especially males, grew up with a sense of patriarchal indignation at the colonial characterization of (male) Africans as "a people with no guts or political acumen, whose future depended entirely on the pride and prejudices of the white minority."[26] The tragedy, of course, was that even among those with the "privilege of an education," such as Vambe, few had Madzidza-like "brave words" for the missionaries or colonial authorities. Few stood up to colonial privilege and abuse, reminding the colonizer that they too were citizens and no one had the right to lean on (white) ancestral privilege alone to claim full citizenship in the colony/country.[27]

Madzidza's dislike of the new settlers was typical of the older generation, who believed that the newcomers (the British) were no good, compared with the Portuguese, who had made their way into the interior in earlier centuries. As Vambe remembered, "Grandmother's strong dislike of white people in general seemed to have its origin in the treacherous role played by Selous and other white men who paved the way for the white occupation of Zimbabwe. 'We fed them, but they bit us afterwards,' was her eternal song."[28] That sense of betrayal was also expressed decades later by chiefs at a meeting with the British government minister Gordon Walker. Walker had traveled to the colonies of Nyasaland, Northern Rhodesia, and Southern Rhodesia (Malawi, Zambia, and Zimbabwe) in the 1950s on a fact-finding mission to discover how Africans viewed the proposed Central Africa Federation, which was to turn the three contiguous colonies into one large colony or federation of colonies. As one large (white-ruled) federation, the colonies stood a greater chance of achieving dominion status—like South Africa, Canada, Australia, or New Zealand—something Southern Rhodesia, unlike the Union of South Africa, had not yet achieved owing to its small white population and its being landlocked. In fact, in a 1923 referendum among settlers, Southern Rhodesia had rejected becoming part of the Union of South Africa in favor of self-rule because of the "Afrikaner problem."

Consequently, three decades later, when Southern Rhodesia took the lead in forming a federation with Northern Rhodesia and Nyasaland, there was great concern, as the British Empire in general was moving toward decolonization. Gordon Walker, therefore, had traveled to the colonies to meet with African chiefs (among others) to hear their views firsthand. Vambe and a fellow African journalist covered that meeting. Vambe's memory of it, ironically, reflected the new educated elite's belief that the colonial system could be reformed to accommodate Africans. For that meeting, the Rhodesian government chose a white native commissioner from the Native Department who was a fluent Shona speaker, rather than an African, to translate for the chiefs and the visiting British minister. *I was indescribably furious that the British Minister was not being properly informed of what the African Chiefs thought, not only about the Federation, but more important still, about the whole [chain] of events which had turned Southern Rhodesia into a pocket edition of South Africa without the mighty British Government raising a finger,* Vambe lamented. And since he could not speak at that meeting, his memoirs were his way of correcting *the record of the feeling of our representatives, so that historians would know that the Africans of Southern Rhodesia were totally against race segregation [in the colony and proposed Federation]. . . . The chief spoke to this effect: "In one of your laws of international conduct, you stipulate that a conquered nation should pay an agreed sum of money to the conqueror over a period of years, say twenty-five years. When this and other conditions have been fulfilled, you forgive each other, and live as friends afterwards. You did this to the Germans after the First World War. And even after the recent war, you did not seem to bear a grudge against the Germans. You certainly did not segregate or discriminate against any German. But you have not shown this human and Christian attitude to us black people. We fought you in the 1896 rebellion and that is a very long time ago. Yet you have not forgiven us. Why don't you exact some punishment on us as imposed on the Germans? We are prepared to pay whatever fine . . . , as long as we know that this will buy back our freedom in the only country God gave us."*[29]

Vambe clearly shows that he shared the assertive but soft-spoken chief's views on racism in the colony. Yet, Vambe could not find any "brave words" within himself to support the chief in challenging authority. At that meeting, he behaved in much the same way that he described his elders as behaving when Grandfather Mizha was arrested. Vambe, it seems, had internalized oppression, for he could not openly express protest even if it meant only agreeing with the eloquent speaker. Vambe was not alone in his decision not to speak out; his fellow African journalist, who was just as angry and also felt cornered, encouraged silence. He reminded Vambe that if he or they spoke up against the colonial official misrepresenting African political views, Vambe "could create a crisis which would result in my losing my job." More importantly, his fellow journalist reminded him that his (Vambe's) reputation would be tarnished and he would never be able to find another job in his chosen profession—or any job of middle-class standing open to Africans—in the colony: "I took his advice and said nothing; I sat in mortified silence, but raged inwardly."[30] So it was that Africans and Rhodesians could never equally represent themselves to their superiors from London. The worst of it was that Africans tended to complain "to each other, which made no difference at all to their problems"[31]—an ironic observation considering that the Shona- and English-speaking African journalists had not raised their voices at the meeting between the chiefs and the minister. The settlers, for their part, had come to think that "it was [their] right to be respected by every African."[32] This scenario clearly illustrates Madzidza's concerns. It also affirms Frantz Fanon's analysis that "in a colonial context, the settler only ends his work of breaking the native in when the latter admits loudly and intelligibly, the supremacy of the white man's values" and representations.[33] Through their silence, Vambe and his colleague confirmed to the white authorities present that the settlers had the power. The Rhodesian authorities knew they had "broken the native in" when neither man spoke out even though it was obvious that they knew that mistranslation was occurring at that critical meeting.

Aaron Jacha Contests Vambe's "Tribal History"

The intergenerational gendered experiences of colonialism that Vambe remembered involving his family and his people, while shared as collective history and memory among many Africans as "natives" in the colony, were not uncontested. That is, in Vambe's imagine-nation of vaShawasha's social and collective memory was the idea that they were a "tribe *always* known by the totems Murehwa and Soko."[34] The politico-cultural nationalist Vambe assumed that Shawasha "tribal" identity was timeless, pure, and unsullied by anyone, including the Ndebele, who had settled in what became southwestern Southern Rhodesia four or so decades before European occupation in 1890 or 1893. However, if people like Vambe remembered their "tribal" history as pure, others (even among the Shawasha) remembered different narratives of Shawasha/Shona history and ethnic identity, including relations with the Ndebele. An example is the narrative of Aaron Jacha, an African man educated at a Methodist mission, who told a different version of the history of "an ill-fated people." Unlike Vambe, who was educated by Catholic missionaries, Jacha was educated by Protestants; and among other likely variables, it seems that each man's view of the remembered and narrated past was colored by the worldview of his missionary mentors. Jacha told his own story of precolonial African history and relations, braided into that of his male forebears, whom he characterized as forward-looking men, able to adapt and thrive in every new generation and situation, right into the colonial period, when he was living up to that legacy by working for the colonial bureaucracy.

By his telling, Jacha was *born in 1899 in the month of October at Epworth mission, which at the time was referred to as the Chiremba area. Even today, that name Chiremba, is still used. It was there that my parents lived; I am the son of Jacha. The name Jacha which I am well known by is not my name, but my father's. My real name by which I was baptized is Aaron. My father belonged to the Rusike country. Rusike is now part of Goromonzi district. Our ancestors were in that country long before the coming of the whites; they were migrating from Muzarabani, an area in Mount Darwin district, the country of the Korekore. In that area is a place called Mabwemachena lying in the Musengezi River Valley. It is at that place that my ancestors lived. As you know, it was the area of the great chiefs, where the Munhumutapas lived. My ancestors migrated from there, and headed south; mainly because of disagreement with others.* Aaron Jacha, like narrators we encountered in the previous chapter, saw history as motion rather than a static memory. Jacha's narration traces a family history not only of migration but also of mixing with other clans and ethnic groups, thereby changing and shifting identities. Yet, like many others whose narratives are in the African History Collection (including Vambe), he connected his family, clan, and ethnic histories to the Munhumutapa kingdom as a way of claiming autochthony longer and deeper than that of the (British) settlers.

Jacha continued his narrative of Shawasha autochthony in that part of Southern Rhodesia, emphasizing that the main reason why *tribes separated was because of failure to agree with each other, and others felt they were not well settled and so decided to migrate. When they settled down, they were initially commoners, just as the others; but because of their industrious-*

ness and magical powers, they proved they were clever. You see, [my people] were nicknamed Rusike people by the Rozvi because the Rozvi realized these people could make fire [more easily]. Rusike means the one who makes fire by friction, taking two sticks and rubbing them against each other in dry tender grass; the sparks from the two sticks caught and a fire started. The sparks are called magora. So they were nicknamed Rusike, and his praise poem became Wadyegora (fire eater). The Rozvi themselves used to confer chieftainship and [my ancestors] were given the chieftaincy called Rusike. So today, our country is Rusike, and our praise poem is Wadyegora. Our original mutupo (totem) was nzou (elephant) but when my ancestors got here, they became Moyo [heart, after the Rozvi totem], and our new name Wadyegora.[35] Jacha also told of (older) African patron-client relations that had nothing to do with skin color but were based on industry, ethnicity, and mobility, all flexible categories subject to change over time.

Unlike Vambe, Jacha did not seem bothered by the shifting identities in his people's history; nor did he seek a primordial existence unchanged over time. Jacha relished telling how his ancestors had started in the northeastern part of the country, the land of the "Korekore" and the "original Nehanda." But after moving, they had taken on a new identity among the Rozvi, including the Rozvi totem of Moyo and a new praise poem, Wadyegora (Fire Eater). Cultural nationalists like Vambe did not like that kind of remembering, for it sullied the imagined "purity" of the nation/tribe. Jacha's narrative, on the other hand, suggests that those able to adapt to the new situation—including taking on new totems and praise poems—were better able to narrate not only the "ill fate" of their people's history but also the memory of their resilience and ability to thrive. Jacha's family and ethnic identities had changed not only in the distant past but also in recent times. His own father was one of the first Africans to accept Christianity [Methodism] when the whites came into this country. That is why many of us, of the Mutaiko house [clan] were educated. We went to school, and we, by far, outdid those of the other [clans,] who have only recently begun to attend school. We began going to school long back.[36]

Jacha's narrative obviously presents his own family history as that of men able to live with the ambiguity and fluidity of individual, ethnic, and national identities—including a racialized colonial one that he could turn to his advantage. For that reason, he did not find it devastating that his father, along with his brothers, had once lived among the Ndebele. In fact, he enjoyed retelling his father and uncles' colorful history: My father *and his brothers, after the death of their father, Chakuvinga, were captured by the Ndebele and were taken to Lalapanzi. Once there, because they were intelligent, they were told to join the Ndebele impis (army regiments). Some went with their wives, but others did not have wives. Once there, they had their ears pierced to make them look like the Ndebele. However, the spirits of their homeland did not want them to stay there, and so they made a plan to go back to their home. In fact, they ran away. They were pursued, but not recaptured. My father, Jacha himself, had a long story of this escape. He said when they escaped, they were followed, and they were scattered all over with others, making it out through different channels. My father realized that the Ndebele had caught up with him, so he went into an ant-bear's hole. He had a small body, so he managed to hide in the ant-bear's hole. The Ndebele went past looking for him but they failed to find him. The other brothers, China-kidzwa and Mutunhire wondered where he was; and seeing that the Ndebele had gone back, they searched for him. Just before dawn, they came across him, for he was following their trail, and together they trekked to Wedza.*[37]

Jacha seems not to have denied the ethnic differences between the Shona and the Ndebele. Indeed, the Ndebele had a caste system based on place of origin, with those who had come from farther south (Zululand) having a higher social status. In reality, however, because those of the south (the Ndebele) were outnumbered by those among whom they finally settled (the Shona), it was more practical to incorporate and assimilate than to impose an all-out (African) colonial system. Thus, most Shona from further north who had been captured by the Ndebele in their raids, like the Shona of Jacha's father's generation, were assimilated into Ndebele life and culture. As Jacha told it, *the Shona among the Ndebele had homes for they lived there quite a number of years, being Ndebelized. They could speak the language. My father told me when they lived among the Ndebele they were not made to work, they simply lived there in their own houses, and did some agriculture, including looking after cattle. They used to kill those cattle that had been seized in raids. Otherwise they lived normal lives, they were not taken as captives who were made to work, but there were normal people who had been made to grow up among the Ndebele. Don't you notice those of the Ncube totem [among the Ndebele] are the very Mbire [Shona] people who had been of the Soko totem in Wedza. The Ndebele word for the Shona word Soko is Ncube; and both translate to Monkey. So, by calling themselves Ncube, the Shona were Ndebelizing their totem. What made them escape was the power of their ancestral spirits which told them they could not possibly live there. They resettled on the other side of the Wedza mountain near Manhandida Mountain.*[38] In fact, Hwata, of Charwe's dynasty, also spent time among the Ndebele,[39] and according to Jacha, whether one was royalty, as Hwata was, or ordinary folk, as Jacha's kin were, most Shona adopted the culture of Ndebele society. The Ndebele, in turn, also absorbed Shona practices. Jacha's narrative demonstrates that the historian looking for African-produced voices of the past must cast a wider net. Vambe's memoir, while important as a text of its time, telling us what and how Africans were remembering, is also limited by the storyteller's inability to contain the rich complexities of African responses to colonialism.

Contrasting Jacha's brief memories with those of Vambe highlights an ironic twist to the title of Vambe's memoirs, *An Ill-Fated People*. It would seem that the tragic fate for the Africans was not only the clutches of physical colonialism but also the long-term crisis engendered by psychological colonization. Reading Vambe's memoir, one is haunted by how psychological colonialism stamped itself deep into the psyche of the colonized. That experience was not unique to Southern Rhodesia; it was shared by many in the British colonies in Africa and elsewhere. The Kenyan intellectual Ngũgĩ wa Thiong'o wrote for many when he remembered his own humiliating colonial education, especially learning the English language, which displaced his native Gíkũyũ.[40] What was more, "English became the measure of intelligence and ability in the arts and sciences, and all other branches of learning. English became the main determinant of a child's progress up the ladder of formal education."[41] Wa Thiong'o's critique is important because it helps us to understand both the rupture and the resilience experienced by Vambe's generation of Africans, who would become ardent nationalists.

Fighting Colonialism with One Hand, Upholding Sexism with the Other

Lastly, and perhaps most important to this book's gender analysis of masculine nationalist memory, texts like Vambe's *An Ill-Fated People*, while important as evidence of Africans documenting their own history or fictional imaginations of the past, brought to the fore the corrosive nature of gender-biased memory. Both white and black male nationalists tended to uphold patriarchy, keen to fight for the fatherland with one hand while upholding sexism with the other. In the case of white nationalists, white women's pioneer history was muted if not whitewashed in favor of men's narratives. Sexism, also evident, was contested by nineteenth-century African women, for example, in the trial of Kaguvi, in which the women witnesses vigorously defended themselves against African men's patriarchal assertions over women's bodies and lives.

In the case of twentieth-century black nationalists, racism, not sexism, was the "real" enemy. Women who sought to carve out spaces of liberation for themselves were deemed corrupters of "African culture," as exemplified by Vambe's assessment of some women in his village: *One of the first signs of moral corruption in [the African] village was the case of a woman called Misi, who took up prostitution, which the Africans of that day regarded the worst possible human degradation. As far as I know, she was the first woman in Chishawasha to fall from the state of tribal grace, and to succumb to this vice, which was among the first and most loathsome importations of European civilization into Africa. Of course, as white industry expanded and uprooted more and more Africans from the safety of their highly moral tribal environment, prostitution became more common and less shocking, particularly among the Ndebele and Manyika peoples. But at this stage, the otherwise innocent and puritanical people of Mashonganyika were scandalized and angered when they discovered that one of their own womenfolk had fallen this way. The conservative VaShawasha seized on Misi's case as one of the best pieces of evidence they would have against the bad influence of the white man. And they not only made Misi a tribal issue, but also regarded her as a special kind of traitor to the good name and traditions of their tribe. They tried to banish her altogether from Mashonganyika. . . . As I remember only too well, they were not only horrified by Misi's moral depravity, her obvious lack of shame and her defiance, which was shared by her mother. They were also afraid that Misi would lead astray some of the other women in Mashonganyika.*[42] That characterization assumed that women were the moral barometers in African societies; yet it did not analyze the crisis of women's lives and their struggles for equal treatment in African societies and by the colonial government, which sought to contain African women by villagizing and/or traditionalizing them in the rural and urban areas. More importantly, it did not critique the men who patronized those women as corrupters of "African culture."

Vambe's sexist analysis of Misi did not begin with background on how and, especially, why she came to be a prostitute. Rather, it began with the story of a contaminated woman about to infect her society with what she carried between her legs and of the values of female self-assertion, which suddenly seemed "un-African." Vambe cast Misi as a woman who "had all the necessary ingredients for making a success of her calling, and she did. She had great beauty. She had brains, and charm, and ruthless craftiness."⁴³ Not only did Misi brazenly work as a prostitute but Vambe would see her returning home laden with gifts for her family. "On these periodic holidays at her home . . . , exactly as the village sages had anticipated and feared, these emancipated ladies greatly excited local men of the younger set whose simple, work-worn wives and sweethearts were not as alluring or as well-washed, sweetly scented, and finely dressed as their arrogant rivals from the towns."⁴⁴ Only later in the narrative did Vambe remember that Misi had not always been a prostitute; she had been "a respectable woman, married with three sons." Trouble had started when on weekends men penned up in the townships of nearby Salisbury wandered into neighboring peri-urban and rural spaces looking for fun, a taste of home, and sex, since they lived in bachelor pads, or dormitories, with little privacy and were not allowed to have their wives with them. That Vambe chose to emphasize Misi's moral depravity rather than the blow that had devastated African societies—even as there were few openings for new forms of self-expression—tells us that nationalism's memory tended toward a patriarchal reclamation of power rather than an emancipatory ideology for all. After all, Misi had come from a family that Vambe characterized as "[typifying] Shona adaptability." And in the same fashion that he contrasted his grandfather with his grandmother at the beginning of the book, he gave the men of Misi's family a better assessment than he gave the women.

Misi's family, and especially the men, Vambe wrote, "were an extraordinarily intelligent people. Her father had seen something of the Rhodesian world because he had worked in different parts of the country. Although he was getting on in age, and was regarded as one of the elder statesmen of the tribe, he was a liberal and progressive man who accepted the inevitability of social changes."⁴⁵ Her brothers were doing well for themselves, one as a tradesman, the other as a builder, "while her two sisters were trend-setters in the world of dress fashions." The mother, according to Vambe, was the worst, for "she worshipped anything implied in the word *chirungu*—Europeanism" and all the baggage that came with it, including her fear of witches, which led her to inflict a serious wound on herself in an effort to ward off a nonexistent witch. That fear of witches—a combination of African and European nervosas—went hand in hand with the fear of *ngozi* spirits, which could be used to hex those doing well for themselves because of their assimilation into European modes of being.

Vambe's memoir is important for understanding how individual, social, and collective memory interacted, reproduced, and canceled one another out. It is also shows the paucity of Western education for Africans in the colonies. For rather than broadening the mind and affording students the chance to travel the world, if only through books, colonial education in Southern Rhodesia tended to cultivate in some an insular provincialism, landlocked as the colony itself was—a mind-set shared with the Rhodesian settlers, who clung to imagined ancestors, as we have seen. The ill fate of the people of colonial Zimbabwe, then, was the past that strangled Africans, especially women, who they demanded behave "properly," even as most were deprived of opportunities to reach their full potential and contribute as full citizens in the new colony/nation. "Nationalism," Partha Chatterjee observed, "fostered a distinctly conservative attitude toward social beliefs and practices,"[46] an observation to which Vambe's case bears testimony. Vambe tended toward imagined histories that reinforced real and invented gender dynamics, including the denial that prostitution ever existed in African societies—much like the argument against homosexuality articulated and critiqued by Marc Epprecht in his wonderful work *Hungochani: The History of Dissident Sexuality in Southern Africa.*[47]

Through the lens of one family, this chapter illustrates the impact of colonialism on three generations of Africans. Members of the older generation, though still bitter about their defeat in the 1896–97 wars, were anchored by the memory of another time when Africans had had more control over their lives. The experience of colonialism was remembered differently by members of the middle generation, the ones with one foot in the African past and another in the colonial present. That schizophrenic identity, or double-consciousness, produced a generation seeking to make the best of a vanishing (African) history, while still grappling to understand the exclusionary and racialized colonial system. The youngest generation in Vambe's memoirs most fully demonstrated the effects of Christian mission education and colonial ordered life, which produced cultural nationalists who were eager to show off their "modern" skills yet wanted to bottle a vanishing African past that they had ignored until it was almost too late. Lastly, this chapter shows the perils of defining African culture in patriarchal terms, which often meant that women were treated unfairly, as happened in a nationalist movement discussed in the next chapter.

7 Educated Political Prisoners, a Guerrilla Matron, and the Gendered Pursuit of Independence

The fluidity of history, memory, and commemoration practiced by settlers and recounted by the autochthons in earlier chapters crystallize in this last chapter's four case studies. For much like Occupation Day, which only gained prominence and power over time, Nehanda-Charwe and the African past also gained currency in African nationalist rhetoric once it became clear that invoking the ancestors—and the stolen land—resonated with the majority of Africans in the cities and in the countryside. The case studies deal with (a) the educational experiences of elite political prisoners and their families; (b) the unintended consequences of the colonial government's sponsorship of an African novel, *Feso*, by Solomon Mutswairo; (c) gender discrimination in the nationalist movement; and (d) contestations over the "real" Nehanda in the early 1980s.[1] The ideas and actions of cultural and political nationalists discussed in this chapter affirm the political scientist Benedict Anderson's thesis that print culture, especially the turn from sacral language to the vernacular, was a critical impetus for the "origin of national consciousness."[2] Using the Reformation as an example, Anderson told how "in 1517 Martin Luther nailed his theses to the chapel door in Wittenberg, printed in German translation [not Latin]."[3] By so doing, Luther opened up a new way of being that bypassed the powerful structures of and in Rome, creating a new community bound together by what went on to become "standard" everyday German. I argue that the same processes occurred in African (and Other) settings as the colonized sought greater expression of their political ideas outside the purview of imperial control, especially by turning the oral past into the written vernacular present, to appeal to nationalist sentiment among intellectuals and the masses.

Finally, in contrast to much of the historiography that has articulated postindependence politics in much of Southern Africa as deeply shaped by socialist and communist Europe and the communist Soviet Union, China, and Cuba, this chapter shows that the rising African political elite were much more attuned to expressions of exclusionary Rhodesian memory that celebrated Occupation Day and heroes at Mazoe, which excluded African voices and histories. Rhodesian memory practices were the African nationalists' models, more than a mere imitation of communist or socialist ideology elsewhere. For that reason, I analyze the rise of Charwe as (Mbuya) Nehanda in nationalist thought, especially how she went from being a regional name in the ethnic memory of central Mashonaland to being an icon known beyond Zimbabwe and Southern African borders. Charwe as Nehanda was African nationalists' counternarrative to settler Rhodesia's Rhodes. Nehanda-Charwe was the instrument of African memory, the ancestor who stood for all the nameless and faceless ones.

Political Prisoners, Quaker Activism, and the Pursuit of Freedom through Education

By the 1930s, ethnic-bound politics, while still dominant, were beginning to shift as Africans in urban areas bound together by working-class labor conditions not only demanded better wages and working conditions but also challenged the premise of a race-based society that privileged some on the basis of skin color and ethnicity. The rising political elite of Southern Rhodesia began to form broader political parties, galvanizing the urban working classes with promises of better working conditions and wages and the landless peasants with the promise to take back and redistribute the stolen land. The responses of successive colonial regimes to those African political parties were to ban them and imprison the leaders in the hope that chopping off the heads of the movement(s) would kill the resistance. Languishing in prison in the 1950s and 1960s, many political activists and leaders took to reading educational and religious materials. Many decided to advance their education level—their levels ranging from basic literacy to advanced university degrees. That educational endeavor, as we will see, did not include a pronounced memory of the African past. Rather, it manifested itself as attempts to fit into the colonial system by learning about things European. For those incarcerated, the prison system became a campus, where those with higher levels of (Western) education taught those with lower levels.

The colonial government was not too pleased with that scenario and often sought to curtail, rather than encourage, the intellectual development of Africans, whom they perceived as subjects, not citizens. That intellectual development often fell to white foreigners who took an interest in the lives of imprisoned Africans in what was, by the mid-1950s, the Central African Federation of Rhodesia and Nyasaland (today's Zambia, Zimbabwe, and Malawi). George Loft, an American Quaker activist and resident representative of the American Friends Service Committee (AFSC) to the Federation in sub-Saharan Africa, was one of those outsiders. The AFSC, a branch of an international service agency of the Religious Society of Friends (Quakers), had offices in Salisbury, where Loft served from 1957 to 1960.[4] Loft's story is important, as it offers a counterpoint to Howell Wright's imperial flag-waving. Loft's Quaker code of ethics moved him to help those in dire straits for political reasons. He was also acutely aware that some of the African political prisoners he was assisting were the potential ruling class should Southern Rhodesia become fully independent. In contrast to Howell Wright, who sought out the Rhodesians and their stories of conquest, Loft was sought after by the Africans, some of whom poured out their hearts to him. Loft's story brings into sharp focus the reality that history was grayer than nationalists would have us believe. Just as white nationalists tried to present a history of "discovering" Rhodesia with no help, the Africans offered their counternarratives.

In this chapter we see that black nationalists later tried to control the narrative of how the movement was nurtured, portraying the nationalists as inspired and buoyed by the ancestors, when in fact a combination of factors were at work. Those factors included access to Western epistemological forms and resources such as those of the AFSC, which allowed them to read and write about the Western past and so turn toward their own "forgotten" African past. Loft's presence in this first case study reminds us, again, that outsiders played a part in the articulations and uses of history and memory in nationalists' making of Zimbabwe—even though both Black and White nationalists would have preferred that that historical detail be forgotten.

The AFSC, though religious in tone, was not a missionary organization in the conventional sense but a society that sought to promote peace through nonviolent means.[5] Loft and his wife, Eleanor, took their charge toward Africans, and especially political prisoners, very seriously. They built relationships with those (mostly) men, corresponding with them and their families, as well as with a wide variety of people across the color line in the Federation of Rhodesia and Nyasaland. The correspondence between George Loft and many elites of African nationalism illuminates the graspings of a younger generation who, having failed to convince settler society that Africans were human—as opposed to "gyrating barbarous tribes"—sought to acquire a Western education, which clearly opened doors for those who possessed it. That need for more and better educational opportunities and support meant that most political detainees in Southern Rhodesia's prisons wrote to Loft and the AFSC seeking support. They wanted material and financial support afforded to themselves or to family members, whose education had been curtailed because they, as the breadwinners, were imprisoned. As one prisoner wrote to Loft, *You will be very much surprised to receive a letter from me seeing that you have never heard of me before. I have come to know you because of the fame of your good name and your good deeds. I have some troubles which are above my powers of thought; one of them, which I am submitting to you for any help or assistance. I have a son and two brothers all passed their standard six examination to attain one form, but they have failed to have room in Nyasaland secondary schools.*[6] The letter's author was A. S. Musukwa, a Malawian political prisoner held in Southern Rhodesia. Musukwa had heard from other prisoners that Loft was a fixer of prisoner's problems, especially helping them with educational opportunities and/or financial assistance.

Help in obtaining educational financial assistance was the main request Loft received from political prisoners—and (some of) their family members—during his tenure in Salisbury, as well as after he his return to the United States. In fact, earlier in April of the same year, before he received Musukwa's letter, Loft (or his office) had compiled "Thumbnails of Some Key Detainees Imprisoned in S. Rhodesia" from around the Federation. The detainees included Hastings Kamuzu Banda, Dunduza Chisiza, Orton E. Chirwa, and David Rubadiri, all of Nyasaland (Malawi). Also included were Robert Chikerema, George Nyandoro, and Paul Mushonga, all of Southern Rhodesia.[7] What is striking about these two groups is that those from Nyasaland were more (highly) educated than their Southern Rhodesian counterparts. Banda, who was fifty-four years old, had received his medical education in the United States, Scotland, and England and had had a private practice in England before returning to the Federation. Chisiza, recorded as an economics graduate of Fircroft College, in Birmingham, England, and the "first African advocate in Nyasaland," had lived at Hope Fountain Mission in Bulawayo (Southern Rhodesia) before returning to the colony of his birth (Nyasaland). Lastly, Rubadiri, a reputed poet and an eloquent speaker, was a graduate of Makerere University, in Uganda, and had done graduate work at Bristol University in England. His wife, Gertrude, who had the same level of education as her husband, was not listed. Rather, she was written into the biographical index of her husband, which means that her story is in her husband's shadow in Loft's archive. Loft was (unwittingly) participating in the creation of male heroes whose memories would make Malawi's narrative of African liberation at women's expense.

The Southern Rhodesian prisoners were distinguished by their relatively younger age, averaging thirty-three and a half years; their primary education had been confined to their home colony's missionary schools, with high school in South Africa. Chikerema had gone to a Catholic mission school for his primary education and to South Africa for high school. Nyandoro had attended an Anglican mission school and received his high-school education through private study. Reputed as the "best African bookkeeper in Southern Rhodesia," as well as an effective speaker, Nyandoro had traveled outside the colony to Ghana in 1957. Mushonga had also attended a Catholic mission school, and with the education ceiling rather low for Africans, he had become an entrepreneur, with a store in the African township of Highfields, in Salisbury. Those men and their educational levels are important, because most of them later used their access to Western education to turn toward the African past. That turn was fueled by their realization that even their Western education and assimilation did not spare them from racial discrimination. They had all along assumed their "lack of education" was the main reason for exclusion as "uncivilized."

Loft did not only deal with prominent male figures. As he wrote to friends and well-wishers in the United States, he was dealing with "men and women representing a fair cross-section of the colony's Africans— ranging all the way from relatively unlettered reserve-dwellers to sophisticated urbanites. Some probably cannot read at all; others have rather advanced tastes in literature."⁸ Among the books detainees requested were texts on politics, economics, poetry, and "authoritative histories of the United States and other countries; books on agriculture, Adam Smith's *The Wealth of Nations*; and *Socialism, Capitalism and Democracy* by Schumpeter."⁹ The book requests speak volumes about people hemmed in by provincial and limited colonial education, which allowed Africans only so much education and no more. Also striking is that the books detainees requested had little to do with Africa, its history, geography, or otherwise, illustrating that African knowledge systems were not part of the Western curriculum in most schools and universities, even in the United States.

Detainees' book requests tell their own tale of the quest for educational and intellectual independence, along with political independence, which was an African right in many African countries by the 1960s and 1970s. It is also telling that Terence O. Ranger's history classic, *Revolt in Southern Rhodesia, 1896–97: A Study in African Resistance*, discussed earlier, was published in 1967, a time when most Africans had woken to the exclusion of their own history in the colonial education system and in public displays like Occupation Day. Ranger's book therefore became a foundational text for most nationalists, who leaned on it to buoy their fledgling liberation movements, which needed a narrative of spirited African resistance, which may have ended in defeat in the 1896–97 war but was resistance worth celebrating as nationalist resistance of old, with lessons for latter-day nationalists. Ranger's book was important because it offered an alternative (imagined) collective memory of Africans collaborating across ethnic lines to resist settler colonialism—in contrast to the colonial narratives of splintered African "tribalisms" that the Europeans had ended, hence the need for colonialism.

Ironically, the harsh prison system provided an opportunity for an education—at all levels—for the Africans of Southern Rhodesia, whose opportunities had been limited to mission schools, which the colonial government funded poorly, if at all. The AFSC assigned its members to meet each detainee's needs, from checking up on family at home, to addressing health issues, and most importantly, to filling requests for books. On November 10, 1959, the three Zimbabwean political detainees in Selukwe Prison—Chikerema, Nyandoro, and Mushonga—along with others, including Josias Maluleke, Peter Mtandwa, and Edson Sithole, asked for more literature, including *Life* and *Time* magazines, Bibles,

H. A. Guy's *Life of Christ,* and books on social and industrial history, modern economics, Greek, Roman, and British history, and British politics. Sithole, for example, was taking a correspondence course in journalism, and in order to get a higher-level diploma, he needed to publish articles as part of his coursework, but those articles had to be nonpolitical, as the government would not allow otherwise. Like many of his imprisoned compatriots, Sithole was doing his correspondence studies with an institution in South Africa; others did theirs through institutions in England.[10] All those men's names are important, because they became key nationalists in Zimbabwe's history and memory.

Individual detainees cultivated personal relationships with George Loft, his wife, Eleanor, and other (affiliated) like-minded people. In the letters, George Loft comes off as an affable, effective, and resourceful man committed to the cause of peace and to the Africans, whom he considered victims of a terrible colonial system that he—and his comrades— could change only by offering the best nonviolent support to the detainees, their families, and the larger anticolonial movement.[11] It is ironic, as will become clear below, that Loft did not see it as his place to challenge the colonial government's race-based policies, policies and laws that had put most of those men (and some women) behind bars in the first place. Be that as it may, because of the work he and the AFSC were doing with the Africans in the rural and urban areas, as well as in the prison system, Loft earned the trust and friendship of many. One of those was Didymus E. Mutasa, who wrote his first letter to Loft in 1958. On St. Faith Mission Farm letterhead, Mutasa wrote a note thanking Loft for his visit and for the literature he had left at the mission farm. The visit and the gift had moved Mutasa beyond words: "It is always difficult to find words that can express people's gratitude for anything that would have been done for them. This is more so with me who has very poor vocabulary and command of the English language. But I would like to thank you very much for coming to stay with us at Chiwetu and for the literature that you sent me."[12] The young Mutasa and fellow members of the Makoni Students' Association were deeply touched by Loft's visit, which they regarded as a "sign of fellowship and brotherhood, and to us, your talk and life was as though our Lord had come down again." Whatever literature Loft had left with Mutasa was appreciated, as it was literature not easily available to an average African (in the rural areas) in those days.

For Mutasa, an important nationalist, his correspondence with Loft resulted in his having to overcome far fewer limitations related to educational opportunities, mentorship, and threadbare professional networks than most Africans in order to obtain a decent—sometimes even just basic—education. Most of those Africans ended up being deemed too old for scholarships, since getting the necessary qualifications took too long and often meant personal or familial expenses beyond the means of most. Loft networked on Mutasa's behalf in an attempt to obtain a scholarship from the Indian government that seems to have eventually allowed him to study in Birmingham, England.[13] Mutasa took his family along and wrote Loft to let him know how they were getting on. "Our family is very well, thank you very much, and seems to have adjusted to the British way of life with all its individualism," Mutasa informed Loft. The children were doing better than the parents, as "Gertrude and I wish for a more communal society but realize we cannot have it here. So we make the best of what there is." And they did, keeping alive the friendships they had started in Rhodesia with blacks and whites alike.[14] Most important was the news that "Gertrude will bring us a seventh member of the family. This will give us all great joy despite the fact that our neighbors think that our family is already too big as it is at the moment. We need more 'freedom fighters' so we must breed whilst we can." We will never know whether Gertrude Mutasa agreed that she was "breeding" more freedom fighters, but what is clear is that the Mutasas managed to leave Rhodesia for further studies abroad, an opportunity that not many got.

Of those who studied abroad, history, politics, economics, and law were the popular disciplines. Others focused on skills needed to take over the new country, such as agriculture and other "practical" subjects, especially for women. It is striking that in their letters most of the young men made no mention of their country's history before colonialism. Granted, letters to and from prison were censored, but it is quite telling that none of the letters I read had "brave words" for colonialism. Instead, what emerges is a group of imprisoned political strivers of the late 1950s into the 1960s.[15] The letters that the young political activists and some of their wives wrote to George Loft are sobering, revealing their earnest quests for an education and for the independent use of their minds and time, something the Rhodesian government could not take away. That first generation born and raised under colonialism, much like Vambe in the previous chapter, devoted their lives to proving themselves as capable as any white settler. Thus, even after he had returned to the United

States, Loft continued to receive letters from detainees (and their wives) seeking financial assistance and study material.

Overwhelmed by the need, and sometimes dipping into his own pockets, as he did for one Michael Mawema, Loft wrote to the local AFSC for advice on how to handle cases of those he could not personally assist, as he did with the case of a "letter from Robert Mugabe asking for assistance with his studies and enclosing an application form for the University of South Africa."[16] On June 28, 1967, Mugabe had written to Loft in response to a letter from Loft after a prison visit. Loft had told Mugabe that he had been able to find some money for another prisoner, Michael Mawema, to study with the Chartered Institute of Secretaries in Johannesburg. Mugabe was pitching for the same opportunity in his reply, hoping to get funding to continue his studies and so distract himself from the tragedy that had befallen him and his wife, Sally: the loss of their only young child. Their individual letters to Loft tell an interesting gendered story in the nationalist movement. For example, Robert wrote one to two lines of acknowledgment of the tragedy and moved to other issues: "Yes, my wife told me that she had received from you. Last Xmas was a very sad time for us. We lost our only child on 26th Dec., rather unexpectedly. My wife and I, however, became used to the loss."[17] Robert and Sally's story about the loss of their only child reminds us what was important to nationalists at the time before Nehanda-Charwe and the heroes of the 1896–97 war became the central focus and message of the movement in the 1960s. The Mugabes' story and, indeed, the stories of all Loft's nationalist correspondents also tell that the transformation of Charwe into Mbuya Nehanda, a "national" figure, was an almost mirror image of the slow transformation of Occupation Day in settler consciousness from a localized (Salisbury) event into a colonywide holiday. Similarly, Charwe went from being the medium of Nehanda in central Mashonaland to being a national figure with resonance beyond the cultural and ethnic memory of Nyamhita among the Shona and finally an anticolonial figure who transcended ethnicity, geography, and political affiliation. Women's and men's different needs in the nationalist movement—as exemplified by Sally and Robert—tell us that we need to revisit nationalist historiography to reevaluate its fissures and write new histories of its achievements and limitations.

Robert's and Sally's letters also serve as a reminder that what motivated some male nationalists (nation first) may not have been what motivated some female nationalists (family first), yet both were committed to a life without colonial/settler rule. For example, Robert may have been speaking for himself when he wrote about getting used to the loss of their child, for Sally clearly felt differently, although she tried to sound cheerful in her letter from her native Ghana, where she was at the time. *Dear Mr. Loft*, Sally began her letter, *I write to break the long silence—I always wish to write you but keep postponing for no reason. I guess you heard of my mishap, the death of my son on Dec. 26th. This brought a lot of hardships on me and for some time I felt out of the world. I have been trying with great difficulty to be myself again, but I see it would take time. It was a great shock to Robert in prison, but he being a man, braved it up and he is well by God's grace. I can safely say I am better now and hope to be myself again.*[18] The gendered nature of grief and its tending in the nationalist movement tells us of more than just a husband and wife telling their different perspectives on the loss of their only child in the middle of a historic resistance for freedom. It also shows how patriarchy and the ideals of manhood infused personal life and political activity. These sorts of responses also had an impact on how men and women responded to colonialism—and especially on their later memories. Nelson Mandela's nationalist autobiography is an excellent example of (mostly) men putting nationalist ideology and the liberation struggle before personal (familial) issues. In Mandela's case, it led to the dissolution of his first marriage, to Evelyn, and a prolonged separation from his second wife, Winnie, as he was condemned to life imprisonment at Robben Island shortly after they were married.[19]

To return to Sally's story, Loft rallied a friend of his, David, who was living in West Africa, to either write or call on Sally, as she was mourning the death of her son, with her husband imprisoned, unable to be with her at their time of great loss. Loft, though a committed humanitarian and Quaker, was generally conscious that any of the detainees were potential leaders of future independent countries, so he treated all with respect. As he wrote to David, he had been corresponding with Mrs. Sally Mugabe, whom he had yet to meet personally, since visiting her husband in prison. "Robert Mugabe," according to Loft, "is generally considered one of the potential African leaders of Rhodesia, if that unhappy country gets to the point where Africans, in fact, have an opportunity to lead." Loft thought it would be "helpful to Sally if someone could call on her or at least write to her from close by to express sympathy and fellowship."[20] Loft's consciousness of the elite political prisoners is evident in the collection of

his papers at Stanford, in which the correspondence is largely with political leaders and those whose wives, like Sally, corresponded directly with
him. Sally stands out in many ways, similarly to Molly Marshall-Hole,
whom we encountered in chapter 3, who was able to self-represent and
so record her own voice in the archive instead of being spoken for by her
husband and other men.

Loft was not off the mark in assessing Robert Mugabe as a "potential
African" leader, for Mugabe, like many nationalist leaders of that time period, generally focused on the liberation struggle first and family matters
second. An example of Mugabe's dedication is expressed in a letter he
wrote to Loft in June 1967: *Since you last saw me, I have gone through quite
a hectic time. I did about three and a half months at the Wha Wha detention
camp. Then I was removed to Salisbury to do my month gaol sentence. After
the sentence, in June 1965, I was sent to Sikombela Restriction Area under a
five year restriction order. In November of the same year, but three days before
U.D.I. (Unilateral Declaration of Independence), I was then removed back to
Salisbury prison where I still am. Although I have lost some weight, I am still
quite fit. We try to keep ourselves as busy with reading and studies as possible.
I have been reading law, economics, and administrative law. I was helped by
a friend in Britain in my first year of the course. I wonder whether you could
help me in getting assistance for the rest of my course stretching up to the end
of 1967. I'll send you the details as soon as I hear from the University. Everyone is doing something. The lowest amongst us is doing Standard IV. Those
who are more highly educated amongst us try to assist those in junior grades.
In this way, we day to day try to keep our minds occupied with something
useful.*[21] It is telling that almost none of the preserved letters and lists
shows any budding sharp-tongued or critical-minded Marxist-Leninism,
the philosophy that would be the mantra of their radicalized guerrilla
movement, as discussed below. True, the prisoners were writing to Loft,
a white male, a Quaker, and, though liberal in his worldview, a product
of the same global racial hierarchy that had seen him as the missionary
to the political prisoners, and they beggars for opportunity. Thus, rather
than an articulation of their ideas in an equal exchange with Loft, what
comes through is that most of the books they requested or read were
rather conventional, mostly British or even American.

Mugabe wrote again to Loft in December of the same year, wondering
why he had not heard back from him about his University of South Africa
course. Was Loft having some difficulty raising the fee of sixty pounds

sterling for registration?, he asked.[22] All he needed to know was whether it was possible to raise "only partial payment of say £15 or £20, and the rest in installments. But should it prove absolutely difficult to raise any amount, do not hesitate to inform me before time elapses." Mugabe then suggested that Loft contact another friend of Mugabe's, Tom Melady, who "could assist in raising the requisite fee." While all that was going on, Robert wrote to Loft that Sally was "now in London on a scholarship and will be studying a Domestic Science course. She seems to like it there." Sally, always the cheerful and more open correspondent, wrote to Loft from London in January 1968. She had arrived in London on November 17 the previous year "and went straight to school. It gave me very little time for any correspondence. I, however, wrote my husband to inform you of my stay in Britain. Sorry if it escaped him."[23] Sally found the winter in London "awfully cold"; the roads were icy, and she had even fallen while boarding a bus, helped to her feet by some kind strangers. She considered herself one of the lucky ones in that she had not been injured. Her other looming hardship was the high cost of living in London, which was going to be for a long stretch, as she hoped to "stay for 2 years for some courses, end of which I hope to return to Ghana if the situation in Rhodesia is still no better." The absence of her husband and her return to her country of birth, Ghana, allowed Sally to be her own person in ways not easy or accessible to many married women at the time. Also, women who, like Gertrude Mutasa and Sally Mugabe, were able to travel overseas with or without their husbands had more educational opportunities and got a better education than they would have had in the colony. Others, like the nationalist Ruth Chinamano or Evelin Mushonga, were not so lucky, as they, like their husbands, were often imprisoned, leaving their children without parental or material comfort.[24]

Sally's narrative is particularly important in light of the next section, on women in the nationalist movement, because it reminds us that women were not exceptionally attuned to the past of their foremothers. Women were just as eager as men to make the most of the practical present rather than focus on the sacred/mythical past, with its seemingly fewer lessons to be drawn from women who had thrived in spite of colonialism. Sally's representation of the practical nationalist woman reminds us that memory making for a nationalist purpose was invoked once the (female and male) nationalists could speak the language and engage the culture of the colonialist. In fact, that Sally came from the African country that was most admired by nationalists on the continent and in the diaspora is itself of significance because it shows that much like their male counterparts, nationalist women were eager to "modernize" rather than look back to their "oppressed" mothers' histories. Indeed, the pull of the past (history) and the push of the present (memory) formed the paradox of nationalism. For African women like Sally Mugabe, moving forward meant acquiring Western domestic science in order to be of use when "things got better in Rhodesia" rather than looking to their foremothers, whose knowledge did not come from books and was not written down anywhere and so did not count for much at the time.

Last, and just as important, whereas the overwhelming number of Southern Rhodesian (Zimbabwean) elite detainees were advancing their education while in prison, some had already gotten their education in South Africa, Britain, or the United States and engaged Loft on a more equal footing. Such was the case with Herbert Chitepo, the first African barrister in Southern Rhodesia, who did not do prison time but was an active nationalist in the colony. In fact, Chitepo served as attorney to many Africans seeking legal representation, including political prisoners. In his minimal correspondence with Chitepo, we see another side of Loft, who sought to take the middle road in the politics of Southern Rhodesia. In Chitepo we also see the fear of the Rhodesian government realized, for he was a well-educated African man who not only understood the Roman-Dutch law practiced in the colony but had taken to penning the African past, and in an African language, as in the epic poem *Soko risina Musoro*.[25] Loft, who wanted to be seen by the Rhodesian authorities not as collaborating with the African nationalists but as a neutral facilitator, preemptively wrote then prime minister Edgar Whitehead telling him that he would testify as an "expert witness" at detainee trials, in which Chitepo played a key role. Loft's stand on neutrality did not sit well with Chitepo, who did not trust Loft as much as some Africans did, especially those imprisoned, who often unburdened themselves to the American Quaker.[26]

To be sure, Loft was no Howell Wright. In Loft's correspondence with many of the African nationalist leaders we see how pragmatic they were. In their letters they tended to write about the practical present (an education) rather than the historical injustices of the past that had led to their imprisonment. True, prison correspondence was censored. Indeed, many of their letters were written on Her Majesty's Prison stationery, stamped as approved (and read) by the authorities. All the same, it does say something that the leading lights of colonial Zimbabwe's resistance movement in one political party chose to shelve the past for later, while claiming Western tools of knowledge that would come in handy when they had to use the past (history) to move the present (memory) forward. As we will see in the next two sections, nationalists, guided by Nehanda-Charwe, later retooled their history of activism to show their uncompromising resistance to colonialism. The nationalists acted within certain parameters without jeopardizing their lives; in imagine-nation, they were perpetual resistors who acted as Charwe did, resisting "everything" European to the bitter end.

The Eye of the Storm: Rebranding Charwe as Mbuya Nehanda, the Guerrilla Matron

The muted collective memory seen in prisoners' correspondence with Loft turned radical once many of them were released from prison and rejoined their guerrilla movements, now parked in neighboring countries, especially Zambia and later Mozambique. Firebrand African nationalists and ordinary folk took to shaking their own trees of local and "national" history, gathering enough fruit to see them through the dark winter of war from the late 1960s into the late 1970s. They were fighting, they argued, for the land of their ancestors and for equality. It was during that time that the public memory of the 1896–97 wars, including their heroes and heroine, was reinvigorated and began its ascendancy as Africans grew confident in their past, which they now realized had been wrongly excluded from the Eurocentric definitions of history. For African youth in particular, the discovery of the writings of Herbert Chitepo and Solomon Mutswairo, who tapped into African oral traditions and wrote about them in African languages, was particularly exhilarating. Chitepo's epic poem *Soko risina Musoro* (A tale without a head) and Solomon Mutswairo's novel *Feso* resuscitated and popularized the memory of an African past when Africans had ruled themselves and the idea of a potential return of that freedom through ancestors like Charwe, who had lived through settler colonialism and resisted it until their death.

The spiritual support (memory) of those 1896–97 heroes buoyed nationalists' passion for independence in ways similar to the ways that the memory of the Pioneer Columns had buoyed settlers' sense of entitlement to Rhodesia as their (white) inheritance. Through both Chitepo's and Mutswairo's writings, poetic lamentations directed at the African ancestral spirits gave young people a voice and words with which to imagine a future in which the past—the spirits of the dead—would once again unite with the living to form a cohesive society no longer ruptured by colonialism. After all, the spirit medium had functioned in society as a channel, or bridge, between the living and the dead; and the works of Chitepo and Mutswairo—among others—echoed the dis-covery of their (African) cultural identities, as well as their voices and practices denigrated and/or banned by the state and the church.[27] Those writings and other expressions, such as public orations of praise poetry and per-formances of folk dances, became the shelter from the political storm created by the 1965 Unilateral Declaration of Independence by Ian D. Smith's Rhodesia Front. Charwe, reimagined as Mbuya Nehanda—Ancestor Nehanda—was the eye of that nationalist storm.

Ironically, the reclamation of the lost cultural past and all its "wonder-ful" traditions was often the reclamation of a masculinized past that gave the frontrunner nationalists a sense of being men too, men with a past to rival and/or surpass that of the settlers, whose forefathers had come to the country less than a hundred years earlier. The poem in Mutswairo's *Feso* titled "O Nehanda Nyakasikana" was a quintessential example of resistance poetry of the period. However, it was also a masculine rendi-tion of oppression that struck a gendered line across the past and pres-ent, making women the "breeders" of a future nation, to borrow from Mutasa in the previous section. Mutswairo's poem read, in part: *O Ne-handa Nyakasikana! / How long shall we, the Vanyai, groan and suffer? / Holy tutelary spirit! / How long shall we, the Vanyai, suffer oppression? / We are weary of drinking our tears / . . . / The young ones our women bear, / given us by you—Great Spirit—who should be inheritors / of our hard-earned sub-stance, all have an uneasy time in their own land / . . . / Where is our freedom, Nehanda? / Won't you come down to help us? / Our old men are treated like children / in the land you gave them, Merciful Creator! / . . . / What foul crime have we committed / that you should abandon us like this? / Nehanda Nya-kasikana, how long shall it be / That we, the Vanyai, must suffer? / Holy Tu-telary Lion Spirit! / How long shall it be / That we, the VaNyai, must suffer oppression / By this cursed Pfumojena who is devouring our / people and our land?*[28]

The novel, including the poem, was translated by Mutswairo himself and edited by D. E. Herdeck. The English translation is quite striking in its gendering of otherwise differently gendered ("genderless") chiShona pronouns. In English the poem almost has a different meaning because of the gendered English pronouns, which amplify the fault lines that are implied, muted, or nonexistent in chiShona. Because of their education, truncated as it was in most cases, Africans had to do their best to tell their own histories with the tools available to them at the time.[29] Though Mutswairo's novel was historical fiction set in the seventeenth century, and the Nehanda therein a medium of that time period, to young nationalists Mutswairo's novel, especially that poem, was a lamentation to Charwe, the late-nineteenth-century Nehanda medium of the Mazowe.

Thus, Chitepo's and Mutswairo's writings were expressions of a historical consciousness no longer content to stay under the colonial radar. Rather, it sought and was buoyed by popular collective memory among Africans who remembered their own dynastic, ethnic, and regional heroes, much as the settlers of Mazoe did. Charwe had been a clan, ethnic, and regional figure, and it was the nationalists who turned her into a "national" figure—into Mbuya Nehanda for all. Individual African writers and thinkers were tapping into their historical consciousnesses and personal experiences of colonialism and linking them with those of previous generations, all the way back to 1890, in an attempt to create cohesive Africans narratives of their right to be in Rhodesia—Zimbabwe— even though such a country had not existed in that form before 1890. And there lay the rub. Settler narratives that celebrated Occupation Day made it seem as though whites had a perfect ancestral solar system, with Rhodes and the Pioneers as the sun around which all other (planetary) narratives orbited, sustaining life in the colony into the infinite future.

The African nationalist leaders who spearheaded the rebranding of Charwe as a national Mbuya Nehanda were mostly from north-central and northeastern Zimbabwe, people who had grown up not only in districts with strong Nehanda traditions (before Charwe) but with successive Rhodesian governments fearful of the emergence of another female medium in Mazowe with power and influence similar to Charwe's or claiming to channel Charwe's spirit. Each Occupation Day celebration reminded the Africans of the 1896–97 wars. The colonial government did not allow them to hold their own celebrations remembering their heroes and their heroine, Charwe. Those African nationalists perhaps unconsciously showed their political savvy by recognizing the imagined nature of settler myths around which the colony/nation orbited. For Africans to succeed in creating a pan-African identity across ethnic lines, nationalists reasoned, precolonial "nationalist" figures needed to be put forward. However, none fit the bill better than Charwe, whose refusal to convert to Christianity became the hallmark of her anti-imperialism.

African and multiracial political parties, which had been banned or had irrevocably fractured because of ideological differences and power struggles, increasingly turned to the past to find symbolic cannon fodder with which to wage the war of liberation. A splinter group from the established Zimbabwe African National Union (ZANU) added "Patriotic Front" to its name to create a new political party, the ZANU-PF. That new party took on a hard-line black nationalist tone. To further burnish its credentials, it (later) adopted Charwe (a.k.a. Mbuya Nehanda) as the matron saint of the political and military wings of that nationalist movement. By choosing Charwe, the party effectively reified and colonized the most visible figure of the 1896–97 wars, and the only woman so visible at the trials. Another reason why African nationalists chose Charwe as their matron saint, apart from Mutswairo's *Feso*, I argue, was that many of them in that movement came from her part of the country and had perhaps grown up with colonial anxiety at the mention of the name Nehanda.

The nationalist movement's claims to Nehanda were also bolstered by Terence Ranger's *Revolt in Southern Rhodesia*, a (British) professional historian's study of African resistance to colonialism that used the very same colonial archives that had been touted as having no African representation. Through Ranger's book, a "people without a past" suddenly had proof of it—written by one of them (the whites/British), no less. Thus, the fact that many in the political and military wings of ZANU-PF (and the Zimbabwe African National Liberation Army, ZANLA) were from Charwe's general geographic region in central and northeast Mashonaland, along with the fact that many from other regions were educated and had read the then contemporary books by Chitepo, Mutswairo, and Ranger, affirmed the memory and power of the legend, history, and memory of Charwe—and of the ancestors writ large.[30] Thus, by interpreting Charwe beyond central Mashonaland and its ethnic memory, the nationalist movement had found its biggest gun with which to fight the psychological warfare that had been missing in its military strategy until then.

Nehanda's "Granddaughters" Pursue
Female and African Independence

Concomitant with the adoption of Nehanda as nationalist matron, along with other spirits and mediums, into the guerrilla movement in the 1960s was women's agitation to be recruited as equal participants on the military front lines of the movement.[31] Some did not shy away from leaning on Nehanda-Charwe as their reason for wanting to fight as gun-wielding guerrillas rather than "helpers." For those young women, Mbuya Nehanda, a woman, had participated in the 1896–97 war, which meant that they had a right to participate in the twentieth-century war. Equally. The issue of women's frontline participation was a contentious one, as (most) male leaders of the movement remembered their hero ancestors of the 1896–97 war as mostly male, but for the "exceptional" Nehanda. Women's participation could have remained a contentious issue with little support within the movement, as the mind-set at the time was that there was no historical precedent of African women participating in wars. What turned the tide in women's favor was that the 1960s saw a large shift in favor of women's equal rights in many parts of the world. The shift occurred not only in the West but also in the East, where aspirant socialist and communist states and governments sought to promote equality among the sexes, albeit with differing results. The year 1975 was declared the United Nations' International Women's Year, and the decade 1976–85, the UN Decade for Women.[32]

ZANU-PF's response to both internal pressure and external realities with regard to women's issues was to mount stilted campaigns about women's involvement in the movement in the organization's bimonthly magazine, the *Zimbabwe News*. In addition to policy statements by the leadership about women's place in the struggle, women (who did not hold many positions of power) also registered their opinions in the magazine, either in letters to the editor or in commissioned articles that appeared in the magazine from time to time. Some letters made explicit reference to Nehanda-Charwe and precolonial women who took part in the 1896–97 uprisings, while others urged women to participate on the front lines by taking up the gun instead of continuing with feminized forms of protests such as strikes, demonstrations, and financial and material support of the combatants.

One such letter to the editor was written by one Winnie Muderere, who emphatically told women that they needed to "fight together with the men."[33] In her gendered we-women-must-fight-beside-our-men tone, she gave examples of countries where women were fighting or had fought alongside men: Kenya, Algeria, and Vietnam. She argued that those examples should inspire Zimbabwean women to join the armed struggle. Muderere's letter was, however, silent on the patriarchal nature of nationalist discourse, which gave rhetorical but not real power to women, especially women not connected to the political elite by kinship, marriage, or birth. Muderere saw it as women's "duty to study our political problems carefully and to keep ourselves as fully informed of the enemy as our men, and like men think how best we can crash Smith's [Rhodesia Front]." "Fellow women," she concluded, "it is high time we shouldered our guns and took part in Chimurenga; it is time to fight and not to sit and knit."[34]

A woman who shared similar sentiments about women's frontline participation was one Mai (Mrs.) Masenda, whose letter called for "Zimbabwe women to play an even greater role in the struggle for liberation."[35] While acknowledging that women had participated as women and mothers, she considered those contributions to "have been largely restricted to the field of peace time politics"—activities like organizing mass demonstrations and making donations to the movement in cash and/or kind. Such participation, Mai Masenda maintained, was not enough. Women needed to show that they meant business by joining the armed struggle "in the jungles of Zimbabwe to show our resolve. This is what other women are doing all over the world—in Vietnam, Thailand, Korea, and Latin America. Why not ourselves?"[36] Mai Masenda's condemnation of women's "peace time contributions" to the struggle for liberation is striking for its feminization of certain kinds of contributions to the struggle compared with the "ultimate contribution"—holding a Kalashnikov, the popular AK-47, on the front lines of battle.

If the letters of Winnie Muderere and Mai Masenda did not make any reference to Nehanda-Charwe or women's involvement in the 1896–97 war, an article in the same magazine in March 1968 took a different tone. Titled "Women and Chimurenga," the article began by invoking the history and memory of Nehanda-Charwe, albeit in embellished tones that exaggerated historical facts. *The history of our struggle for liberation shows that women have not been [a] dormant section of the Zimbabwe nation*, the assertive author declared. *Even the first Chimurenga fought in 1896–97 is not without examples of women who distinguished themselves as heroic fighters for the liberation of the motherland. For instance there may not be any Zimbabwean who has not heard of Nehanda. This woman urged a number of chiefs around Salisbury to rise against the colonial usurpers who had just started spreading themselves in their midst. As a result of her activities Chimurenga began in these areas with the wiping out of an enemy patrol unit and spread about like wild fire. Eventually Nehanda was captured in a cave and sadistically murdered by fascist troops.*[37] The projection of Charwe as an unrelenting anti-imperialist is striking, as is the omission of her unpalatable side of doing business with settlers. Just like the Rhodesians, who chose to project Rhodes as a benevolent founder, not a rabid imperialist and racist, the Zimbabweans chose Mbuya Nehanda the benevolent and uncompromising ancestor, not the shaky spirit medium looking out for her own interests as well. Unsurprisingly, the invocation of Nehanda-Charwe in anti-imperialist nationalist terms saw more and more young people, especially women, claim her for themselves. She became a symbol for young women, who were denied participation on the front lines because of their gender. It was through Nehanda-Charwe that many young women legitimized their demands to participate as full combatants, instead of supporting actors, beasts of burden, and/or comfort women for male combatants, who were deemed the "real" guerrillas.[38]

Granted, the foregoing letters by Muderere and Masenda did pack a feisty propaganda punch. Masenda's last letter, however, demonstrates that the liberation movement's reference to women's historical presence in the fight against imperialism was often perfunctory in the rush to tell the story of Nehanda-Charwe, the star heroine. The heavy reliance on one local heroine to inspire Zimbabwean women contributed to women's failure to wield real power within the nationalist movement and after independence. Men (in positions of power) often generalized the struggle in gendered terms, invoking "our forefathers" as the victims whose land had been taken by the imperialists (also men) and needed to be reclaimed. African men made comparative leaps between the twentieth-century struggles and those of 1896–97, treating them as if the two events had happened in the same time period. As one of them wrote in the *Zimbabwe News* in February 1969, *The Smith regime believes that the only effective way of purging the Zimbabwe Liberation Movement of its relatively new revolutionary dynamism is to remove, by murder, the man most responsible for this dynamism: [Ndabaningi] Sithole. The fascists in Rho-*

desia will not be allowed to get away with their planned murder of our leader.
If anything else, the trial of this most dedicated leader has only served to show
Zimbabweans that those true qualities of revolutionary leadership so ably dis-
played by our forefathers in the 1890–96 Chimurenga wars of resistance are
not dead.[39]

Women, on the other hand, often received a limited education in general, but especially on the subject of women's history, on which they could have leaned—as the men did—to argue their case against discrimination on the basis of their gender. It would have made the nationalist movement more representative of vigorous intellectual activity about the past by men and women on an equal footing. Far fewer women than men in the liberation movement had had access to (higher) education in prison or outside, which often meant that women were at a disadvantage when it came to articulating and critiquing the blend of Marxist socialism and African political thought that the mainly male leaders of the movement articulated.[40] As we have seen, it was mostly male political prisoners who pursued their education, courtesy of George Loft and his kind, either in prison or abroad. Ironically, many of the same leading men, as well as the vast majority of rank male cadres, were not keen on seeing "women's rights" become an integral part of the liberation movement.

The leadership, however, was not unaware of the changing winds in favor of women internationally. Moreover, many of the leading men had traveled to communist as well as Western countries and had realized that if they ignored the "woman question," it would be at their own peril, as much of their financial and military support came from the West and East, respectively. The strategy ZANLA adopted was to mount a massive campaign focused on "women combatants" in order to tell the world that their liberation movement was indeed a progressive political and military movement. That translated into marketing strategies such as staging photographs of gun-wielding female combatants, giving the illusion that women were participating on the (combat) front line, as eloquently argued by Josephine Nhongo-Simbanegavi.[41] In reality, women were largely assigned "female" tasks, especially providing (sexual) "comfort" to the "real" guerrillas, the men.[42]

The exception to the male-centered ZANLA military wing came with the establishment of a token Women's Detachment, whose base was— *Yes!*—named after Nehanda.[43] This, perhaps, was the most important juncture, when Nehanda-Charwe entered the nationalist discourse as both woman and symbol, since before that she had been primarily an ancestor (symbol). As one woman ex-combatant later remembered about her experience of the guerrilla war and Nehanda's importance, the war was difficult for everyone, but for some women there was the Nehanda base, the only female military base, where "life was different, and we were put into platoons to be trained to operate guns. I preferred to go back to Nehanda for training—training to be a fighter, to use a gun."[44] The commander of the base's Women's Detachment was also a woman, Joyce, whose aliases were Teurai Ropa and, most tellingly, Comrade Nehanda.[45] Comrade Nehanda invoked Mbuya Nehanda as a revolutionary and a symbol, though, ironically, she was articulated in male nationalist terms rather than woman-centered nationalist ones. Had Nhongo (alias Comrade Nehanda) articulated a woman-centered Nehanda, it might have facilitated the opening of intellectual spaces for vigorous debates on women's rights within the nationalist liberation movement and, by extension, within an envisioned democratic Zimbabwe.[46]

Teurai Ropa Nhongo, though a high-profile female representative within ZANLA's power structure, was limited in the power she wielded because of her gender and age. However, as ZANLA pushed her forward to be the face and spokesperson of the liberation movement's women's wing, there was a clearer drive by ZANLA toward connecting the memory of Nehanda-Charwe and late-twentieth-century women's place within the nationalist movement. For example, in a speech addressing the Eighth Congress of the Women's Union of Albania, Nhongo brought the force of Nehanda-Charwe's imagined history and its importance to women and "revolutionaries" (i.e., men) in the struggle. In that speech, Nhongo invoked the name of Nehanda, asserting that she was women's raison d'être in the struggle. By extension, if it had not been for Nehanda, women would not have been able to claim full legitimacy to participate in the struggle as combatants. In her speech Nhongo tried to strike a balance between portraying women as oppressed by men and portraying a patriarchal culture and reiterating that men too had experienced oppression under colonialism. "There can be no doubt that Zimbabwean women have stood up," Nhongo told her audience in Albania. "We have won our rights and place in the Revolution not by anyone's pity, but through our own determination, devotion, and bravery in our *Chimurenga* [war of liberation]." Instead of leaving it at that, she went on to undermine her articulation by suggesting that women "owe a lot to our progressive male Comrades who have stood by us, fought for our rights, and *allowed* us a *degree of freedom* to contribute to . . . a National cause."[47] Yes, she was equally emphasizing women's and men's place in the struggle, but she seems to have considered it more important not to offend men rather than to assert women's central, rather than marginal, place in the movement. Either that or her speech was a statement of the standard party line on the status of women within ZANU-PF and ZANLA, or perhaps it was written for Nhongo, as it defies logic that she could in one sentence undercut her own articulation of women's nationalism as determined by them in their own right rather than as the charity of "progressive male comrades."

Nhongo, like many women (and men) in the liberation movement, had received a basic formal education through the colonial system, which had offered very limited educational opportunities for Africans, especially African women. For that reason, I am inclined to theorize that she was reluctant to fully articulate a women-centered nationalism because of a combination of factors, including her own and other women's limited education, fear of reprisal, dependence on men for access to power and leadership positions, and inability to independently maneuver and form a powerful women's wing within ZANLA. A strong and independent women's caucus (and voice) within that liberation movement might have revolutionized the war. As Lois A. West reminds us, feminist nationalist movements are "social movements simultaneously seeking rights for women and rights for nationalists within a variety of social, economic and political contexts."[48] Nevertheless, toward the end of her speech, Nhongo paid tribute to Nehanda, acknowledging continuity, change, and possibility for women in Zimbabwe's future. As Nhongo put it, *We, the Zimbabwean women in struggle are the heirs of Mbuya Nehanda, that Revolutionary heroine, who inspires every Zimbabwean woman with feelings of great patriotism. Mbuya Nehanda was an exemplary freedom fighter during the first Chimurenga. She fought gallantly and refused to give in to the colonialists. Although the racist colonialists executed her by hanging her at the gallows in what is now known as Salisbury's Maximum Security Prison in 1897, her spirit is still fresh in the minds of many Zimbabwean women. Her exemplary heroism is the spirit that guides every Revolutionary Zimbabwean. Her spirit lives forever.*[49] Ah, the esthetics of manicured memory!

As the foregoing quotation attests, at the end of her speech Nhongo was arguing that the memory of a nineteenth-century "Zimbabwean" woman legitimized twentieth-century women's presence in the combat zone and in the liberation movement. Charwe, the late-nineteenth-century Nehanda medium of the Mazowe, had moved from the periphery to the center of the nationalist stage. She was now a full-fledged *symbol* who inspired women (and men) to participate in the armed struggle of Zimbabwe. The larger message, therefore, was that women had a right to be in the struggle, because they were "heirs of Mbuya Nehanda," the "great patriot." Never mind that Charwe, while a dogged anti-Christian, was also an ambiguous historical character, as we saw earlier. History was messy, but the nationalists manicured a messy past to please the eye in the present. In Nehanda-Charwe the Africans had found their Rhodes equivalent; Nehanda became the sun around which the guerrilla movement orbited, boosting numbers in rural and urban areas. By a nationalist telling, Zimbabwe was to belong to (Mbuya) Nehanda's black children!

Updating Nehanda from Ancestor to Comrade Nehanda

Nhongo's speech, incidentally, was reproduced in an edition of the *Zimbabwe News* that carried several textual and photographic references to Nehanda-Charwe, including a full-page article titled "Nehanda Died for Zimbabwe. Will You?" The article exemplified how African nationalists had come to use the history of the 1896–97 war much as the settlers had used Occupation Day—as a badge of honor and a mark of true autochthony. That 1978 article began: "One of Zimbabwe's most celebrated revolutionaries and guerrilla leaders was Comrade Nehanda Nyakasikana," confusing the spirit with its late-nineteenth-century medium. Though the Nehanda alluded to in the article was Charwe, the invocation of Nyakasikana was a nod to the deep past, much as the poem in Mutswairo's *Feso* had been. Political nationalists—like cultural ones—took liberties with historical fact in the name of moving the revolution forward. Which name belonged to which Nehanda was not important; what mattered was that the past was serving the needs of the present. Moreover, giving Charwe the title "Comrade Nehanda" tells us that she was updated and portrayed as "one of us," one who understood imperialism and fought with latter-day nationalists—not so much Nyamhita, the "traditional" Nehanda. The updating of Charwe to Comrade Nehanda is much like Fox's articulation of Rhodes's grave as sacred to settlers. In the case of African nationalists, updating Nehanda to comrade status was also a way of dealing with the political crises of the war in the 1970s, a time when divisions within and among the nationalist movements had taken nasty turns. The Zimbabwe News article remembered Nehanda-Charwe in very male terms, and no other name in the litany of fallen comrades memorialized a woman. The only other general reference to women came at the end of the article, when the unnamed author stated: "Comrade Nehanda taught Zimbabweans . . . that men and women are truly equal and inseparable partners in the struggle for national liberation as well as in the post-war period of national reconstruction and development."[50] Nehanda had moved from being a rain spirit to being a robust war heroine and, finally, a symbol of reconstruction and especially new gender relations in the envisioned Zimbabwe.

On May 21, 1979, as the war was clearly coming to an end, Robert Mugabe addressed a ZANU-PF seminar in Xai Xai, Mozambique, on women's issues. He largely cast precolonial African women as victims, except for "Nehanda the first heroine and martyr[, who] was obviously a distinct and exceptional character."[51] Casting Nehanda-Charwe in exceptional terms in a speech addressed to a largely female audience, Mugabe painted the majority of women, in an undefined precolonial period, as victims, a strategy that pandered to the idea that only exceptional women like Nehanda could and would reach the top.[52] The question Mugabe's statement raises is whether in Teurai Ropa Nhongo, alias Comrade Nehanda, the liberation movement had already chosen its "distinct and exceptional character." Teurai Ropa was increasingly the "voice of women" in the elected but more often appointed offices of the party's power structures. The nationalist movement's limited knowledge of women's history in general and the limited spaces and voice given to women within the movement tell us that for nationalists at the time, women's rights and issues seemed to be borrowed concepts—much like the Marxist-Leninist ideology that drove the whole movement in the final war years, though in contrast to feminism, Marxism was never cast as a "foreign" ideology.

Beginning the morning of April 17, 1980 (and continuing for the rest of the day), the soon-to-be Zimbabwe Broadcasting Corporation (ZBC) transmitted radio and television news about the momentous event of Zimbabwe's independence. It was a "new" and free African nation. Among those who got prime attention from the broadcasters were the heroes of the 1896–97 uprisings, in particular Mbuya Nehanda. Again, she was the sole female remembered by name in a long line of heroes who had suffered and/or died during the 1966–79 war. Nehanda became a bridge between the past and the present, connecting the young nation with its "ancestors." Charwe was remembered not only in the ZANLA liberation camps but across the country. Her part was documented in the popular songs people composed on the fly and sung not only at guerrilla-organized rallies in the countryside but also in the cities, where political rallies were often held.[53]

Reclaiming a "National" Ancestor for Mazowe: The 1980s and Nehanda's Claim to Power

As the newly independent country celebrated its universal franchise, its newly elected leadership, and its freedom, claimants to the position of Nehanda abounded around the country, causing confusion among those who thought they had a corner on that spirit—and the benefits that would accrue after independence. More than two women were claiming to be Nehanda. The tradition of two simultaneous Nehandas—Nehanda's Head and Nehanda's Feet—was accepted, as we saw earlier, but more than two was problematic, bringing us back to the questions I posed in the introduction. Was the spirit claimed by nationalists that of Nehanda (Nyamhita) or of Charwe? Were both Nyamhita's and Charwe's spirits competing for influence, not only in the Mazoe but throughout the new country? Academic or theoretical as these questions may sound, they are important to ask, as the issue of spirits, and especially the spirit of Nehanda (Charwe), became quite political, as evidenced by the interviews with the claimant to the position of Nehanda and her gatekeepers in the Mazowe in January 1982. The issue of spirits—familial, regional, and national—is still as vexing in postcolonial Zimbabwe. The land-reform program of the first decade of this century has been posited as the third liberation war, after those of 1896–97 and 1966–79.

In nationalism's various iterations of its history, the heroes of 1896–97 are still the top symbols of heroic, if failed, nationalism. In a way, the story of the postindependence Nehanda medium's grasping attempts at power (told below) speaks to how (ordinary) people on the margins of power in the newly independent country tried to find ways to influence the (newly) powerful, who were beginning to distance themselves from the "primitive and backward" past, the very past they had leaned on during the liberation struggle. The tellers of the Nehanda tale are from the African Oral History (AOH) Collection. Like the storytellers we encountered in chapter 5, they were eager to tell their version of history, especially of the 1896–97 war and its famous heroine. They were eager to tell not only about their spirit's past but also about what that spirit of the heroine Charwe wanted in the postindependence period.

The keepers of Charwe's memory in the Mazowe in the 1980s, it turned out, had sent a present to the new "king"—then prime minister Robert Mugabe—in the hope of opening a channel of communication similar to those of earlier days, when spirit mediums had been ex-officio members of the ruling circle, with the power to influence policy and important decisions. That had been the case with any Nehanda in history, and indeed any senior regional spirit medium or lowly familial one. The gatekeepers of the Nehanda (Charwe) of Mazoe—Mavhunga and Mhindurwa—saw in the civil servant Dawson Munjeri, who had visited them to collect oral traditions and histories, not a bureaucrat doing his government duties, but a representative of the state. Because they saw Munjeri as representing the state rather than the government, they were eager to learn about the gifts sent by the Nehanda medium to the new leadership. They asked Munjeri, "What happened to the beasts that were sent to Salisbury [by Nehanda]? For two days there was pandemonium in Salisbury and Mbira music was played but did you not hear of these animals, a head of cattle? When is the acknowledgment coming [from the new leadership]?"[54] The gatekeepers also wanted to know more about the vexing issue of multiple Nehanda medium claimants around the country, at the same time arguing that their medium (in Mazowe) was the "true" Nehanda. They believed that unless their "true" Nehanda was recognized by the new leadership and nation, the whole postindependence project would not go well. The gatekeepers were using a tactic of claiming power in a situation that was obviously structured in (Western) European terms rather than African.

The need for acknowledgment of gifts sent by the spirit of Nehanda (Charwe) to the new leadership is interesting because of the human and earth-bound nature of those spirits' references. For example, although the gatekeepers (all men) were in a trance, they did not speak in the language of the nineteenth-century Charwe, who would have called Salisbury by its precolonial name, Harare, known by the spirit at the time. When the interviewer failed to come up with an answer as to why the state had not acknowledged the Nehanda's gift—for he was a government employee, not a state official—the gatekeepers turned to the issue at hand: the many who claimed to be Nehanda. This issue was important because not only would its investigation involve tracing a long lineage of Nehanda traditions in the Mazowe valley but it would establish the supremacy of Charwe as *the* Nehanda. As one of the gatekeepers put it, *What I can say is that if there were many Nehandas in this country, the mountain called Shavarunzi is there to help you. That mountain holds the possessions of Nehanda for that was Nehanda's dwelling site. Their spirit did not come for fame, no, it did not come for prestige. There is no one who, even after a long absence comes back and forgets to trace where he left his possessions. Nehanda should be able to trace [her] possessions. Today Nehanda is here because of the suffering of the children. She is here to unite you and show you the right path and bring about peace. The spirit has explained to the (political) leaders all these things, but no one has come here to follow up on this. I went to Dande where a similar case [of another Nehanda] was going on. We went to Dande because we wanted to have the country established. We then met with a man called Muzenda (then deputy Prime Minister). You people are trying to fool us, you are trying to save yourselves. We gave the message that Dzivaguru, a great spirit, had said, "Nothing is difficult in this, simply go to Shavarunzi—I mean all those who claim to be the Nehandas should come together. It is that mountain that will decide. No one can forget what [she] left in that mountain.["]*[55] The push and pull of real and imagined history is fascinating, as we see the people of the Mazoe now fully claiming the "right" to Nehandaship, even from its place of origin, Dande.

While the story of Nehanda and her gatekeepers' encounter with the civil servant collecting oral traditions might be read as bizarre, it has to be understood as part of ordinary people's attempts to grasp at the hem of power as it was rising to heights beyond their reach. The nationalists may have ridden the wave of populist Nehanda sentiment—and ancestral power—during the war, but now that they had achieved independence, they were uncomfortable with those same traditions, which appeared "backward" and "primitive." Now that power was theirs, they had to appear "modern" not only in their dress but in the practice of government as well. Thus, the Mazowe's claim to having the "true" Nehanda was also a claim to a memory embedded in another history (of Dande in the northeast). Nehanda had now acquired new meaning through the tradition of accepted mediums in the region, who were also using the

memory of Charwe to claim the power of the real Nehanda and passing it off as their own. Put another ("universal") way, the actions of the
people of Mazowe were similar to Europeans' use of Christianity as their
"tradition" and culture, divorced from its Jewish roots. But in fact, Christianity had started in Palestine mostly among Jews, and as the movement
had grown, its message and adherents had spread beyond Palestine into
North Africa and the far reaches of the Roman Empire. Christianity became the religion of the powerful of Europe, synonymous with European culture and traditions. Indeed, Europeans claimed it as their own,
spreading it far and wide across the globe, such that when it reached
the African interior, such as Chishawasha, it was laden with European
symbolism rather than with its original Jewish traditions. Thus, when the
Nehanda gatekeepers in Mazowe sent a herd of cattle to the new head of
state (Prime Minister Mugabe), they were attempting to revive a history
of power sharing between the state and the church, as it were.

The Nehanda gatekeepers also emphasized that sending cattle to the
"new king" was not new, but a tradition accorded any new leaders in
the land by the reigning Nehanda medium: *When the whites first came
into the country, Nehanda [Charwe] gave them a black heifer. She accepted
them [the whites] because she felt they were her (relatives), but she said she
knew her own choice would come. When we were still in captivity [under
colonialism], Nehanda already knew who the future leader (of the country)
would be and we the Hera accepted that. [At that point, one spirit chided
the other saying,] Nyashanu, why go into all that detail? I will wait until the
whole country has accepted the true Nehanda, before I go into the sort of
detail you are going.*[56] That statement about Nehanda (Charwe) accepting
the colonizers and giving them a heifer could also have been a reason
that the new "king" did not acknowledge the gift from *the* spirit of the
land, Nehanda. In fact, the idea may have seemed absurd to the nationalist guerrillas–turned–new rulers, who had invented the idea of Comrade Nehanda, the anti-imperialist, for ZANU-PF and ZANLA nationalist
ideology and propaganda. Although the spirits tried not to burden the
bureaucrat with "detail," they could not help insisting that their Charwe,
the nation's Mbuya Nehanda, had to be recognized through the accep-
tance of its current medium in Mazowe as the "real" and only Nehanda
of the new nation.

The first spirit insisted that the state and ordinary people had to establish new relations with the current Nehanda medium instead of playing games. As the spirit/medium put it, *People come here saying they have been sent here by the authorities, I tell them all they want but when they go back they are like a cockroach that has dropped into a pail of milk (meaning they never come back). Each and every one of them says they want details on Nehanda and I give them, but then having obtained this information the people concerned disappear. You yourself are going to behave likewise; you will be like a cockroach in a pail of milk. Like a crocodile you will simply consume because [what]ever falls in a pool of deep waters will always belong there (i.e. it disappears).*[57] I can also tell you, earthling, the second spirit, who had sworn no great details until the "true" Nehanda was acknowledged, interjected, asserting that *things have changed, indeed, you have changed things, but if the dead were to [rebel] against you, who will you ask? When you took the country, you should have asked for guidance. That is the time you should have come to Nehanda and ask[ed] for the proper directions. It told you the spirit of Nehanda has always insisted it is responsible for rain. White people came before the fighting broke out [in 1896–97] and asked Nehanda to provide guidance, but Nehanda said, "No, my responsibilities are for rain." Nehanda there and then demonstrated this power and rain fell, the whites acknowledged that Nehanda was the rain master.*[58] The second spirit continued: *The reason we always have to look for Hwata and Chiweshe is because when she was there (in captivity), she showed her powers in the presence of the two. They (whites) tried to say that Chiranda was the true spirit, but Chiranda refused and said Nehanda was responsible for [rain]. The whites asked her to show the powers and she did by summoning the rains to fall. She took a bet from the whites and they acknowledged it and asked her to stop the rain and she did. Nehanda was executed because of her powers which she demonstrated and the whites believed it, and to this day they come and are shown these powers.*[59] Although the spirit had not wanted to give away too many details before the "true" Nehanda was acknowledged, he could not resist giving more details, showing that he was confident that he was on the right side of history, as it were. From his narrative, it is clear that the spirit of Nehanda referred to was the spirit of Charwe, even though occasional flashes invoke the older tradition of Nyamhita, the spirit of fertility and rainmaking. What the gatekeeper spirit Mavhunga said also sounds more like oral history becoming tradition, but a tradition that was still much younger than that of the original Nyamhita. Even more interesting, none of the Nehandas before or after Charwe were acknowledged by the spirits—only the exceptional Charwe. This was constantly reinforced by the stories told that only had to do with her, and the 1896–97 war.

Perhaps the most important thing about the foregoing story of Nehanda is that it was the story of the spirit of Charwe. It was—dare I say it?—an *ngozi* spirit pleading for a final return home to a restful repose after wandering in the vast universe unable to find release and comfort elsewhere. By the gatekeepers' telling, the spirit of Charwe was gravitating toward our speck of a planet, guided by the sun, which marked her place in the Mazowe she had known. As the reticent male spirit, speaking through the medium, told the interviewer, *Nehanda is a captive spirit because it wants to go back to its mountain. It wants to stay at its old site because short of that it remains a strolling beggar. I know Nehanda, that I cannot deny, and I have observed the spirit. I have always said that if there is anyone claiming to be a Nehanda, take that person to the [Shavarunzi] mountain. I have confidence in my Nehanda, because all I need to prove is the rain.*[60] If the spirit of Charwe was "a strolling beggar," aiming for its old home, then its medium, on whose behalf the aforementioned spirits/ mediums were speaking to Munjeri, was a rather puzzling figure, if not a letdown. She sounded more like a "tribal conservative," to borrow from Vambe, if that could pass as a description for anyone, really.[61] I say that because after some lengthy negotiations Munjeri was allowed to interview the medium of Nehanda while he medium was in a trance.

What transpired between Munjeri and the Nehanda medium highlights a rather consistent pattern of incoherency in the thoughts and/ or records of most Nehandas we have encountered, especially Charwe. Unlike in most of the other interviews, rather than let Munjeri act as the assertive interviewer, the medium/spirit took charge and asked the first question: "Have you not heard of a *binga-nyika*? that the land needs to be cleansed through a [girl] child?" Munjeri responded in the negative. According to that 1982 Nehanda medium of Mazowe, the success of post-independence Zimbabwe required (1) a *binga-nyika* and (2) the banning of the color red in any form: *When Nehanda first came into this land, she came as a* binga-nyika. *Her brother was also a* binga-nyika *[the ritual incest discussed in chapter 1]. So, a girl is needed to* pinga-nyika, *and until that is done, nothing will go well. A ceremony should be held so that the land can be cleansed. It was for this reason that I donated a [herd] of cattle and a sheep so that whoever received it would come and seek more information. Then* without warning, she turned to another vexing issue for spirits, people's wearing the color red. *Why do people wear red, tell me? Red symbolizes blood. When [a government representative] came here, it was mentioned that Mugabe should ban red in this country. If I see red, I go "blind." I do not want the red cloth, do you hear me? You go and do what I have told you, and everything will be all right. First, a binga-nyika must be produced, and after that, let's see if your country will not go right. In the old days, if you wanted chieftainship, you would take a child into the forest, and if the child was eaten (by wild beasts), then you would know your chieftainship would be perma-nent. Have you people given a* binga-nyika *you know the country is in turmoil with many contestants for power. This "King" will produce the* binga-nyika, *a young girl who will die a virgin. She is never married. This is what used to happen in the old days when things weren't alright. A* binga-nyika *had to be produced. It is like the spirit of Nehanda on me. It was a* binga-nyika, *it does not like men. From the very day it took possession of me, I have never known men, and once I engage in that, I die.*[62] The teller of this narrative comes off as more human (medium) than spirit, though the two tremble toward each other with no embrace.

The authority of the human channel and religious power conflate to make demands of memory on the living in the name of history. The con-scious medium spoke as a spirit rather than let the spirit speak for it-self through the medium—illustrating the confusing nature of the spirit world, which often conflates history with memory, the medium with the spirit. What is the difference, one might ask, between the pope and the Catholic Church, the Dalai Lama and Tibetan Buddhists, the spirit and its medium? A lot; yet the idea that those institutions are, by definition, represented by the human as spirit—not just a representation—is quite powerful for those who lean on those religious institutions and traditions for nation-building.

Lastly, it is important to reiterate that the evidence suggests that the 1982 spirit being talked about in this last narrative was the spirit of Charwe, executed on behalf of the British government in 1898. The whole transcript makes evident that despite attempts by successive colo-nial governments to excise Charwe from history, her memory was alive not only in nationalist rhetoric but also among her people in the Ma-zowe, who had turned her spirit, rather than the spirit of Nyamhita—which Charwe and other mediums before and immediately after her had channeled—into Nehanda. The spirit of Charwe, as the rest of the narrative suggests, had turned into an *ngozi* spirit, which was then placated with the payment of a "blood child." The family of those implicated in Charwe's execution by the British still owed an outstanding debt, and as the medium put it, *If you kill someone, you must pay for that. What is needed is human compensation* (binga-nyika), *like the one I have here. That child was given to me as payment because the child's relatives presented false evidence that led to the execution of an innocent* mudzimu *[ancestor]. The issue has now been resolved, and the spirit of Nehanda [Charwe] can be satisfied. That child is a blood child, given as compensation. They have not yet brought the necessary cattle so there are crimes still pending against the Hera. The person responsible came out of his own accord and admitted that he had given false incriminating evidence against Ambuya Nehanda. He said he did that because he was afraid of being hanged, that is why he persecuted Ambuya to save his own skin. The person is now dead.*[63] These statements support my argument that the spirit upheld in nationalist discourse was the spirit of Charwe, not Nehanda Nyamita Nyakasikana. Charwe's spirit loomed largest in the nationalist movement's imagination; the nationalists made Charwe into a larger-than-life "exceptional" figure, a matron saint of their guerrilla movement. For that reason, it makes sense that the spirit mediums of Mazowe were seeking acknowledgment as they, perhaps without recognizing it, were asking the nationalist movement–turned–ruling elite to compensate for the use of their ancestor as "national" ancestor in the newly independent country. It was a request, if not to pay history's debt, then to satisfy memory's hunger for recognition in the present.

This chapter demonstrates that memory is socially constructed to serve the needs of the living in each generation. As we saw at the beginning of the chapter, nationalists were not too concerned with the past or with Charwe as Nehanda, as they sought to furnish themselves with Western educational skills that would facilitate their transition into a world governed by Western modes of knowing and being, with African ones serving as a historical backdrop. However, with the turning of local and regional oral traditions into written texts in African languages, representing the African past writ large, an "imagined community" of Zimbabweans was born. In that moment of black consciousness, none was better suited to be the symbol of an affirming African past than Charwe wokwa Hwata, medium of Nehanda, also known as Mbuya Nehanda. The nationalist movement's use of the historical Charwe as Nehanda had the unintended

consequence of turning young women into assertive (feminist) nationalists who claimed a place on the front lines of battle, just as Nehanda had
done in 1896–97, and not as "helpers." The failure to fully integrate an
inclusive nationalism meant that political and cultural nationalist ideology was keen to fight racist imperialism with one hand while holding
tight to patriarchal values with the other. Lastly, the power of the memory of Charwe as Nehanda went beyond political nationalist circles to
reach ordinary people, especially women, who saw in her example an
opportunity to claim historical (traditional) power for themselves by asserting that they were the "true" Nehanda. Charwe as (Mbuya) Nehanda
may have been the raft to the shores of independence, but once there,
new national heroes, those who had done time in colonial prison and/or
on the front lines outside the colony during the recent war (1966–80)
were eager to write a new script of a "modern" nation. That new nation
needed its own "site of memory," a place where the remains of the new
founding fathers would rest in peace. But for how long?

Conclusion
An Acre of Land for Heroes of the Land

Just as Rhodes and Rhodesians created colonial sacred burial grounds at Matobo and elsewhere in the colony, the new leaders of independent Zimbabwe reproduced rather than challenged the real ancestor worship of nationalism—the ascent of men as heroes of the land. In the new postcolony/nation, focus turned from Matobo to a hill five miles west of Zimbabwe's capital, Harare. On that hill is the national monument—"The Shrine," as those in the know like to call it, or The National Heroes' Acre Monument, or simply Heroes' Acre. Heroes' Acre sits on a hill with a splendid view of Harare, its western suburbs, and the highway that leads to other major towns and cities to the south and west of the capital. The National Heroes' Acre Monument was built as a final resting place for the new founders of the nation—a turn away from what nationalists (now) considered "fuzzy" heroes and heroines of the 1896–97 war, whose supposed representatives were demanding *binga-nyika*, as discussed in chapter 7. Heroes' Acre would represent the new heroes, whose credentials and status were unambiguous, documented in writing and photography, and who could be certified as "true" nationalists. Opposite Heroes' Acre, to the north of the highway, is the National Sports Stadium. The fact that the national shrine, with its restricted entry, is right across from a space of national gatherings, sports, or other major events (with both free and paid entry) had never struck me as provocative until one afternoon in August 2009, during my last research trip for this book. As I stood atop the hill taking in the view, I reflected on the resilience and creativity of the people in the face of devastating crises as the country attempts to become postcolonial politically, economically, and socioculturally.

I received permission to visit Heroes' Acre, intending to study the few women buried there and what their presence represented in the nation's memory. Once I was there, it occurred to me that the whole site was a wonderfully ironic metaphor for ending this book on memory in the history of Zimbabwe. The idea that struck me as most ironic was that those buried at Heroes' Acre had earned their place there because they were said or known to have fought, militarily and/or otherwise, for the liberation of the country, *the land*. Yet here they were, their remains confined to an acre of land in all of Zimbabwe's 150,804 square miles. Of course, some of those buried there had participated in shaping what became a "national" site of memory, a contested burial site for the new ruling elite and some of their wives. Burial at the site was politicized from the start, favoring mostly the elite, even within the ruling party, as many scholars have shown.[1] Norma Kriger has insightfully documented the parliamentary debates on the meanings of that site for Zimbabwe and especially on the definition of a hero: What qualified a man—and his wife—to be buried there, when so many others who had sacrificed themselves but were not given the same reward?[2]

The site, then, is a poignant symbol of elite nationalist memory imposed on the majority as "national" memory, much as the Pioneers became shorthand for white entitlement in the (Southern) Rhodesian colony. It also reminds one of the fact that Rhodes's racism was not questioned by settlers and their descendants, who chose to remember his "national" founder status instead.[3] By contrast, the postcolony did not seek to locate and reinter Nehanda-Charwe's bones—or those of any heroes of the 1896–97 wars from anywhere in the country—at Heroes' Acre (or elsewhere). Rather, Heroes' Acre became a place to memorialize the new founders of Zimbabwe. Zimbabweans have talked, and continue to talk, about Heroes' Acre with the announcement of each new "hero." Increasingly, the site is seen as a burial site for those who at the time of their death are in the good books of ZANU-PF's elite, which has made the already contested "real hero" status even more questionable. The declaration of hero status is still dominated by men naming mostly other men national (and provincial) heroes. The process is controlled by a ZANUP-PF party that predominantly considers political party credentials (conferred by the president and the party's politburo rather than by a representative body not affiliated with any political party). This is reminiscent of Pioneer status, which was contested in Rhodesia; who could claim pioneer status and the benefits thereof was not decided by law until later. In the past decade or so, Heroes' Acre has also become the background for President Robert Mugabe's railing against real and phantom enemies at home and abroad. The site, therefore, is representative of the perils of making and remaking ancestors in a country that has seen such violence in the name of the past since its founding as a colony in 1890.

Heroes' Acre, therefore, is an appropriate site of memory to end this story—of many stories—of a country still searching for its place in the sun. The representations of "the people" in the bas-reliefs and the statue to the Unknown Soldier at a sacred site full of singular men (and some women) speak of the nationalist impulse to include the nation's ordinary "saints and martyrs," much as stained-glass windows in medieval cathedrals remember not only Christ and angels but the pantheon of saints as well. Some scholars have argued that Heroes' Acre was modeled predominantly on monuments like those to communist leaders such as Mao or Lenin, but it is likely that Zimbabwe's nationalists were also inspired by monuments that they had grown up with in colonial Rhodesia—and perhaps resented for their exclusion of African historical figures. The Heroes' Acre iconography mirrors that on the Matobo Hill monuments to Rhodes and the Shangani Patrol—as directed by Rhodes. In his last will, Rhodes directed his trustees to "erect or complete the monument (the bas-reliefs) to the men who fell in the first Matabele war at Shangani in Rhodesia. [Furthermore,] I desire the said Hill to be preserved as a burial place, but no person is to be buried there unless the Government for the time being Rhodesia . . . , but a vote of two thirds of its governing body says that he or she has deserved well for his or her country."[4] Heroes' Acre uses the same motif, I argue, and the criteria for deciding who can lie there as a hero mirror those used by Rhodes to determine who deserved to be buried at Matopo after himself. At Zimbabwe's National Heroes' Acre, ordinary people who gave their lives in the fight for freedom are represented by a giant statue portraying a trinity of figures, one female and two males, at the center of the site, and two bronze bas-reliefs depicting colonial life and the promise of independence, each topped with a Zimbabwe bird, on walls to the north and south of the statue. To the east rises a column carrying an eternal flame.[5] The statue and the two walls evoke the country's recent history, rather than its deep past, representing heroes of the new nation in the image of the monument's creators, ZANU-PF.

The statue honoring the Unknown Soldier is the site's coat of arms, as

Figure 13. Heroes' Acre, statue to the Unknown Soldier. (Photographed by author, August 2009, with permission of the National Museums and Monuments of Zimbabwe)

it were. It is also a wonderful paradox, in that while it portrays three figures, two men and a woman, it is named for a single soldier. The female soldier carries in her right hand a Kalashnikov, the AK-47, that symbol of the revolution, while an end of the flag, presumably the national flag, is tucked under her left arm. Of course, in the hierarchy of the sculpture she is not first; she is the second in line—up or down—but I choose to invoke her first. The first male, at the bottom of the trinity, wields an antiaircraft missile in his left hand; his right hand, on his belt, appears relaxed but determined, ready to load his missile from the ammunition on his belt. The second male, at the top, is the flag bearer, who holds his left hand in a tight fist, ready to raise it in that symbol of (Black) power and unity. All three figures strike a resolute pose. They stand firm in their conviction that they are on the right side of history, affirmed by the symbolism of the stones on which they stand, stones representing Great Zimbabwe, from which the (new) country took its name. The same symbolic stone and architecture graces the burial site, especially the terraces where the dead are buried, as though evoking the days of glorious kings who ruled a great African kingdom of old.

The trinity statue greets the visitors as they crest the steep hill. The statue is imposing, impressive in its size and the three larger-than-life figures, who stare into the distance in quiet determination. That impression quickly melts as one is struck by the incongruence of an AK-47-carrying female dressed in a skirt, dress shoes, and socks rather than battle fatigues and boots to match. The statue not only mocks the idea of women as guerrillas but effectively domesticates women who would challenge their prescribed place in the newly independent society. That domestication of women in a place that celebrates African sacrifice and freedom seems to say that good women during war were those that wore gender-appropriate apparel even when it was not practical. Thus, if only that statue survived as evidence of women's participation in the historic war, the (professional) historian and interested person would only have that gendered representation of women in Zimbabwean history, when their lived experiences carried many more (forgotten) stories. In a way, the statue is representative of the oral tradition of Nehanda. What remains of that tradition is attached to men—her father and her brother—and a few shards of evidence from which I tried to make sense of that world. The statue to the Unknown Soldier not only represents the immediate memory making of postcolonial Zimbabwe but also speaks volumes about the construction of women as never first in the history of the nation nor representative of the nation—in the past or the present. Thus, the articulation of the national identity of women, whether women in the Mutapa kingdoms, where we encountered Nyamhita Nehanda, or the ex-combatants of the new nation today, has tended to reflect the lives of men more than women's own lives and historical experiences. The same can be said of settler women, as in the example of the three Mazoe women discussed in chapter 4.

If women in Zimbabwe's recent history had not told their stories—or written about their experiences—then this sculptural representation of a thoroughly domesticated gun-carrying female soldier would be the only public narrative available for studying women's combat history during the war of liberation.[6] That narrative's dominant message is that women were "only the help" during a war that defined the new nation, for they only carried, but never used, the guns that won the war. This statue, then, epitomizes attempts by the aspiring state to construct a narrative about the new nation's founding that recalled the narratives of old African kingdoms, whose women were hangers-on rather than active agents in and of history. I insist on a feminist analysis of the history of a postcolonial nation like Zimbabwe as portrayed in this book, and in architectural and artistic representations such as those at Heroes' Acre, to maintain the claim that it is the historian's duty to "run a knife between the tree [history] and the bark [memory]"[7] to reveal the narrowness of an imagined-nation based on patriarchal exclusions.

The two bronze bas-reliefs are the most densely packed artifacts of national history turning into national memory. Relief 1, to the north, tells the story of the past (colonialism). Relief 2, to the south, tells the story of the future (independence). The two, representing the "perfect" tension between history and memory, form the gate through which one passes to visit the graves of the dead heroes. The bas-reliefs each have three panels mounted on a wall to provide one long narrative of history and memory. Relief 1 is read from right to left, the first panel telling the story of colonial brutality, the police dogs that attacked ordinary people, even women with babies on their backs. The panel invokes the polarized history of white settler brutality and African victimhood; it is an undeniable narrative of what occurred. Yet, as we have seen, settler society's attempts to limit African agency was always subverted by overt and subtle forms of resistance. If this panel tries to invoke polarized black and white histories, the stories told in this book affirm and rupture that narrative. The stories told in this book crack the "pure" white history of conquest and the "pure" black history of victimhood. What emerges is certainly a history of colonialism, but a complicated colonialism, as most of the actors, including the creators of Heroes' Acre's narrative, had complicated relations with white and black people in their own journeys to liberation, as we saw in the stories of white missionaries trying to make amends at Chishawasha, of blacks' friendships with the American George Loft, and of the young women who invoked Nehanda in order to serve in the guerrilla army.

The second panel shows a consciousness-raising process as those in the know articulated the issues and the armed struggle needed to undo

Figure 14. Heroes' Acre, bas-relief 1, telling the story of the past (colonialism). (Photographed by author, August 2009, with permission of the National Museums and Monuments of Zimbabwe)

the oppression depicted on the first panel—much as the better-educated prisoners tutored those with lower levels of education in Rhodesia's political prisons. The young (males) appear in the forefront, with the women and the peasants (as men) listening attentively, their thatched huts in the distant background. The third panel shows the decisive moment of action. The bare-chested, Kalashnikov-wielding young man on bended knee, presumably to the ancestors, seeks a blessing and guidance as he goes off to war. Other young men are bidding farewell to family or friends and preparing for war. A woman marches along at the front of the line—dress, headcover, and all—carrying a gun for war. Yes, she carries while he wields; that is how the nation's memory was imagined. To round it all off, that panel of action invokes "tradition," with African material culture represented by musical instruments like the marimba, the clay water or beer pot and drinking gourd in the foreground. The three panels paint a rather uncomplicated linear progression of history, a history that celebrates the violence of the war that brought independence and universal suffrage, as though violence were the only option.

Relief 2 shows nationalism in all its triumphalism—unlike Relief 1,

Figure 15. Heroes' Acre, bas-relief 2, telling the story of the present and the future (postcolonialism). (Photographed by author, August 2009, with permission of the National Museums and Monuments of Zimbabwe)

which, though masculinized in its representation of agency and leadership, attempts to "equalize" oppression and leadership. Relief 2, on the other hand, depicts the memory of a visionary leader, one who is neither unknown nor ambiguous. It is Robert Mugabe himself, with the people but above them as they all march toward the future, to the new nation. A Kalashnikov is held high; the national flag flutters in the air, heralding the arrival of a new nation on the world stage. The future is unknown, but it beckons. A woman with her own AK-47, slung over her right shoulder, embraces a child; another woman holds up high a child, the future. Hope. Tellingly, none of the men hold children in their arms. Most either hold guns or raise fists into the air in triumph. Other women and men bring up the rear, carrying all manner of things on their heads and in their arms. The future calls, and the one and only leader marches forward, leading his people into the unknown. On the panels of relief 2, all the ugliness of colonial history is gone. A "pure" black nation is born, devoid of white people, as none are visually represented. Independence—a glorious moment!

Relief 2 is fascinating for its creation of the single-leader mythology. White settlers, as we saw, put their stock in Cecil John Rhodes and his minions; Africans put theirs in Nehanda and those (mostly) men remembered from the wars of 1896 and 1966. At the beginning of the postcolonial era, Robert Mugabe fashioned himself the single undisputed leader. That only he is recognizable, larger in size than all the other figures on the bas-relief, perhaps foretold the tragedy of the future. Relief 2, while celebrating the history of the erstwhile oppressed, also inscribed a gender problematic in that it has no space for the complications of history. It assumes that a nation has one version of the remembered past. However, in the words of Jeffrey Olick, "Memory is never unitary, no matter how hard various powers strive to make it so. There are always sub-narratives, transitional periods, and contests over dominance."[8] Remember Molly Marshall-Hole and the Rhodesian memory? Remember Aaron Jacha and his version of inter-African relations at the moment before colonialism? Heroes' Acre tries to stretch history, assuming that memory will smooth over the gaps and incompleteness of history and its contradictions. But it cannot, as nationalism has created its own "founding right of state," which excluded and trampled on Others' memories of how Zimbabwe was made.

This book does not, of course, answer all the questions it raises. As a first book of its kind, it focuses on a small place and region of the country to the exclusion of others. My hope is that it blazes a trail for others to follow and that others will chart new courses in telling other narratives of the uses and abuses of history in postcolonial nations in Africa and elsewhere. This book shows that memory is never a fixed historical phenomenon, that memory itself produces its own history too, as each generation seeks meaning from the ever-expanding past, fed by the living's need for memory. The history and memory of the spirit of Nehanda is the best in this history of layers of memory, as that spirit turned from an ethnic history and memory of a people to a nationalist memory much removed from its "original" story of fertility and rain. Maybe spirits never die.

I close with a poem I wrote to my mother, a woman who loved history. Both my parents were conditioned by the same colonialism that shaped the lives of many of the Africans encountered in this book. The muted history lessons my parents taught me inspired this book, and this poem can be read as my own mythmaking in honor of a woman who did not have much book learning but who could debate philosophical ideas about the past with the most learned.

Believe It or Not . . .

. . . It was my "illiterate" mother
Yes, you heard right; I said it was the illiterate
Who taught me how to recycle and reuse
Before I went to school and
Learned how to spell *r-e-c-y-c-l-e*!

Do I trace a cynical smile on your face?
Well, believe it or not,
It was my illiterate mother who taught me
How to use *appropriate technology* for farming
So the soil would retain its soul, and life giving self
When the rain lashes down with the impatience of a full bladder.

Oh, yeah, believe it or not,
It was my illiterate mother, who said to me,
Baby girl, you go to school.
And it is my illiterate mother, who says to me,
Do well in school my child,
Learn, share, and compare yourself with nobody else
Because you are not them, and they are not you.

But believe it or not,
Some of what my illiterate mother taught me
I have seen and been reading in the learned books
And some of it has not been much different from what she taught me
And what her illiterate mother taught her . . .

I got a letter from my illiterate mother the other day,
Believe it or Not . . .
She wanted to know how her baby girl was doing.
She wrote the most beautiful letter an illiterate mother
Could write to her literate daughter.

You go baby mine, my illiterate mother wrote me.
Learn what the books say and

What the educated people say.
Only, don't lose nor forget who you really are.
I raised you the best I knew then,
I learned it from the university I attended:
The University of Life Experience.
I wrote back and said:
You know what Ma, I have learned and am learning a lot,
But believe it or not,
What I learned from your illiterate self has been the best foundation
For whatever education I have been having and will ever have.

I read in some of the books what you are,
An *environmentalist.*
I read in some of the books the patterns you learned and observed
    over time,
That way, you learned what works and what doesn't in raising me
And believe it or not, you were *theorizing . . . !*

Of course, some of what you taught me might belong to museums
    now,
But heck, much of it is still applicable,
And is making such a comeback you won't believe it.

Take heart Ma,
What you taught me I will not squeeze between my thighs
As I sit in the citadel of knowledge,
Because the citadel of knowledge *is* because of what
You and all other illiterates have shared
With *literates* who have made a name for themselves studying your
    experiences.
And believe it or not, I have joined their ranks,
Yet remain so illiterate in so many ways that you are literate . . .

And believe it or not, Ma,
What is in some of the books I read,
Comes from what illiterates like you
Have shared and share with literates like me!

Don't worry Ma,
I will not shy away from saying I learned it from illiterate you,

Who learned it from her illiterate mother,
Who also learned it from her illiterate mother, . . .
Whose illiterate mother passed it down to her.

And believe it or not, Ma,
You and I will reclaim what You, Your Mother,
Her Mother, her Mother's Mother . . .
And many illiterate Mothers did not or could not write.

You and me, Ma,
Will be coauthors in Memory of the Forgotten Memory
Those connoisseurs in the art of knowledge and money making
Have not only drawn from,
But copyrighted!

Notes

Introduction

1. The gains Zimbabwe made in the first decade and a half after independence are in sharp contrast to its current state—politically, economically, socially, and culturally. Many of the gains made in those first fifteen to twenty years, including the production of a well-educated and skilled class of young people, most of whom now live abroad—are being reversed by internal and external economic and political pressures.

2. Cush, "Tale of Two Countries."

3. Michel-Rolph Trouillot articulated the paradoxes of history in *Silencing the Past.*

4. Chatterjee, *Nation and Its Fragments,* 10.

5. Ibid., 5.

6. David Martin and Phyllis Johnson's focus on leaders of the guerrilla movement in northern and eastern Mashonaland is useful here. See Martin and Johnson, *Struggle for Zimbabwe,* chap. 5.

7. Godwin and Hancock show that white Rhodesians were more differentiated than even they liked to admit. *Rhodesians Never Die.*

8. Aschwanden, *Karanga Mythology;* Shoko, *Karanga Indigenous Religion in Zimbabwe.*

9. This issue is fully explored in the last section of chapter 7.

10. I am grateful to Terence Ranger for his invitation to participate in the British Zimbabwe Society's Research Days in June 2010, whose theme was religion in contemporary Zimbabwe.

11. Julie Cairnie critically analyzed this phenomenon in her essay "Women and the Literature of Settlement and Plunder."

12. The documentary film *Mugabe and the White African,* www.mugabeand thewhiteafrican.com, captures this phenomenon of colonial forgetting very well. Also, Ranka Primorac analyzes the rise of Rhodesian identity in her essay "Rhodesians Never Die?"

228 Notes to Pages 7–15

13. See esp. Catholic Commission for Justice and Peace, *Gukurahundi in Zimbabwe* (original report 1997). For a broader historical context, see esp. Ranger, Alexander, and McGregor, *Violence and Memory*.

14. Ricoeur, *Memory, History, Forgetting*, 21, emphasis in original.

15. Hobsbawm, "Introduction: Inventing Traditions," 1.

16. Ricoeur, *Memory, History, Forgetting*, 25.

17. Atwood, "In Search of Alias Grace," 176.

18. Confino, "Collective Memory and Cultural History," 1386.

19. Ibid., 1387.

20. Ricoeur, *Memory, History, Forgetting*, 56.

21. Ibid., 96.

22. Halbwachs, *On Collective Memory*, chap. 4. See also Ricoeur, *Memory, History, Forgetting*, 121.

23. Olick and Robbins, "Social Memory Studies," 110. The omission of African history's contributions to memory studies in this review essay is rather glaring.

24. I borrow the phrase from Morrison, "Unspeakable Things Unspoken."

25. Fanon, *Wretched of the Earth*, 53.

26. Amadiume, *Male Daughters, Female Husbands*; Mohanty, "Under Western Eyes"; Barkley Brown, "What Happened Here"; McFadden, "African Feminist Perspectives of Postcoloniality"; Oyewùmí, *Invention of Women* (for a shorter, sharper version, see Oyewùmí, "Visualizing the Body"); McCall, "Complexity of Intersectionality"; Boydston, "Gender as a Question."

27. Boydston, "Gender as a Question," 576.

28. Ibid.

29. I am sure that I would not have written the same kind of book if I had stayed in Southern Africa, and not lived and studied in North America, from where I had philosophical and geographic distance. Edward Hallett Carr best articulated the subjective nature of the historian's craft in his lectures. See Carr, *What is History?*, esp. chap. 1, "The Historian and his Facts," 3–35.

30. Noordervliet, "In Defense of Clio's Honor."

31. Ibid.

32. The historiography includes Abraham, "Early Political History"; Randles, *Empire of the Monomotapa*; Garlake, *Great Zimbabwe*; Huffman, *Guide to the Great Zimbabwe*; Beach, *Shona and Zimbabwe*; Bhila, *Trade and Politics*; Mudenge, *Political History*; Livneh, "Pre-colonial Polities"; Chirenje, "Portuguese Priests and Soldiers"; and Pikirayi, "Archaeological Identity of the Mutapa Kingdom."

33. Trevor-Roper, "Rise of Christian Europe," 875.

34. Zeleza, "Gender Biases in African Historiography."

35. See Ranger's "Nationalist Historiography" for his reflections on his career as a historian of Zimbabwe and what has happened to that history. For my

various treatments of the term *pioneer*, see my Note on Orthography, Language Use, and Historiographies.

36. Roberts, "Introductory Comments: History and Memory," 513.

37. Ricoeur, *Memory, History, Forgetting*, 167.

38. One of the most compelling of books that make extensive use of sources, rather than snippets, is Butalia, *Other Side of Silence*.

39. As I finished revisions for this book, I was gladdened by William Cronon's presidential column in the American Historical Association monthly magazine, *Perspectives in History*, titled "Professional Boredom"—and the responses it generated. The essay makes a case for writing historical works that not only engage professional historians but are accessible to a wider audience. Cronon, "Professional Boredom."

40. Noordervliet, "In Defense of Clio's Honor."

41. I borrow the phrase *sites of memory* from Nora, "Between History and Memory," 18–19.

42. Mamdani, *Citizen and Subject*; Mamdani, *When Does a Settler Become a Native?*; Mamdani, "Beyond Settler and Native."

43. Teresa Barnes eloquently articulated this postcolonial paradox of the uses and abuses of history in her article "History Has to Play Its Role."

44. The full quotation reads: "Hegel remarks somewhere that all great world-historic facts and personages appear, so to speak, twice. He forgot to add: the first time as tragedy, the second time as farce." Marx, *Eighteenth Brumaire*, 1.

1. Far from the Tree

1. Even though I focus here on colonialism by Europeans in Southern Africa, I subscribe to a broader definition of colonialism that is not always centered on the European experience. See, e.g., Chakrabarty, *Provincializing Europe*.

2. Garbett, "Disparate Regional Cults," 56–57.

3. Herbert, *Iron, Gender, and Power*, chaps. 2 and 3.

4. See esp. Berger, *Religion and Resistance*. For a gendered definition of spirit mediumship, see Charumbira, "Spirit Possession."

5. For example, someone born in an Eland family had to marry outside the Eland totem; someone from a Lion family had to marry outside the Lion totem; and so on. The northern Hera, from whom Gutsa, Shayachimwe, and Nyamhangambiri descended, were of the Mhofu/Shava (Eland) totem. Like all others within their totem group, they had praise poems (*zvidawo*; sing., *chidawo*) that distinguished them from within as descendants of this or that brother. Thus, once the two brothers and nephew settled in central Mashonaland, they assumed new *zvidawo*. Shayachimwe, who founded the Hwata

dynasty, in which Nehanda-Charwe was born, kept his Mhofu/Shava totem but assumed the new praise name Mutenhesanwa.

6. For a detailed historical study of Shona dynasties, see, e.g., Beach, *Zimbabwean Past,* esp. secs. 2 and 3. My own assessment of Beach's work is similar to Zilberg, "Review."

7. For an ethnography of northern Zimbabwean spirits, including the spirit of Nehanda, see Garbett, "Disparate Regional Cults."

8. For archaeological and anthropological studies, see, e.g., Summers, *Inyanga;* and more recently, Jacobson-Widding, "Pits, Pots, and Snakes"; Herbert, *Iron, Gender, and Power,* chap. 2; Huffman, *Snakes and Crocodiles;* and Beach, "Cognitive Archaeology."

9. See esp. Hodza and Fortune, *Shona Praise Poetry.*

10. I reconstruct this narrative of Nyamhita's story from David P. Abraham's oral-tradition methodology in "Early Political History."

11. On incest in African folklore, see Jacobson-Widding and Van Beek, *Creative Communion;* and Jacobson-Widding, "Pits, Pots, and Snakes," 10–15.

12. The term *Ambuya* or *Mbuya* has varied meanings, including "grandmother," "mother-in-law," and "ancestor," which I use in this book. It is also used as an honorific title for any female elder regardless of affinity. The male equivalent term is *Sekuru.*

13. Fontein, *Silence of Great Zimbabwe,* 157–65.

14. Borg, *Meeting Jesus Again,* 13.

15. I use this analogy to convey not the grandeur of the religions those men spawned but the idea that they were Spirit people who changed their societies. To fully grasp my comparison, see, among other works by Jesus scholars, ibid., 32–36.

16. David Beach's rendition of that oral tradition tilts toward a Marxist materialist perspective. See Beach, *Shona and Zimbabwe,* 95–105, 313–17.

17. National Archives of Zimbabwe (hereafter NAZ)/S2929/2/3/1, "Revised and Amended Delineation Report on the NeChinanga Community of Chief Makope, Chiweshe Tribal Trust Land, Mazoe District," Jan. 1968, 7. In the report, *Charwe* was spelled *Chargwe;* I update the spelling here for consistency. The 1965 delineation report did not make any reference to Nehanda(s) in the Mazoe District, though it did note the importance of religion and spirit mediums to people of the area. See NAZ/S2929/2/4, 4.

18. Kerr, *Far Interior,* 138. Another manuscript describing nineteenth-century Mazowe is at Rhodes House, Oxford: Francis Gamaliel Phillips, "My Journey to and Experience in Mashonaland," Mss. Afr. s. 608, 11, Bodleian Library, Rhodes House, Oxford University. A librarian at Rhodes House verified in the summer of 2005 that the date "189?" is written in pencil on the typed manuscript.

19. For an excellent essay on the role of religion in collective memory, as

well as on the construction of sacred sites of memory in the "Holy Land," see Halbwachs, *On Collective Memory*, chap. 6 and pt. 2.

20. The Mazowe valley is still an important site of memory and contestation. See, e.g., Sadomba, "War Veterans in Zimbabwe's Land Occupations," chaps. 4 and 5.

21. Axelson, *Portugal and the Scramble for Africa*, 186.

22. Thompson, *History of South Africa*, chaps. 1–3. Essays in Elphick and Giliomee, *Shaping of South African Society*, bring various perspectives illuminating the *longue durée* of South African race relations, especially since European settlement.

23. Elphick and Giliomee, *Shaping of South African Society*, chap. 4. See also Thomas, *Rhodes*, chaps. 10 and 13.

24. Keppel-Jones, *Rhodes and Rhodesia*, 121–22.

25. Thomas, *Rhodes*, chap. 15.

26. See Selous, *Sunshine and Storm in Rhodesia*.

27. Keppel-Jones, *Rhodes and Rhodesia*, 2–15.

28. For a recent history of the Ndebele, see, e.g., Ndlovu-Gatsheni, *Ndebele Nation*.

29. See, e.g., Keppel-Jones, *Rhodes and Rhodesia*, 189–224; and Newitt, *History of Mozambique*, chap. 14.

30. Mudenge, *Political History*, chaps. 6 and 7.

31. Capt. M. D. Graham to Mashonaland Administrator, "The Guerold Murder Case," in Great Britain Colonial Office, *Correspondence Relating to the British South Africa Company*, 17. Note that the settler's name seems to have been spelled variously, *Guerolt* in on-the-ground documents and *Guerold* in upper-chain-of-command documents.

32. Henry B. Loch to Knutsford, 15 Feb. 1892, in ibid., 11.

33. The colonial administrator of Southern Rhodesia at the time was one of Rhodes's closest friends, a Scottish medical doctor by the name of Leander Starr Jameson.

34. See Phimister, *Chibaro*.

35. *Rhodesia Herald*, 29 Oct. 1892. It took more than a decade to change the laws, especially as relating to Africans in the Cape Colony, where Rhodes was premier from 1890 to 1896.

36. I choose *wars* or *insurrection*, instead of the contentious terms *uprising* and *revolt*, terms that have dominated the historiography. Terence Ranger wrote the first history of that period, a "national" history of the colonial encounter, in his *Revolt in Southern Rhodesia*. See also Ranger, "Connexions between 'Primary Resistance' Movements." Beach contested Ranger's interpretation of that history in *War and Politics* and "An Innocent Woman, Unjustly Accused?" Other critiques of Ranger's original work tended to be nationalistic, taking issue with Ranger's European bias in rendering the story of the revolt. They

include Mutunhu, "Nehanda of Zimbabwe"; and Tsomondo, "Shona Reaction and Resistance," 11–32. Julian Cobbing was another voice of criticism, but his criticism was directed at Ranger's rendition of Ndebele history. See Cobbing, "Absent Priesthood." David Lan, another respondent to the Ranger theory, was probably closest to Ranger in arguing for the importance of religion in war, as shown in his closely hewn ethnography, *Guns and Rain*. My own work engages the historiography's gender biases, and this is exemplified in my piece focusing on Beach's assertion that Nehanda was "An Innocent Woman, Unjustly Accused." That response appeared as "Nehanda and Gender Victimhood."

37. Ricoeur, *Memory, History, Forgetting*, 79.

38. Brown, *On the South African Frontier*.

39. For comparative studies in other countries in the region, see, e.g., Pieres, *The Dead Will Arise*; and Gewald, *Herero Heroes*, esp. chap. 4.

40. NAZ/BO/11/1/1, Henry J. B., "Letter to his Mother," 28 Apr. 1889; Fitzpatrick, *Through Mashonaland*, 32–33.

41. Phillips, "My Journey to and Experience in Mashonaland," 11.

42. Ibid., 13.

43. NAZ/N1/1/9, A. C. Campbell, "Quarterly Report Salisbury District," 29 Jan. 1896.

44. "Our Native Troubles," *Rhodesia Herald*, 17 June 1896.

45. For a recent innovative discussion of how Africans interpreted colonialism through naming, see Lukaka, *Naming Colonialism*.

46. The growing historiography of first contact in North America and the Pacific region is a useful literature that could enrich African historiography by tracing the entanglements of the past to illuminate the present. See, e.g., all the essays in Lutz, *Myth and Memory*.

47. NAZ/A1/12/26, H. Marshall Hole, "Report of the Civil Commissioner, Salisbury, October 29, 1896," 17–18.

48. NAZ/N1/1/9, A. C. Campbell, "Quarterly Report Salisbury District," 29 Jan. 1896.

49. Ibid.

50. *Rhodesia Herald*, 24 June 1896.

51. "Our Native Troubles," ibid., 17 June 1896. A significant number of company reports on the rebellions first appeared in the *Rhodesia Herald*. For this reason, I have tracked that paper much more than previous scholars on the subject.

52. In the south, where the Ndebele had gone to war in March 1896, the BSAC, for example, had a negotiated settlement led by none other than Cecil Rhodes himself. Ranger, *Voices from the Rocks*, pt. 1.

53. Alderson, *With the Mounted Infantry*, 130. See also Gann, *History of Southern Rhodesia*, 133–39; and Ranger, *Revolt in Southern Rhodesia*, 271.

54. NAZ/AL/1/1/1, "Messengers from Mazoe—Dispatches from O. C. Fort Alderson," 15 Nov. 1896.

55. NAZ/W/18, "Report of the CNC of Mashonaland on Kagubi and Nianda," [1896?].

56. Ibid.

57. McMahon, "Clearing the Granite Range."

58. Ibid., 185.

2. War Medals, Gendered Trials, Ordinary Women, and Nehandas to Remember

1. Connerton, *How Societies Remember*, 6. Karl Marx's *Eighteenth Brumaire* is the best example.

2. Connerton, *How Societies Remember*, 7–9.

3. Mamdani, *Citizen and Subject*, chap. 1.

4. Lutz, "Introduction: Myth Understandings," 1–2.

5. It should be noted that Carrington was grateful for Portuguese support in neighboring Mozambique through the governor of Beira, Colonel Machado, and his underlings. Erstwhile colonial competition over territory was momentarily abandoned as it became important to save white lives in the varied battles in Rhodesia and the war became too big to lose.

6. Carrington to Rosemead, National Archives, United Kingdom, WO 32/7840. Unless otherwise noted, this section relies on documents in the cited folder, as well as copies of the same and other letters in folders WO 32/7842 and WO 32/7843.

7. I am not a military historian. Those with the interest and expertise may challenge me on this point; better yet, they could work on the cited archive and see what conclusions they draw.

8. I cannot think of a better patriarchal symbol of empire.

9. Ricoeur, *Memory, History, Forgetting*, 79.

10. MacDonald, *Language of Empire*, 4.

11. I paraphrase from Billie Holiday's song "Strange Fruit," on lynchings in the United States, especially the southern states. That photograph was to be the subject of a beautiful memorialization by Yvonne Vera in her novel *Butterfly Burning*, giving name to those who died unnamed. Vera, *Butterfly Burning*, 10–15.

12. The other men poised for awards in the first category were sergeants; lieutenants; captains; the elite 7th Hussars, who included a prince; and the native commissioners.

13. National Archives, United Kingdom, WO 32/7840; see also WO 32/7842.

14. S.W. (under secretary of state, Colonial Office) to High Commissioner Rosemead, Mar. 1897.

15. National Archives, United Kingdom, WO 32/7840.

16. Carrington list of men of "Conspicuous Gallantry in Action," ibid.

17. Halbwachs, *On Collective Memory*, 134. The whole chapter (120–66) is

actually important for understanding the dynamics of social class in the making of collective memory.

18. Ibid.

19. *War Office Gazette*, 7 May 1897.

20. Nesbitt's award, like those of some other men, was contested. See "Cable News: The Mazoe Patrol," *Rhodesia Herald*, 1 July 1896; and letter to the editor, ibid., 9 Dec. 1896.

21. NAZ/AL/1/1/1, "Messengers from Mazoe—Dispatches from O. C. Fort Alderson," 15 Nov. 1896.

22. NAZ/N1/1/6, NC Mazoe to CNC, 30 Oct. 1897; *Rhodesia Herald*, 18 Aug. 1897.

23. *Rhodesia Herald*, 13 Oct. 1897.

24. Ibid., 27 Oct. 1897.

25. NAZ/N1/1/6, NC Mazoe to CNC, 29 Oct. 1897.

26. Ibid., my emphasis.

27. NAZ/N1/1/6, NC Mazoe to CNC, 30 Oct. 1897.

28. NAZ/W/18, "Report of the CNC of Mashonaland on Kagubi and Nianda," [1896?].

29. NAZ/S401/253, "Preliminary Examination of Kagubi," 29 Oct. 1897.

30. NAZ/S401/252, "Preliminary Examination of Nianda," 12 Jan. 1898.

31. It is important to reiterate that at this point in the colony, many of the bureaucrats were acting officers, as those in office had either died in the war or shipped out to South Africa. After the war, the colony set out to restructure and outfit most of its posts with "trained Civil servants." Marshall Hole, *Making of Rhodesia*, 380. On imperial women workers in Rhodesia, particularly nurses in the 1890s, see, e.g., Charumbira, "Administering Medicine without a License."

32. NAZ/S401/252, "Preliminary Examination of Nianda," 12 Jan. 1898, my emphasis.

33. Ibid.

34. Beach, "An Innocent Woman, Unjustly Accused?," 45.

35. Ibid., 53.

36. I use *Kunyaira* when discussing African references to him, and *Pollard* for European references.

37. I am grateful to Hannah C. Wojciehowski for the suggestion of torture as a possible explanation.

38. NAZ/AOH/17, "Interview with Mr. Rakafa," 17 Aug. 1977, 37–38. The abbreviation AOH is for the African Oral Histories Collection.

39. The problems of the colonial archive have been and continue to be addressed by Africanist scholars. Studies on Southern Africa closest to this book's subject are, among others, the erudite Hamilton, *Terrific Majesty*; and Lalu, "Grammar of Domination."

40. For commentary on the insurrection trial sessions, see Wood, "1898 Criminal Sessions."

41. Gutsa and Zindoga, Nehanda-Charwe's codefendants, along with forty-four other men, escaped jail on Friday, 25 February, five days before the trial. "The Escape of Prisoners," *Rhodesia Herald*, 2 Mar. 1898. The general sense of dis-ease among the settlers was quite palpable.

42. My longer discussion of Charwe's and other women's active participation in the 1896–97 war in central Mashonaland can be found in Charumbira, "Nehanda and Gender Victimhood."

43. NAZ/S401/253. Unless otherwise stated, the discussion here is based on this court record. I have not yet figured out what the women's names mean; in this form they do not make much (Shona) sense to me.

44. "The Escape of Prisoners," *Rhodesia Herald*, 2 Mar. 1898.

45. For more on this phenomenon of death and water, see Pwiti and Mahachi, "Shona Ethnography."

46. Charlie's wife, Chikunda, testified against some men charged with the murder of the gold prospector William Birkett, killed in or near the Mazoe. NAZ/S401/258, "Preliminary Examination of Mabidsa, Rowanga, Mawonira and Gamanya," 21 Dec.1897.

47. On using women as pawns in the late nineteenth century, see Schmidt, *Peasants, Traders, and Wives*, 30–35.

48. NAZ/S401/252, "Preliminary Examination of Nianda," 12 Jan. 1898; NAZ/S2953, "Regina vs. Nianda," 2 Mar. 1898; "The High Court," *Rhodesia Herald*, 9 Mar. 1898.

49. NAZ/S2953, "Regina vs. Nianda," 2 Mar. 1898. See also NAZ/S401/252, "Preliminary Examination of Nianda," 12 Jan. 1898.

50. I borrow the phrase from Hobsbawm, "Introduction."

51. NAZ/S2953, "Regina vs. Nianda," 2 Mar. 1898.

52. Garbett's study of spirit-medium territories in Dande—"Disparate Regional Cults"—is still pertinent. See also Fry, *Spirits of Protest*.

53. Hwata consistently took the position that the witnesses were "telling the truth," which made the process rather difficult for both Charwe and himself. Murphy quit the case because of that testimonial conflict.

54. "The High Court," *Rhodesia Herald*, 9 Mar. 1898.

55. NAZ/N1/1/6, NC Mazoe to CNC, 29 and 30 Oct. 1897.

56. "The High Court," *Rhodesia Herald*, 9 Mar. 1898.

57. Richartz, "End of Kakubi." The quotation is from 54; the image that is figure 5 also appeared in the report.

58. Catholic priests' prominent role in an otherwise Protestant colony came about because of Cecil J. Rhodes's great admiration of Ignatius of Loyola, on whose Society of Jesus Rhodes wanted to model a secret society of Anglo-Saxon men who would rule the world. Rhodes, *Last Will and Testament*, 63.

59. Richartz, "End of Kakubi," 53.

60. I did not have access to Richartz's diary while in Zimbabwe. A Jesuit priest said he was working on it and flatly told me there was nothing else to say about the matter of Richartz that had not already been said. He did not think much of women's and gender history; I hope he will change his mind should he read this.

61. Richartz, "End of Kakubi," 55.

62. Ibid., 53–54.

63. NAZ/N3/1/13, E. T. Kenny, Native Commissioner, "District of Mazoe Yearly Report," 19 Apr. 1898, 7–10. See other annual reports in N9/19/12.

64. NAZ/N3/1/13, "Mazoe South District," in confidential letter from Kenny to CNC, 10 Jan. 1907. All quotations in this paragraph, unless noted otherwise, are from this letter.

65. On Mativirira as successor to Charwe as the medium of Nehanda in the Mazoe, see also Beach, "An Innocent Woman, Unjustly Accused?," 28–29.

66. Yoshikuni, *Elizabeth Musodzi*, 2. I will return to the subject of Chishawasha and the memory of Nehanda later.

67. The director of the National Museums and Monuments of Zimbabwe (NMMZ), Godfrey Mahachi, in August 2009 told me that the Nehanda site had been entered into the Registry of Monuments. On problems with preserving precolonial sites of memory in Zimbabwe, see, e.g., Pwiti and Ndoro, "Legacy of Colonialism"; and Mataga and Chabata, "Preservation of Spiritual Heritage in Zimbabwe."

68. NAZ/N3/1/13, E. T. Kenny, "Confidential Dispatch to CNC," 22 Jan. 1907. Unless otherwise noted, all quotations in this section are from this dispatch, both the letter and statements.

69. NAZ/N3/1/13, "Hwata Statement," in Kenny, "Confidential Dispatch to CNC," 22 Jan. 1907.

70. NAZ/N3/1/13, Acting CNC to NC, Mazoe, 11 Feb. 1907.

71. NAZ/N3/1/13, A. B. Randins to Acting CNC, 11 Feb. 1907. On the number of missionaries to South Africa (which included Rhodesia then), see Brigg, "Salvation Army."

72. "The Rising in Rhodesia," *Times*, 29 June 1896; see also "The Mazoe Relief," *Rhodesia Herald*, 8 July 1896.

73. On the memory and quandary of missionaries, including the Salvation Army, as paradoxical imperialists and "saviors" in the past and their place in Zimbabwe's land crises from 2000 to the present, see Chitando, "Sacred Remnant?," 185, 193.

74. NAZ/N3/1/13, Acting CNC to NC, Mazoe, 11 Feb. 1907.

3. Remembering Rhodes, Commemorating Occupation, and Selling Memories Abroad

1. Terence Ranger wrote a definitive history of the Matobo Hills from colonial times to the present. Ranger, *Voices from the Rocks*, chaps. 1, 3, and 4. See also Daneel, *God of the Matopos*.

2. For other examples of non-British Europeans or people of European descent, see Ernst and Scheurer, *History of the Swiss in Southern Africa;* and Brown, *On the South African Frontier*.

3. An insightful study of the calendar as a social construct that changes over time, a tradition that English settlers carried with them, if unconsciously, is Cressy's *Bonfires and Bells*.

4. Ricoeur, *Memory, History, Forgetting*, pt. 2, chaps. 1–3.

5. See esp. Ranger, Alexander, and McGregor, *Violence and Memory*.

6. Howard A. Arnold to Howell Wright, 20 May 1937, Howell Wright Collection (MS 565), Manuscripts and Archives, Yale University Library (hereafter HWC MS 565), Series I, box 1, folder 6. Unless otherwise noted, all citations to this collection are to Series I.

7. Ricoeur, *Memory, History, Forgetting*, 82.

8. Fox, "Rhodesia and the War," 348.

9. Ibid., 349.

10. Ibid.

11. For some historical context, see also Keppel-Jones, *Rhodes and Rhodesia*, esp. chap. 4.

12. NAZ/H15/2/1, Pioneer Association, "Frederick Clayton Trust Act, Chapter 17:02, Ord. 10/1918." The act included (almost) complete lists of all the men who served, which can be cross-checked with lists in the National Archives, United Kingdom, and the Howell Wright Collection at Yale.

13. Paul Maylam's short history of the historical memory of Rhodes is a great summary. See Maylam, *Cult of Rhodes*, esp. the introduction and chaps. 2 and 5.

14. "Occupation Day," *Rhodesia Herald*, 25 Aug. 1893.

15. "Matabeleland," ibid., 9 Nov. 1894.

16. "Gymkhana Club Meeting, Occupation Day," ibid., 18 Sept. 1895.

17. "Occupation Day," ibid., 9 Sept. 1896, my emphasis.

18. "Occupation Day," ibid., 16 Sept. 1896.

19. Ibid. At the time, Southern Rhodesia was considered part of South Africa. In fact, three years after he made that speech, W. H. Brown published a travelogue that made him famous: *On the South African Frontier*.

20. "Pioneers at Dinner: Echoes of the Past," *Rhodesia Herald*, 10 Nov. 1904.

21. "Occupation Day," *Rhodesia Herald Weekly Edition*, 10 Aug. 1906.

22. Ibid.

23. "Occupation Day: Farmers in Complete Sympathy with Movement for Observance," *Rhodesia Herald Weekly Edition*, 10 Aug. 1906.

24. Mamdani, *When Does a Settler Become Native?*, 4.

25. "Occupation Day: Annual Celebration, Children's Picnic, Pioneer Dinner," *Rhodesia Herald Weekly Edition*, 18 Sept. 1908.

26. Ibid.

27. "Occupation Day 25th Anniversary Speeches by the Administrator and the Mayor," *Rhodesia Herald*, 17 Sept. 1915.

28. Ibid.

29. Fowler, *History of the Class of 1906*, 351.

30. Rosaldo, "Imperialist Nostalgia."

31. Ibid., 107.

32. Ibid., 108 and 107.

33. Ibid., 108–9. Rosaldo reminds us that the word *nostalgia*, whose "origin appears to have been associated with domination," has its roots in western Europe and that nostalgia is not a universal experience. It was originally a medical diagnosis for Swiss mercenaries suffering from a terrible homesickness far away from home on ill-conceived missions. For another take on the definition of *nostalgia*, see Lowenthal, *Past is a Foreign Country*, 10–11.

34. HWC MS 565, http://hdl.handle.net/10079/fa/mssa.ms.0565.

35. Hans Sauer to Wright, 19 Nov. 1937, HWC MS 565, box 34, folder 503.

36. Wright, "Ex Africa Semper Aliquid Novi."

37. Wright to Roger W. Adcock, 7 Nov. 1936, HWC MS 565, box 1, folder 2. This was a standard line in almost every first letter Howell Wright wrote to anyone in connection with the collection he was amassing. He was always quick to point out that it was for Yale, for country (the United States), and for empire in the memory of Rhodes. Adcock's name is misspelled in the finding aid; in fact, Wright himself made the same mistake in his first letter to Adcock, which Adcock corrected by listing his genealogy and his long connection to South Africa and Rhodesia, beginning with his grandfather, who had landed in Port Elizabeth in 1820.

38. Ibid.

39. Wright to Adcock, 25 Feb. 1937, HWC MS 565, box 1, folder 2. Until 1923 Rhodesia was still thought of as part of South Africa, though it was never officially so.

40. Wright to C. K. Allen (warden, Rhodes House), 31 Dec. 1937, HWC MS 565, box 1, folder 5. It is worth noting that Wright expressed this sentiment to many, but it is particularly telling in this correspondence with Allen, who was in charge of Rhodes scholars in Oxford. See also Rhodes, *Last Will and Testament*, 64.

41. Wright to Adcock, 12 Apr. 1938, HWC MS 565, box 1, folder 2.

42. Ibid.

43. Adcock to Wright, 27 Jan. 1937, HWC MS 565, box 1, folder 2. All quotations in this paragraph and the next are from this letter.

44. As we saw in the previous section, 12 September as a date of official occupation was contested.

45. Connerton, *How Societies Remember*, 51.

46. "Pioneers Re-Assemble after 40 Years," *Rhodesia Herald*, 11 Sept. 1930. The tensions surrounding Occupation Day are much like those surrounding the commemorations of Columbus Day in the United States.

47. Southern Rhodesia's status as a British colony is itself the subject of historical debate, though not heated. The BSAC administered it from 1890 to 1922, and then a successful referendum for a self-governing colony took effect in 1923. It has been argued that since Southern Rhodesia was never administered by the British Colonial Office, as was the case with colonies and protectorates, its ambiguous colonial history makes its status as a colony tenuous at best. That argument, in my view, is usually made in response to Robert Mugabe's "anticolonial" rants rather than in response to documented colonial history, of which there is a copious historiography, including this book. Besides, is it not ironic to speak of a "self-governing *colony*"? For British colonial sentiment, see Tawse-Jollie, "Southern Rhodesia."

48. NAZ/A3/18/39/14, "Amendment to the Law in certain respects in relation to Natives," Native Law Ordinance, 1912.

49. Jennings, "Land Apportionment in Southern Rhodesia," 298.

50. For the U.S. version of the same problematic, see, e.g., Sollors, "National Identity and Ethnic Diversity."

51. Huggins, Foreword.

52. See, e.g., Phimister, *Chibaro*; and Barnes, *"We Women Worked So Hard."*

53. "Pioneers Re-Assemble after 40 Years," *Rhodesia Herald*, 11 Sept. 1930.

54. Ibid. Unless otherwise noted, all quotations relating to the Occupation Day commemorations are from this article.

55. See, e.g., Charumbira, "Administering Medicine without a License"; and Gelfand, *Mother Patrick and Her Nursing Sisters*.

56. Thomas, *Rhodes*, 216–17.

57. Arnold to Wright, 1937–38, HWC MS 565, box 1, folder 6.

58. Ibid.

59. Old Timer, "Salisbury before the Pioneers: Place Names and their Meaning: The Stream at Avondale," *Rhodesia Herald*, 11 Sept. 1930. For Harare's urban history, see, e.g., Yoshikuni, *African Urban Experiences in Colonial Zimbabwe*, 108.

60. Rosaldo, "Imperialist Nostalgia," 108.

61. This could suggest that the Old Timer was a native commissioner or a missionary.

62. Old Timer, "Salisbury before the Pioneers." For a countermemory, see Vambe, *Ill-Fated People*, 92–93.

63. See esp. Mlambo, *White Immigration into Rhodesia*, chaps. 1 and 5; and Shutt and King, "Imperial Rhodesians."

64. Note that some pictures in the box containing figure 9, labeled "Photographs, 1890–1900: Expedition to Mashonaland" (HWC MS 565, Series II, box 32), are from later times, especially the 1930s, while others are reproductions of faded or withheld originals.

65. I follow both Molly's and Hugh's ways of spelling their last name: Molly hyphenated it (Marshall-Hole), while Hugh did not (Marshall Hole).

66. Molly Marshall-Hole to Howell Wright, 10 Jan. 1942, HWC MS 565, box 12, folder 161. This whole section, unless otherwise noted, is based on information in the Hugh Marshall Hole folder.

67. V. W. Hiller to Wright, 6 June 1944, HWC MS 565, box 21, folder 420.

68. Molly Marshall-Hole to Wright, 8 Mar. 1942.

69. Molly Marshall-Hole to Wright, 5 July 1942.

70. Ibid. The book she refers to is McDonald's *Rhodes: A Life*.

71. Hiller to Wright, 8 Dec. 1942. Some copies of letters pertaining to Molly Marshall-Hole can also be found in HWC MS 565, box 21, folders 420–21.

72. Although it was widely read in its time, the report was flawed, as it was hurriedly produced, giving a rather skewed narrative. British South African Company, *'96 Rebellions*.

73. Molly Marshall-Hole to Wright, 10 Feb.1943.

74. Molly Marshall-Hole to Wright, 8 Aug. 1943, emphasis in original.

75. I first encountered the Howell Wright Collection while a graduate student at Yale. In fact, I was attracted to Yale because of its excellent Southern Africa Collection, within the African Collection. The Wright Collection did not immediately appeal to me for its colonial celebration. At the time, I was focused on researching and writing on Nehanda. I did, however, do research in the collection, publishing a paper on colonial nursing in Rhodesia, and when I decided to turn my doctoral dissertation into this book I recalled the collection as a valuable source. I do not think that I was one of the students for whom Wright—and his pioneers—were preserving Rhodesian memory.

76. Hiller to Wright, 10 Jan. 1944, emphasis in original.

77. Molly Marshall-Hole to Wright, 16 Nov. 1943.

78. Hiller to Wright, 6 Mar. 1944.

79. Of course, there were women much more destitute than Molly living in Southern Rhodesia and South Africa, yet few even mentioned their financial circumstances, preferring to celebrate the memories of their pioneer husbands while relying on family to get by.

80. Frank Worthington to Wright, 23 Apr. 1946.

81. Worthington to Wright, 7 June 1946.

82. Hiller to Wright, 1 Aug. 1946.

83. One can follow the trail in the Lord Grey Papers at the University of Durham Library Archives.

84. Worthington to Wright, 17 Aug. 1946.

85. This whole paragraph is based on correspondence between Worthington, Wright, Gray, the Southern High Commission in London, and Hiller and the GRA in Rhodesia, from 11 September 1946 through 2 December 1948. Molly fades from the paper trail.

86. Hiller to Wright, 30 May 1947.

87. Parker Garrett to Worthington, 11 Aug.1948.

88. Worthington to Wright, 12 Aug. 1948.

89. E. Burke to Wright, 18 Oct. 1948.

90. Worthington to Wright, 2 Dec. 1948.

4. A Country Fit for White People

1. W. S. Honey, "Story of the Mazoe Patrol: How They Fought their Way into Salisbury in 1897: 'The Women were Splendid,'" *Rhodesia Herald Pioneer Number*, 12 Sept. 1930, 47. This supplement to the daily newspaper is an excellent example of the formation of parallel memories in the making of the colony.

2. As previously explained, I use the spelling *Mazowe* in the context of African matters and *Mazoe* in the context of European ones.

3. Vansina, *Oral History as Tradition*, 139–46. Vansina's methodology was heavily used and the subject of intense debate when his book was first published. I still find parts of it very usable and illuminating of the (oral) historian's craft and process. See also Ricoeur, *Memory, History, Forgetting*, pt. 2, chap. 1, "The Documentary Phase."

4. See also Bond, *Remember Mazoe*.

5. Because of its fame and contradictions in settler memory, there was even an attempt to "reconstruct" the incident of Mazoe, and that reconstruction included African memories. See ibid.

6. One small biographical entry about a colonial white woman reads: "Mrs. Cass, 1894. Nee Charlotte Ada Griffin. Came to Natal as a child from England. Joined Salvation Army and, as Captain Griffin came to Salisbury to marry Captain E. T. Cass, also of the Salvation Army. She was one of the three ladies who had a terrible experience of being brought into Salisbury laager by the Mazoe Patrol, after her husband was killed by the rebels." Lloyd, *Rhodesia's Pioneer Women*, 16.

7. An insightful essay on this is Jacobs, "Gender Divisions."

8. Honey, "Story of the Mazoe Patrol," 47.

9. Excellent studies of empire, sex, and race in Southern Rhodesia include Jeater, *Marriage, Perversion, and Power*; and McCulloch, *Black Peril, White Virtue*, introduction and chap. 6, "White Women."

10. Harold D. Rawson, "The Mazoe Patrol Recalled by one who Took Part in It: Heroic Telegraphists; Proposed Memorial," *Rhodesia Herald*, 15 Nov. 1935.

11. NAZ/BL/1/1/1, J. L. Blakiston to his father, Jan. 1896.

12. Ibid.

13. Ibid. See also Mlambo, *White Immigration into Rhodesia*, chap. 5.

14. NAZ/BL/1/1/1, J. L. Blakiston to his mother, 17 June 1896.

15. Rawson, "Mazoe Patrol Recalled."

16. Editor's note to ibid.

17. Rawson, "Mazoe Patrol Recalled."

18. Anderson, *Imagined Communities*, esp. chaps. 4 and 11.

19. See, e.g., Bhebe, *Christianity and Traditional Religion*.

20. NAZ/BL/1/1/1, H. M. Moffat to E. S. White, 1935.

21. NAZ/BL/1/1/1, James E. Nicholls to White, 28 Nov. 1935.

22. After the deaths of Blakiston and Routledge, the laagered community, fearing for their lives if help did not come (for they did not know whether any message had gotten through), decided "after some discussion that we were not strong enough to fight our way into Salisbury, so it was necessary to get further relief. Salthouse offered Hendricks, one of our drivers of the ambulance, one hundred pounds if he would get through in the night and take a dispatch to Salisbury." Rawson did not say whether Hendricks ever got his one hundred pounds, and he hinted that Hendricks survived the dangerous mission, though wounded as the rescued force, along with the relief party, fought their way back to Salisbury. Rawson, "Mazoe Patrol Recalled."

23. NAZ/BL/1/1/1, Nicholls to White, 4 Dec. 1935.

24. NAZ/BL/1/1/1, Nicholls to White, 5 Dec. 1935.

25. NAZ/BL/1/1/1, Nicholls to White, 16 Dec. 1935.

26. NAZ/BL/1/1/1, Nicholls to White, 18 Dec. 1935.

27. NAZ/BL/1/1/1, White to Nicholls, 21 Dec. 1935.

28. NAZ/BL/1/1/1, Nicholls to White, 25 Jan. 1936.

29. NAZ/BL/1/1/1, Priscilla Singer to Nicholls, 7 Feb. 1936.

30. NAZ/BL/1/1/1, White to Singer, 25 Feb. 1936.

31. NAZ/BL/1/1/1, Nicholls to White, 14 Mar. 1936. It is worth noting the mundane but amusing fact that Nicholls used letterhead paper from both the Associated Members of the 1890 & 1893 Columns and the Blakiston-Routledge Memorial Committee for his correspondence.

32. NAZ/BL/1/1/1, Singer to White, 17 Mar. 1936.

33. NAZ/BL/1/1/1, M. Gillespie to Blakiston-Routledge Memorial Committee, 19 Mar. 1936.

34. NAZ/BL/1/1/1, Blakiston-Routledge Memorial Fund, Receipts and Payments Account.

35. NAZ/BL/1/1/1, E. C. Alderson to White, 15 Apr. 1936.

36. NAZ/BL/1/2/1, "The Family of Blakiston of Staple-on-Tees," Nov. 1928.

37. Correspondence relating to the naming of the school in Blakiston's honor is in NAZ/BL/1/2/2. In Harare (the colonial and postcolonial name of Salisbury) both the school and the street retain Blakiston's name.

38. "Plaque Unveiled at Post Office: Story of Heroic Feat at Mazoe," *Rhodesia Herald*, 22 June 1936. See also "Story of Blakiston and Routledge: Stirring Episode in the Colony's Early History," ibid., 19 June 1936.

39. Mlambo, *White Immigration into Rhodesia*, chaps. 2 and 4.

40. "Heroic Deed of Mashona Rebellion Commemorated: Monument at Mazoe to Blakiston and Routledge: Unveiling by Governor: Pioneers Worth of Honor," *Rhodesia Herald*, 22 June 1936. Before the ceremony, on 19 April, the same newspaper had carried a story of the arrival of Mrs. Gates and her daughter on behalf of their elderly (grand)mother, who could not attend.

41. Again, the mention of a "Zulu native" and "Cape boys" highlights the visible presence of African immigrants and migrants in the history of Southern Rhodesia's settlement as a colony. Such stories call for a full study of the history and memory of their contributions, muted by settler and native narratives of "pure" settlement—or autochthony.

42. "Heroic Deed of Mashona Rebellion Commemorated."

43. For a Rhodesian view, see Smith, *Great Betrayal*.

44. Ibid.

45. "Heroic Deed of Mashona Rebellion Commemorated."

46. For other paternalistic examples, see Shropshire, "Native Development in Southern Rhodesia"; and Huggins, "Southern Rhodesia." For a recent scholarly take on Rhodesian anxieties, see Bonello, "Development of the Early Settler Identity."

47. On imperial women, especially in Rhodesia, see Cairnie, "Women and the Literature of Settlement and Plunder"; Goebel, *Gender and Land Reform;* Strobel, *European Women;* and Kirkwood, "Settler Wives of Southern Rhodesia."

48. "Legacy Left by Pioneer Women: Heroines of the Mazoe Patrol," *Rhodesia Herald*, 26 June 1936.

49. Boogie, *Experiences of Rhodesia's Pioneer Women.*

50. Burke, *Lifebuoy Men, Lux Women*, 3.

51. NAZ/BL/1/2/3, A. S. Hickman, "Isolated Graves at Mazoe: 1896 Rebellion," 26 Oct. 1953.

52. Ibid.

53. See also Steyn, *"Whiteness Just Isn't What It Used to Be,"* esp. preface, introduction, and sec. 1; and Cairnie, "Women and the Literature of Settlement and Plunder," 174–76.

5. Re-Membering African Masculine Founding Myths in the Time of Colonialism

1. The official reference for these interviews is African Oral Histories Collection (AOH), NAZ.

2. Portelli, "History-Telling and Time," 54.

3. The men were selected (by the National Archives) on the basis of, among other variables, their age and/or social status—a significant gender choice, considering that not many women were interviewed. I read through thirty such oral histories and chose the six represented here for what they tell us about Charwe, the complicated nature of memory, and its uses of history in constructing individual, social, and collective memory. I edited each story— faithful to each transcript—to create a narrative flow that allows each individual to represent himself. I offer analysis and commentary at the beginning, in the middle, or at the end of the narrative or in footnotes, but I try to let these men speak for themselves—with few other voices from the archives. At some points I allow the interviewer, Dawson Munjeri, to enter the picture, if only to illuminate the process of memory making that he was involved in, consciously and unconsciously. However, often I minimize even his presence in order to allow the narrative, with all its contradictions, to illuminate the processes of remembering and forgetting the history of colonialism and the wars of 1896–97 as those men understood the events.

4. Luise White articulates the importance of understanding historical evidence and not prejudging it in her insightful "Telling More."

5. See Beach, *Zimbabwean Past,* esp. secs. 2 and 3. I share Zilberg's perspective on Beach's work. See Zilberg, "Review."

6. Morrison, "Site of Memory," 87.

7. Here and in the following chapters, I give the complete titles of the interviews as they appear in the transcripts. In the interviewees' narratives, which are italicized, square brackets enclose my own insertions and comments, while parentheses enclose commentary by Munjeri or the transcriber. I urge anyone wanting to follow my trail of evidence to read the whole transcript, as sometimes—though not often—I piece the narrative together (as one would a quilt) from noncontinuous pages in the transcript, supplying pages numbers for the sections in the notes. I do this because the flow of an interview was sometimes interrupted by the interviewer seeking to clarify a point immediately rather than let the interviewee speak for a while before asking another question. The interviews are a great resource, as the interviewer employed the best oral-history techniques available to him at the time and often noted other primary and secondary sources that a researcher could or should consult.

8. NAZ/AOH/72, "Interview with Mr. Isaac Chiremba," 29 Oct. 1981, Epworth, 1–20.

9. Ibid., 6–7.

10. Ibid., 8–9.

11. Ibid., 10.

12. On the self-construction of Selous, see, e.g., Mandiringana and Stapleton, "Literary Legacy." Selous's tales are well known and worn, so I will only mention some of Selous's journal articles, which say as much as they leave out

and are often overlooked as source material, as the books tend to get more attention. See Selous, "Recent Journey in Eastern Mashona Land."

13. See also Norris-Newman, *Matebeleland and How We Got It*, 162–65.

14. NAZ/AOH/25, "Interview conducted by Dawson Munjeri with Mr. Nyamadzawo Maruma," 5 Oct. 1977, 1–27.

15. Antonio Manuel de Souza was a Portuguese-Goanese man with a colorful story in the history of Southern Africa, especially present-day Zimbabwe and Mozambique. The Africans called him Gouveia, one from/of Goa. For a biosketch, see Lipschutz and Rasmussen, "Sousa, Manuel Antonio de (Gouveia)."

16. NAZ/AOH/25, "Interview conducted by Dawson Munjeri with Mr. Nyamadzawo Maruma," 1–4.

17. Ibid., 5–7.

18. Information and quotations in the preceding two paragraphs and in this paragraph to this point are from ibid., 5–7, 19–23.

19. Ibid., 24–25.

20. Many "discoverers" of what became Rhodesia married or had sexual liaisons with African women, including the German man who led Karl Mauch to the Great Zimbabwe; the American Harvey Brown, mayor of Salisbury in 1910; and many a native commissioner. As Lawrence Vambe remembered of the fruit of Selous's African marriage: "I take pride in having been a personal friend of Selous junior who died only a few years ago and who was an intelligent man. . . . He lived in the 'Hunter's Lodge,' a house built by his father at the bottom of the Harare Kopje in Salisbury and bequeathed to him by the famous man." Vambe, *Ill-Fated People*, 90.

21. NAZ/AOH/90, "Interview with Munotyei Mashayamombe," 7 Apr. 1982, 1–7.

22. Ibid., 8–9. Information and quotations in the remainder of this paragraph and in the next two paragraphs is from ibid., 10–13.

23. Ibid, 9.

24. Ibid., 16–19. For another narration of the causes of the 1896–97 wars, see ibid., 80–85.

25. NAZ/AOH/17, "Interview with Mr. Rakafa," 17 Aug. 1977, 1–2.

26. Ibid., 19–21. For Rakafa's family history, see ibid., 3–18.

27. For Africans who purchased farms in the "Native Purchase Areas," see, among other interviews, NAZ/AOH/41, "Interview with Munyukwi Samson Chibvongodze," 14 July 1978.

28. NAZ/AOH/17, "Interview with Mr. Rakafa," 37–38.

29. Ibid., 39.

30. Bertha Ruth d'Almeida, quoted in Yoshikuni, *Elizabeth Musodzi*, 2, from the *Sunday Mail* (Salisbury), 3 Feb. 1983.

31. NAZ/AOH/34, "Interview with Chief Marufu Chikwaka," 6 Feb. 1977,

1, 36–38. *Gomba* means "valley," "deep cavity," "small hole," or "big hole." On Mapondera's rebellions and importance, see, e.g., Isaacman, "Social Banditry in Zimbabwe"; and Beach, "From Heroism to History."

32. NAZ/AOH/22, "Interview with Mr. Chidamahiya Chimatira," 7 Sept. 1977.

33. See also Duri, "Hero or Villain."

34. NAZ/AOH/22, "Interview with Mr. Chidamahiya Chimatira," 30.

35. Ibid., 31.

36. There was a crisis of so-called sellouts, or spies, in most of Southern African's liberation movements. See Suttner, *ANC Underground in South Africa*; and Leys and Brown, *Histories of Namibia*.

37. NAZ/AOH/22, "Interview with Mr. Chidamahiya Chimatira," 32–33.

38. Ibid., 34–35.

39. Ricoeur, *Memory, History, Forgetting*, 171.

40. Crane, "(Not) Writing History," 21.

6. African Autobiography

1. Vambe, *Ill-Fated People*.

2. Audre Lorde made one of the first and best conceptualizations of "biomythography" in her memoirs, *Zami, A New Spelling of My Name*.

3. Chatterjee, *Nation and Its Fragments*, 138.

4. Crane, "Writing the Individual."

5. Morrison, "Site of Memory," 85.

6. White, "Telling More," 11.

7. On mental colonization, see Iweriebor, "Psychology of Colonialism."

8. Among the prisoners of war in 1896–97, quite a few Africans besides Nehanda-Charwe resisted converting to Christianity, as noted by Fr. Richartz as well as by another Jesuit priest in Matebeleland, Fr. Victor, in his "Condemned in Matabeleland," 51.

9. Vambe, *Ill-Fated People*, 5.

10. Ibid., 6.

11. Ibid., 6–7. In African nationalist narratives, Nehanda (Charwe) too was famous for refusing Catholic baptism.

12. Ibid., 7.

13. Ibid, 11. For a gendered description of Madzidza and Mizha's characters, see ibid., 24.

14. Ibid., 14. For African life on mission lands, see, e.g., Comaroff and Comaroff, *Of Revelation and Revolution*, chaps. 1 and 2; and Landau, *Realm of the Word*, esp. pt. 1.

15. Fanon, *Black Skin, White Masks*, introduction and chap. 2.

16. Ibid., 18.

17. Vambe, *Ill-Fated People*, 17.

18. Ibid., 20–21.

19. Marx, "Contribution to the Critique."

20. Vambe, *Ill-Fated People*, 146.

21. Ibid., 22.

22. Ibid., 23.

23. Ibid., 29.

24. I discuss the novel and its (nationalist) impact in chapter 7.

25. Vambe, *Ill-Fated People*, 29.

26. Ibid.

27. It was, indeed, a hard argument to make in a country that was more a colony than a (modern) nation that embraced all its citizens equally, but that did not stop many from trying. See, e.g., Ranger, *"Are We also Not Men?"* For a gendered take, especially from women's history, see Barnes, *"We Women Worked So Hard."* See also M. West, *Rise of an African Middle Class*, esp. chaps. 1 and 2; and Scarnecchia, *Urban Roots of Democracy*, esp. chap. 4.

28. Vambe, *Ill-Fated People*, 89.

29. Ibid., 32–33; the quotations are from 33.

30. Ibid.

31. Ibid., 103.

32. Ibid., 104.

33. Fanon, *Wretched of the Earth*, 43.

34. Vambe, *Ill-Fated People*, xxiii.

35. NAZ/AOH/14, "Interview with Aaron Jacha, Marirangwe Purchase Area," 14 July 1977, 1, 3–5. I have left out many digressions and interruptions by the interviewer that are not germane to my discussion here.

36. Ibid., 11–12.

37. Ibid., 13–14.

38. Ibid., 14–15.

39. Beach, *War and Politics*, 13–18.

40. Thiong'o, *Decolonizing the Mind*, 11, emphasis in original.

41. Ibid., 12.

42. Vambe, *Ill-Fated People*, 199.

43. Ibid., 200.

44. Ibid.

45. Ibid., 201.

46. Chatterjee, *Nation and Its Fragments*, 116.

47. Epprecht, *Hungochani*. The introduction and chap. 1 are particularly pertinent.

7. Educated Political Prisoners, a Guerilla Matron, and the Gendered Pursuit of Independence

1. Other postindependence Nehandas include those highlighted in the works of Joost Fontein and Marja J. Spierenburg. Fontein's study shows the story of Sophia Tsvatayi (a.k.a. Ambuya Nehanda) to have been similar to that of Charwe, who had a confrontation with authority, although Tsvatayi's was with the postcolonial government, the "grandchildren" of the "real" Nehanda, Charwe. See Fontein, *Silence of Great Zimbabwe,* 157–165; and Spierenburg, *Strangers, Spirits, and Land Reform,* 36–37, chaps. 6 and 7. Other studies of Nehandas from the 1960s on include Lan, *Guns and Rain;* Ranger, *Revolt in Southern Rhodesia;* Daneel, *God of the Matopos;* and Sadomba, "War Veterans."

2. Anderson, *Imagined Communities,* chap. 3.

3. Ibid., 39.

4. "Statement by George Loft," 30 June 1959, George Loft Collection, box 1, folder 35, Hoover Institution Archives, Stanford (hereafter GLC-HIA), copyright of Stanford University.

5. Ibid.

6. A. S. Musukwa to George Loft, 14 Dec. 1959, GLC-HIA, box 4, folder 21, copyright Stanford University.

7. "Thumbnails of Some Key Detainees Imprisoned in S. Rhodesia," 21 Apr. 1959, GLC-HIA, box 1, folder 1, copyright Stanford University. The descriptions below are from these "thumbnails."

8. Ibid.

9. Ibid.

10. "Visits and Requests: Selukwe Detainees," 10 Nov. 1959, GLC-HIA, box 1, folder 1, copyright Stanford University.

11. It is worth noting that in Loft's home country, the United States, the civil rights movement was in full swing, aiming to achieve much the same rights as those of the prisoners he was serving in Rhodesia.

12. Didymus E. Mutasa to Loft, 30 Aug. 1958, GLC-HIA, box 4, folder 22, copyright Stanford University.

13. Loft correspondence with Mr. Ramanathan of the Indian High Commission in Salisbury and to Mutasa, Oct.–Dec. 1959, ibid.

14. One such important friendship to the Mutasas was with Arthur and Molly Guy Clutton-Brock, the activist missionaries who had been deported from Rhodesia in 1971 because of their work with African nationalists. Clutton-Brock is the minority white national hero whose body is buried at the National Heroes Acre in Harare. See Judith Todd, "Obituary: Guy Clutton-Brock," *Independent,* 16 Feb. 1995, accessed Dec. 2010,http://www.independent.co.uk/news/people/obituary—guy-cluttonbrock-1573319.html.

15. Didymus Mutasa, "Recent Developments in Rhodesia," speech delivered at "Rhodesia after Pearce—Betrayal or Freedom?", Anti-Apartheid Move-

ment Conference, London, 24 Feb. 1973, GLC-HIA, box 4, folder 22, copyright Stanford University. See point 2 of the speech.

16. Loft to Alma Harding, 20 Oct. 1967, GLC-HIA, box 4, folder 14, copyright Stanford University.

17. Robert Mugabe to Loft, 28 June 1967, ibid.

18. Sally Mugabe to Loft, 10 Sept. 1967, ibid.

19. Mandela, *Long Walk to Freedom*, pt. 5, "Treason," 205–15.

20. Loft to David [last name not given], 24 Sept. 1967, GLC-HIA, box 4, folder 14, copyright Stanford University.

21. Robert Mugabe to Loft, 28 June 1967, ibid.

22. Robert Mugabe to Loft, 1 Dec.1967, ibid.

23. Sally Mugabe to Loft, 20 Jan. 1968, ibid.

24. Josiah M. Chinamano to Loft, 26 Apr. 1966, GLC-HIA, box 1, folder 29, copyright Stanford University; Loft to Joshua Nkomo, 31 Dec. 1959, GLC-HIA, box 4, folder 30, copyright Stanford University. Chinamano's letter was written from Khami Prison. His wife, Ruth, was at Wha Wha.

25. Chitepo was assassinated, and his death remains a mystery, but his life has entered nationalist mythology. See White, *Assassination of Herbert Chitepo*.

26. Loft correspondence with Herbert Chitepo, 1959 and 1956, and with Edgar Whitehead, 1959, GLC-HIA, box 1, folder 35, copyright Stanford University.

27. On the politics and the cultural renaissance in African music, see, e.g., Berliner, *Soul of Mbira*, chap. 1; Maraire, "Position of Music in Shona," introduction and chap. 1; and Turino, *Nationalists, Cosmopolitans*.

28. Mutswairo, *Feso*, 87–88, my emphasis.

29. I had the opportunity to interview Mutswairo once, but I lost the interview because I left my tape recorder running and the tape was chewed up. He expressed much the same sentiment about his writing of *Feso* and other works that he had when he was interviewed by Angela Williams in 1994. See Zimunya and Mutswairo, "Mother Tongue."

30. For a version of the adoption of the contemporary Nehanda by the guerrillas, see Martin and Johnson, *Struggle for Zimbabwe*, 50, 75–8.

31. Lyons, *Guns and Guerrilla Girls*, 77–84.

32. United Nations, "Global Issues: Women," http://www.un.org/en/global issues/women/.

33. *Zimbabwe News*, 2, no. 7 (1 Apr. 1967): 5. It is worth noting that the January issue had declared 1967 a "historic year" and called on all to take up arms: "1967 is an historic year in the history of Zimbabwe and in the struggle for our freedom and independence. 1967 is the year of decision. . . . Let us resolve to join in the war of Chimurenga and Chindunduma. . . . Let 1967 see Zimbabwe free. We must repeat that 1967 is an historic year in the liberation struggle in Zimbabwe. Let us resolve to do our best in the liberation of our *motherland*."

34. Ibid., 5.

35. Ibid. 3, no. 15 (15 Aug. 1968): 3.

36. Ibid., 3–4.

37. Ibid. 3, no. 5 (16 Mar. 1968): 4.

38. These historical gender dynamics and the attitudes of the male cadres have been ably studied by, among others, Nhongo-Simbanegavi, in *For Better or Worse?*; and Ranchod-Nilsson, in "Gender Politics and National Liberation."

39. *Zimbabwe News* 4, no. 2 (8 Feb. 1969): 3.

40. The letters attributed to Muderere and Masenda may have been written by male cadres as propaganda material to recruit women as combatants in the struggle. I base this suggestion on the fact that two of the letters made references to the same armed struggles in Africa and abroad and women's participation in them.

41. Nhongo-Simbanegavi, *For Better or Worse?*, esp. 4.

42. The feature film *Flame*, directed by Ingrid Sinclair, premiered in 1996 and drew much criticism for its portrayal of female and male relations of combatants, especially issues of sexual harassment and rape. See http://www .zimmedia.com/flame/ for film details.

43. See also Sarudzai Churucheminziva, "ZANLA Women's Detachment," in the pamphlet *The Liberation Struggle in Zimbabwe: African Freedom Fighters Speak for Themselves* (1975), Yale University Library, African Collection, MS 605, box 23, folder 426, 9–12.

44. Nyamandwe, "Carine Nyamandwe talks to Virginia Phiri," 4–5.

45. Ibid. After the war, Joyce was the first and only female to hold a full cabinet post in Mugabe's first cabinet, serving as the minister of women's affairs and community development. Today she is Zimbabwe's vice president and is known by her civilian name, Joyce Mujuru. She is the wife of the retired army general Solomon Mujuru.

46. A full-fledged women's movement—outside the strictures of nationalist politics—only gained momentum and legitimacy in the 1990s, as more women's organizations were formed by women with the financial support of international-development agencies. Some of the founders of those organizations had worked for the Ministry of Community Development and Women's Affairs in its early days. Eloquent analyses of the importance of women advocating for their rights and democratic practices within a nationalist framework during and after the war in Southern Africa include McFadden, "Becoming Postcolonial"; and Hassim, *Women's Organizations and Democracy*.

47. Comrade Teurai Ropa, "Women have Total Involvement in Struggle," *Zimbabwe News* 10, no. 2 (May–June 1978): 30, my emphasis.

48. L. West, introduction, xxx; another compelling essay focused on Southern African in the same volume is Mangaliso, "Gender and Nation-Building."

49. Ropa, "Women have Total Involvement in Struggle," 30.

50. "Nehanda Died for Zimbabwe. Will You?" *Zimbabwe News* 10, no. 2 (May–June 1978): 65.

51. Mugabe, "Role and History of the Zimbabwean Women."

52. See oral histories of some of the women who participated in the liberation movements in, for example, Zimbabwe Women Writers, *Women of Resilience;* Staunton, *Mothers of the Revolution;* and Weiss, *Women of Zimbabwe.*

53. Pongweni, *Songs That Won the Liberation War,* chap. 3, on ancestral spirits.

54. NAZ/AOH/111, "Interview with spirit mediums Mavhunga and Mhindurwa—and their spirits, as well as a live Nehanda medium in Nehanda Village, Mazoe," 30 Jan. 1982, 7–8.

55. Ibid.

56. Ibid., 8.

57. Ibid. The parentheses replace original brackets; the brackets are my own.

58. Ibid., 9.

59. Ibid., 12–13.

60. Ibid., 9.

61. NAZ/AOH/105, "Interview with Mbuya Nehanda at Makwiramiti Village, Chiweshe," 30 Jan. 1982.

62. Ibid., 1–4.

63. Ibid., 8, my emphasis.

Conclusion

1. Many scholars and ordinary Zimbabweans have researched and/or expressed their thoughts and contestations on the meanings of that site of memory since it was opened in 1984. For a recent articulation of that contestation, see Bhebe and Ranger, *Soldiers in Zimbabwe's Liberation War.* See also Fontein, *Silence of Great Zimbabwe,* chap. 6.

2. Kriger, "From Patriotic Memories," esp. 1155–58.

3. For white Zimbabwean responses to Heroes' Acre, see, e.g., Fisher, *Pioneers, Settlers, Aliens, Exile,* esp. chap. 4.

4. Rhodes, *Last Will and Testament,* 4–5.

5. For the history and symbolism of the birds atop these walls, see, e.g., Huffman, "Soapstone Birds"; and Matenga, *Soapstone Birds of Great Zimbabwe.*

6. For some of those stories, see Zimbabwe Women Writers, *Women of Resilience;* and Staunton, *Mothers of the Revolution.*

7. Nora, "Between Memory and History," 10.

8. Olick, "Introduction: Memory and the Nation," 381.

Bibliography

Archival Sources

Bodleian Library, Rhodes House, Oxford University

National Archives, United Kingdom, London

National Archives of Zimbabwe, Harare
  African Oral Histories Collection

Stanford University, Hoover Institution on War, Revolution, and Peace Library
  and Archives
  George Loft Collection

Yale University Library, Manuscripts and Archives
  African Collection
  Howell Wright Collection (MS 565), Series I and Series II

Newspapers and Periodicals

British Broadcasting Corporation
Bulawayo Chronicle
Daily Telegraph (London)
Financial Gazette (Harare)
Independent (London)
New African (London)

Rhodesia Herald
Rhodesia Herald Pioneer Number
Times (London)
War Office Gazette (London)
Zambesi Mission Record
Zimbabwe News

Other Sources

Abraham, D. P. "The Early Political History of the Kingdom of Mwene Mutapa (850–1589)." In *Historians in Tropical Africa: Proceedings of the Leverhulme Inter-collegiate History Conference, September 1960,* 61–90. Salisbury: University College of Rhodesia and Nyasaland, 1962.

Alderson, Edwin Alfred Hervey. *With the Mounted Infantry and the Mashona-land Field Force, 1896.* London: Methuen, 1898.

Amadiume, Ifi. *Male Daughters, Female Husbands: Gender and Sex in an African Society.* London: Zed Books, 1987.

Anderson, Benedict. *Imagined Communities: A Study of the Origin and Spread of Nationalism.* Rev. ed. New York: Verso, 1993.

Armitage, David. *The Declaration of Independence: A Global History.* Cambridge, MA: Harvard University Press, 2007.

Aschwanden, Herbert. *Karanga Mythology: An Analysis of the Consciousness of the Karanga in Zimbabwe.* Gweru: Mambo, 1987.

Atwood, Margaret. "In Search of Alias Grace: On Writing Canadian Historical Fiction." In *Writing with Intent: Essays, Reviews, Personal Prose: 1983–2005,* 158–77. New York: Avalon, 2005.

Axelson, Eric. *Portugal and the Scramble for Africa, 1875–1891.* Johannesburg: University of Witwatersrand University Press, 1967.

——. *Portuguese in South-East Africa, 1488–1600.* Johannesburg: Wits University Press, 1973.

Barkley Brown, Elsa. "'What Happened Here': The Politics of Difference in Women's History and Feminist Politics." *Feminist Studies* 18 (1992): 295–312.

Barnes, Teresa. "'History Has to Play Its Role': Constructions of Race and Reconciliation in Secondary School Historiography in Zimbabwe, 1980–2002." *Journal of Southern African Studies* 33, no. 3 (Sept. 2007): 633–51.

——. *"We Women Worked So Hard": Gender, Urbanization and Social Reproduction in Colonial Harare, Zimbabwe, 1930–56.* Portsmouth, NH: Heinemann, 1999.

Baron, Beth. *Egypt as a Woman: Nationalism, Gender, and Politics.* Berkeley: University of California Press, 2004.

Beach, David N. "Cognitive Archaeology and Imaginary History at Great Zimbabwe." *Current Anthropology* 39, no. 1 (Feb. 1998): 47–72.

——. "From Heroism to History: Mapondera and the Northern Zimbabwean Plateau, 1840–1904." *History in Africa: A Journal in Method* 15 (1988): 85–161.

——. "An Innocent Woman, Unjustly Accused? Charwe, Medium of the Nehanda Mhondoro Spirit, and the 1896–97 Central Shona Rising in Zimbabwe." *History in Africa: A Journal in Method* 25 (1998): 27–54.

——. *The Shona and Zimbabwe, 900–1850.* Gweru: Mambo, 1980.

——. *War and Politics in Zimbabwe, 1840–1900.* Gweru: Mambo, 1986.

——. *A Zimbabwean Past: Shona Dynastic Histories and Oral Traditions.* Gweru: Mambo, 1994.

Berger, Iris. *Religion and Resistance: East African Kingdoms in the Precolonial Period.* Tervuren, Belgium: Musée Royal de l'Afrique Centrale, 1981.

Berliner, Paul. *The Soul of Mbira: Music and Traditions of the Shona People of Zimbabwe.* Berkeley: University of California Press, 1978.

Bhebe, Ngwabi. *Christianity and Traditional Religion in Western Zimbabwe, 1859–1923*. London: Longman, 1979.

Bhebe, Ngwabi, and Terence Ranger, eds. *Soldiers in Zimbabwe's Liberation War*. Portsmouth, NH: Heinemann, 1995.

Bhila, H. H. K. "The 1896–97 Rhodesia War Reconsidered." *Botswana Journal of African Studies* 2, no. 1 (Feb. 1980): 139–62.

———. *Trade and Politics in a Shona Kingdom: The Manyika and their Portuguese and African Neighbors, 1575–1902*. London: Longman, 1982.

Bond, Geoffrey. *Remember Mazoe: The Reconstruction of an Incident*. Salisbury: Pioneer Head, 1973.

Bonello, Julie. "The Development of the Early Settler Identity in Southern Rhodesia, 1890–1914." *International Journal of African Historical Studies* 43, no. 2 (2010): 341–67.

Boogie, Jeannie M. *Experiences of Rhodesia's Pioneer Women: Being a True Account of the Adventures of the Early White Women Settlers in Southern Rhodesia from 1890*. Bulawayo: Philpott & Collins, 1938.

Borg, Marcus J. *Meeting Jesus Again for the First Time: The Historical Jesus and the Heart of Contemporary Faith*. New York: HarperOne, 1995.

Bourdillon, Michael F. C. "'Guns and Rain': Taking Structural Analysis Too Far?" *Africa* 57, no. 2 (1987): 263–74.

Boydston, Jeanne. "Gender as a Question of Historical Analysis." *Gender and History* 20, no. 3 (Nov. 2008): 558–83.

Brigg, Charles A. "The Salvation Army." *North American Review* 159 (Dec. 1894): 709–10.

British South African Company. *The '96 Rebellions, formerly titled Reports of the Native Disturbances in Rhodesia, 1896–97*. 1898. Reprint. Bulawayo: Books of Rhodesia, 1975.

Brown, William H. *On the South African Frontier: The Adventures and Observations of an American in Mashonaland and Matabeleland*. New York, 1899.

Burke, Timothy. *Lifebuoy Men, Lux Women: Commodification, Consumption, and Cleanliness in Modern Zimbabwe*. Durham, NC: Duke University Press, 1996.

Butalia, Urvashi. *The Other Side of Silence: Voices from the Partition of India*. Durham, NC: Duke University Press, 2000.

Cairnie, Julie. "Women and the Literature of Settlement and Plunder: Toward an Understanding of the Zimbabwean Land Crisis." *English Studies in Canada* 33, nos. 1–2 (Mar.–June 2007): 165–88.

Carr, Edward H. *What is History? The George Macaulay Trevelyan Lectures Delivered at the University of Cambridge, January–March 1961*. New York: Vintage, 1961.

Catholic Commission for Justice and Peace. *Gukurahundi in Zimbabwe: A Report on the Disturbances in Matebeleland and the Midlands, 1980–1988*. New York: Columbia University Press, 2008.

Chakrabarty, Dipesh. *Provincializing Europe: Postcolonial Thought and Historical Difference.* Princeton, NJ: Princeton University Press, 2000.

Chatterjee, Partha. *The Nation and Its Fragments: Colonial and Post-Colonial Histories.* Princeton, NJ: Princeton University Press, 1993.

Charumbira, Ruramisai. "Administering Medicine without a License: Missionary Women in Rhodesia's Nursing History." *Historian* 68, no. 2 (Summer 2006): 241–66.

———. "Forgetting Lives, Remembering Symbols: Women in the History of Zimbabwe." PhD diss., Yale University, 2006.

———. "Nehanda and Gender Victimhood in the Central Mashonaland 1896–97 Rebellions: Revisiting the Evidence." *History in Africa: A Journal in Method* 35 (2008): 103–31.

———. "Nehanda, Gender, and the Myth of Nation-hood in the Making of Zimbabwe." In *National Myths: Constructed Pasts, Contested Presents,* ed. Gerard Bouchard, 206–22. New York: Routledge, 2013.

———. "Spirit Possession." In *The Oxford Encyclopedia of Women in World History,* ed. Bonnie G. Smith, 4:28–29. New York: Oxford University Press, 2008.

Chimhundu, Herbert. "Early Missionaries and the Ethnolinguistic Factor during the 'Invention of Tribalism' in Zimbabwe." *Journal of African History* 33, no. 1 (1992): 87–109.

Chirenje, J. Mutero. "Portuguese Priests and Soldiers in Zimbabwe, 1560–1572: The Interplay between Evangelism and Trade." *International Journal of African Historical Studies* 6, no. 1 (1973): 36–48.

Chitando, Ezra. "The Sacred Remnant? Church Land and Zimbabwe's Fast Track Resettlement Program." *Studies in World Christianity* 11, no. 2 (Oct. 2005): 182–99.

Cobbing, Julian. "The Absent Priesthood: Another Look at the Rhodesian Risings of 1896–1897." *Journal of African History* 18, no. 1 (1977): 61–84.

Comaroff, Jean, and John L. Comaroff. *Of Revelation and Revolution: Christianity, Colonialism, and Consciousness in South Africa.* Vol. 1. Chicago: University of Chicago Press, 1991.

Confino, Alan. "Collective Memory and Cultural History: Problems of Method." *American Historical Review* 102, no. 5 (Dec. 1997): 1386–1403.

Connerton, Paul. *How Societies Remember.* Cambridge: Cambridge University Press, 1989.

Crane, Susan. "(Not) Writing History: Rethinking the Intersections of Personal History and Collective Memory with Hans von Aufsess." *History and Memory* 8, no. 1 (Spring–Summer 1996): 5–29.

———. "Writing the Individual Back into Collective Memory." *American Historical Review* 102, no. 4 (Dec. 1997): 1372–85.

Cressy, David. *Bonfires and Bells: National Memory and the Calendar in Elizabethan and Stuart England.* Berkeley: University of California Press, 1989.

Cronon, William. "Professional Boredom." *Perspectives in History: The News-magazine of the American Historical Association* 50, no. 3 (Mar. 2012). www.historians.org/perspectives/issues/2012/1203/Professional-Boredom.cfm.

Cush, Ifa Kamau. "A Tale of Two Countries." *New African* 499 (Oct. 2010): 26–27.

Daneel, Martinus L. *The God of the Matopos: An Essay on the Mwari Cult in Rhodesia.* The Hague: Mouton, 1970.

Duri, Fidelis. "Hero or Villain: A Study of Gumboreshumba, Medium of the Kaguvi Mhondoro Spirit and the 1896–97 Rising in Central and Western Mashonaland, Zimbabwe." Seminar Paper presented at Great Zimbabwe University, Department of Humanities Staff Seminar Series, Faculty of Arts, 7 June 2006.

Ehret, Christopher. *The Civilizations of Africa: A History to 1800.* Charlottesville: University of Virginia Press, 2002.

Elphick, Richard, and Herman Giliomee, eds. *The Shaping of South African Society, 1652–1840.* Middletown, CT: Wesleyan University Press, 1989.

Epprecht, Marc. *Hungochani: The History of a Dissident Sexuality in Southern Africa.* Montreal: McGill-Queens University Press, 2005.

Ernst, Felix, and Kurt Scheurer, comps. *History of the Swiss in Southern Africa, 1652–1977.* 2nd ed. Johannesburg: Swiss Societies of Southern Africa, 1979.

Falola, Toyin. *Nationalism and African Intellectuals.* Rochester, NY: University of Rochester Press, 2000.

Fanon, Frantz. *Black Skin, White Masks.* Trans. Charles Lam Markmann. New York: Grove, 1967.

———. *The Wretched of the Earth.* New York: Grove, 1963.

Fisher, Josephine Lucy. *Pioneers, Settlers, Aliens, Exiles: The Decolonization of White Identity in Zimbabwe.* Canberra: Australia National University Press, 2010.

Fitzpatrick, J. Percy. *Through Mashonaland with Pick and Pen.* Johannesburg: Argus, 1892.

Fontein, Joost. *The Silence of Great Zimbabwe: Contested Landscapes and the Power of Heritage.* London: UCL Press, 2006.

Fowler, George S. *History of the Class of 1906: Yale College.* Vol. 1. New Haven, CT: Yale University, 1906.

Fox, H. Wilson. "Rhodesia and the War." *Journal of the Royal African Society* 14 (July 1915): 345–54.

Frederikse, Julie. *None But Ourselves: Masses vs. Media in the Making of Zimbabwe.* Harare: Zimbabwe Publishing House, 1983.

Fry, Peter. *Spirits of Protest: Spirit-Mediums and the Articulation of Consensus among the Zezuru of Southern Rhodesia (Zimbabwe).* Cambridge: Cambridge University Press, 1976.

Gann, L. H. *A History of Southern Rhodesia, Early Days to 1934.* London: Chatto & Windus, 1965.

Garbett, Kingsley. "Disparate Regional Cults and Unitary Ritual Field in Zimbabwe." In *Regional Cults,* ed. R. P. Werbner, 55–92. London: Academic, 1977.

Garlake, Peter S. *Great Zimbabwe.* London: Thames & Hudson, 1973.

Gelfand, Michael, ed. *Mother Patrick and Her Nursing Sisters, Based on Extracts of Letters and Journals in Rhodesia of the Dominican Sisterhood, 1890–1901.* Cape Town: Juta, 1964.

Genge, Manelisi. "Power and Gender in Southern African History: Power Relations in the Era of Queen Labotsibeni Gwamile Mdluli of Swaziland, ca. 1875–1921." PhD diss., Michigan State University, 1999.

Gewald, Jan-Bart. *Herero Heroes: Socio-Political History of Herero in Namibia, 1890–1923.* Athens: Ohio University Press, 1999.

Giblin, James L. *A History of the Excluded: Making Family a Refuge from State in Twentieth-Century Tanzania.* Athens: Ohio University Press, 2005.

Godwin, Peter, and Ian Hancock. *Rhodesians Never Die: The Impact of War and Political Change on White Rhodesia c. 1970–1980.* Oxford: Oxford University Press, 1993.

Goebel, Allison. *Gender and Land Reform: The Zimbabwe Experience.* Montreal: McGill-Queen's University Press, 2005.

Great Britain Colonial Office. *Copies and Extracts of Correspondence Relating to the British South Africa Company in Mashonaland and Matabeleland Presented to both Houses of Parliament by Command of Her Majesty.* London: Eyre & Spottiswoode, 1893.

Green, Anna. "Individual Remembering and 'Collective Memory': Theoretical Presuppositions and Contemporary Debates." *Oral History* 32, no. 2, Memory and Society (Autumn 2004): 35–44.

Halbwachs, Maurice. *On Collective Memory.* Trans. Lewis A. Coser. Chicago: University of Chicago Press, 1992.

Hamilton, Carolyn. *Terrific Majesty: The Power of Shaka Zulu and the Limits of Historical Invention.* Cambridge, MA: Harvard University Press, 1998.

Hassim, Shireen. *Women's Organizations and Democracy in South Africa: Contesting Authority.* Madison: University of Wisconsin Press, 2005.

Hedges, David. "Review: Reconstructing Shona Histories." *Journal of African History* 37, no. 3 (1996): 492–93.

Herbert, Eugenia W. *Iron, Gender, and Power: Rituals of Transformation in African Societies.* Bloomington: Indiana University Press, 1993.

Hirsch, Marianne, and Valerie Smith, eds. "Gender and Cultural Memory." Special issue, *Signs* 28, no. 1 (Autumn 2002).

Hobsbawm, Eric. "Introduction: Inventing Traditions." In Hobsbawm and Ranger, *Invention of Tradition,* 1–14.

Hobsbawm, Eric, and Terence Ranger, eds. *The Invention of Tradition.* Cambridge: Cambridge University Press, 1983.

Hodza, Aaron C., comp., and George Fortune, ed. and trans. *Shona Praise Poetry*. Oxford: Clarendon, 1979.

Horrell, Georgina. "A White Shade of Pale: White Femininity as Guilty Masquerade in 'New' (White) South African Women's Writing." In "Writing in Transition in South Africa: Fiction, History, Biography," special issue, *Journal of Southern African Studies* 30, no. 4 (Dec. 2004): 765–76.

Huffman, Thomas N. *Guide to the Great Zimbabwe*. Salisbury: National Museums and Monuments of Rhodesia, 1976.

———. *Snakes and Crocodiles: Power and Symbolism in Ancient Zimbabwe*. Johannesburg: University of Witwatersrand University Press, 1996.

———. "The Soapstone Birds from Great Zimbabwe." *African Arts* 18, no. 3 (May 1985): 68–73.

Huggins, Godfrey M. Foreword to Jennings, "Land Apportionment in Southern Rhodesia," 296.

———. "Southern Rhodesia." *African Affairs* 51 (Apr. 1952): 143–49.

Hunt, Lynn. *Politics, Culture, and Class in the French Revolution*. Berkeley: University of California Press, 1984.

Isaacman, Allen. "Social Banditry in Zimbabwe (Rhodesia) and Mozambique, 1894–1907: An Expression of Early Peasant Revolt." In "Protest and Resistance," special issue, *Journal of Southern African Studies* 4, no. 1 (Oct. 1977): 1–30.

Iweriebor, Ehiedu E. G. "The Psychology of Colonialism." In *Africa*, ed. Toyin Falola, vol. 4, *The End of Colonial Rule: Nationalism and Decolonization*, 465–82. Durham, NC: Carolina Academic, 2002.

Jacobs, Susie. "Gender Divisions and the Formation of Ethnicities in Zimbabwe." In *Unsettling Settler Societies: Articulations of Gender, Race, Ethnicity, and Class*, ed. Daiva Stasiulis and Nira Yuval-Davis, 241–61. Thousand Oaks, CA: SAGE, 1995.

Jacobson-Widding, Anita. "Pits, Pots, and Snakes—An Anthropological Approach to Ancient African Symbols." *Nordic Journal of African Studies* 1, no. 1 (1992): 5–25.

Jacobson-Widding, Anita, and W. E. A. Van Beek, eds. *The Creative Communion: African Folk Models of Fertility and Regeneration of Life*. Uppsala: Almqvist & Wiksell International, 1990.

Jeater, Diana. *Marriage, Perversion, and Power: The Construction of Moral Discourse in Southern Rhodesia, 1894–1930*. Oxford: Clarendon, 1993.

Jennings, A. C. "Land Apportionment in Southern Rhodesia." *Journal of Royal African Society* 34 (July 1935): 296–312.

Keppel-Jones, Arthur. *Rhodes and Rhodesia: The White Conquest of Zimbabwe, 1884–1902*. Pietermaritzburg, South Africa: University of Natal Press, 1983.

Kerr, Walter Montagu. *The Far Interior: A Narrative of Travel and Adventure from the Cape of Good Hope across the Zambesi to the Lake Regions of Central Africa*. Vol. 1. London: S. Low, Marston, Searle & Rivington, 1886.

Kirkwood, Deborah. "Settler Wives of Southern Rhodesia: A Case Study." In *The Incorporated Wife,* ed. Hilary Callan and Shirley Ardener, 143–64. London: Croom Helm, 1984.

Kriger, Norma. "From Patriotic Memories to 'Patriotic History' in Zimbabwe, 1990–2005." *Third World Quarterly* 27, no. 6 (2006): 1151–69.

Lalu, Premesh. "The Grammar of Domination and the Subjection of Agency: Colonial Texts and Modes of Evidence." In "'Not Telling': Secrecy, Lies, and History," theme issue, *History and Theory* 39 (Dec. 2000): 45–68.

Lan, David. *Guns and Rain: Guerrillas and Spirit Mediums in Zimbabwe.* London: J. Currey, 1985.

Landau, Paul S. *The Realm of the Word: Language, Gender, and Christianity in a Southern African Kingdom.* Portsmouth, NH: Heinemann, 1995.

Leys, Colin, and Susan Brown. *Histories of Namibia: Living through the Liberation Struggle.* London: Merlin, 2005.

Lipschutz, Mark R., and R. Kent Rasmussen. "Sousa, Manuel Antonio de (Gouveia)." In *Dictionary of African Historical Biography,* 223–24. 2nd expanded ed. Berkeley: University of California Press, 1989.

Livneh, Avital. "Pre-colonial Polities in Southern Zambezia and their Political Communications." PhD thesis, University of London, 1976.

Lloyd, Jessie M. *Rhodesia's Pioneer Women (1859–1896).* Rev. and enlarged by Constance Parry. Bulawayo: Books of Rhodesia, 1974.

Lorde, Audre. *Zami, A New Spelling of My Name.* Trumansburg, NY: Crossing, 1982.

Lourie, Margaret, Domna Stanton, and Martha Vicinus, eds. "Women and Memory." Special issue, *Michigan Quarterly Review* 27, no. 1 (1987).

Lowenthal, David. *The Past Is a Foreign Country.* Cambridge: Cambridge University Press, 2003.

Lowry, Donal. "'White Woman's Country': Ethel Tawse Jollie and the Making of White Rhodesia." In special issue for Terry Ranger, *Journal of Southern African Studies* 23, no. 2 (June 1997): 259–81.

Lukaka, Osumaka. *Naming Colonialism: History and Collective Memory in the Congo, 1870–1960.* Madison: University of Wisconsin Press, 2009.

Lutz, John Sutton. "Introduction: Myth Understandings." In Lutz, *Myth and Memory,* 1–14.

———, ed. *Myth and Memory: Stories of Indigenous-European Contact.* Vancouver: University of British Columbia Press, 2007.

Lyons, Tanya. *Guns and Guerrilla Girls: Women in the Zimbabwean Liberation Struggle.* Trenton, NJ: Africa World, 2004.

MacDonald, Robert H. *The Language of Empire: Myths and Metaphors of Popular Imperialism, 1880–1918.* Manchester: Manchester University Press, 1994.

Mamdani, Mahmood. "Beyond Settler and Native as Political Identities: Overcoming the Political Legacy of Colonialism." *Comparative Studies in Society and History* 43, no. 4 (Oct. 2001): 651–64.

———. *Citizen and Subject: Contemporary Africa and the Legacy of Late Colonialism.* Princeton, NJ: Princeton University Press, 1996.

———. *When Does a Settler Become a Native? Reflections on the Colonial Roots of Citizenship in Equatorial and South Africa.* Cape Town: University of Cape Town, Department of Communication, 1998.

Mandela, Nelson. *Long Walk to Freedom: The Autobiography of Nelson Mandela.* Boston: Little, Brown, 1994.

Mandiringana, E., and T. J. Stapleton. "The Literary Legacy of Frederic Courteney Selous." *History in Africa: A Journal in Method* 25 (1998): 199–218.

Mangaliso, Zengie A. "Gender and Nation-Building in South Africa." In L. West, *Feminist Nationalism,* 130–44.

Maraire, Dumisani A. "The Position of Music in Shona 'Mudzimu' (Ancestral Spirit) Possession." Phd diss., University of Washington, 1990.

Marshall Hole, Hugh. *The Making of Rhodesia.* London, 1926.

Martin, David, and Phyllis Johnson. *The Struggle for Zimbabwe: The Chimurenga War.* Harare: Zimbabwe Publishing House, 1981.

Marx, Karl, "A Contribution to the Critique of Hegel's Philosophy of Right." www.marxists.org/archive/marx/1843/critique-hrp/intro.htm.

———. *The Eighteenth Brumaire of Louis Bonaparte.* New York: International Publishers, 1963.

Mataga, Jesmael, and Farai M. Chabata. "Preservation of Spiritual Heritage in Zimbabwe: The Case of Gomba/Mazowe Landscape." *Zimbabwean Prehistory* 28 (Nov. 2008): 50–58.

Matenga, Edward. *Soapstone Birds of Great Zimbabwe.* Harare: Africa Publishing Group, 1998.

Maylam, Paul. *The Cult of Rhodes: Remembering an Imperialist in Africa.* Cape Town: David Philip, 2005.

Mazrui, Ali A. *The Africans: A Triple Heritage.* Episodes 3, 4, 8. Washington, DC: WETA and the BBC, 1986.

———. "Preface: Black Berlin and the Curse of Fragmentation: From Bismarck to Barack." In *The Curse of Berlin: Africa after the Cold War,* by Adekeye Adebajo, ix–xxviii. London: Hurst, 2010.

McCall, Leslie. "The Complexity of Intersectionality." *Signs* 30 (2005): 1771–1800.

McCulloch, Jock. *Black Peril, White Virtue: Sexual Crime in Southern Rhodesia, 1902–1935.* Bloomington: Indiana University Press, 2000.

McDonald, James G. *Rhodes: A Life.* New York: R. M. McBride, 1928.

McFadden, Patricia. "African Feminist Perspectives of Postcoloniality." In "The Struggle for Zimbabwe," special issue, *Black Scholar* 37, no. 1 (Spring 2007): 36–42.

———. "Becoming Postcolonial: African Women Changing the Meaning of Citizenship." *Meridians: Feminism, Race, Transnationalism* 6, no. 1 (2005): 1–22.

McMahon, Horace W. "Clearing the Granite Range in the Mazoe Valley." In Alderson, *With the Mounted Infantry,* 184–85.

Memmi, Albert. *The Colonizer and the Colonized.* 1967. Reprint. Boston: Beacon, 1991.

Mlambo, A. S. *White Immigration into Rhodesia: From Occupation to Federation.* Harare: University of Zimbabwe Publications, 2002.

Mohanty, Chandra Talhade. "Under Western Eyes: Feminist Scholarship and Colonial Discourses." *Feminist Review* 30 (1988): 61–88.

Morrison, Toni. "The Site of Memory." in *Inventing the Truth: The Art and Craft of Memoir,* ed. William Zinsser, 83–102. 2nd ed. Boston: Houghton Mifflin, 1995.

———. "Unspeakable Things Unspoken: The Afro-American Presence in American Literature." Tanner Lectures on Human Values, University of Michigan, 7 Oct. 1998.

Mudenge, Stanislaus I. G. *A Political History of the Munhumutapa ca. 1400 to 1902.* Harare: Zimbabwe Publishing House, 1988.

Mugabe, Robert. "The Role and History of the Zimbabwean Women in the National Struggle." In *Our Struggle for Liberation,* 20–25. Gweru: Mambo, 1983.

Munochiveyi, Munyaradzi B. "'We do not want to be Ruled by Foreigners': Oral Histories of Nationalism in Colonial Zimbabwe." *Historian* 73, no. 1 (Spring 2011): 65–87.

Mutswairo, Solomon. *Feso.* Ed. Donald E. Herdeck. Harare: HarperCollins, 1995.

Mutunhu, Tendai. "Nehanda of Zimbabwe (Rhodesia): The Story of a Woman Liberation Fighter." *Ufahamu* 7, no. 1 (1976): 60–71.

Ndlovu-Gatsheni, Sabelo J. *The Ndebele Nation: Reflections on Hegemony, Memory, Historiography.* Pretoria: UNISA, 2009.

Newitt, Mayln. *A History of Mozambique.* Johannesburg: University of Witwatersrand Press, 1995.

Nhongo-Simbanegavi, Josephine. *For Better or Worse? Women in Zimbabwe's Liberation Struggle.* Harare: Weaver, 2001.

Noordervliet, Nelleke. "In Defense of Clio's Honor." Lecture, Twenty-first International Congress of Historical Sciences, University of Amsterdam, 22–28 Aug. 2010. http://www.ichs2010.org/documents/in_defence_of_clios_honour.pdf.

Nora, Pierre. "Between History and Memory: Lieux de Mémoire." In "Memory and Counter-Memory," special issue, *Representations,* no. 26 (Spring 1989): 7–24.

Norris-Newman, Charles L. *Matebeleland and How We Got It: With Notes on the Occupation of Mashunaland.* London: T. Fisher Unwin Paternoster Square, 1895.

Nyamandwe, Carine. "Carine Nyamandwe talks to Virginia Phiri." In Zimbabwe Women Writers, *Women of Resilience,* 1–14.

Olick, Jeffrey K. "Introduction: Memory and the Nation; Continuities, Conflicts, and Transformations." In "Memory and the Nation," special issue, *Social Science History* 22, no. 4 (Winter 1998): 377–87.

Olick, Jeffrey K., and Joyce Robbins. "Social Memory Studies: From 'Collective Memory' to the Historical Sociology of Mnemonic Practices." *Annual Review of Sociology* 24 (1998): 105–40.

Oyewùmí, Oyèrónké. *The Invention of Women: Making an African Sense of Western Gender Discourses.* Minneapolis: University of Minnesota Press, 1997.

———. "Visualizing the Body: Western Theories and African Bodies." In *African Gender Studies: A Reader,* ed. Oyèrónké Oyewùmí. New York: Palgrave Macmillan, 2005.

Phimister, Ian. *Chibaro: African Mine Labor, 1900–1933.* London: Pluto, 1983.

Pieres, Jeff. *The Dead Will Arise: Nongqawuse and the Great Xhosa Cattle-Killing Movement of 1856–7.* Bloomington: Indiana University Press, 1989.

Pikirayi, Innocent. "The Archaeological Identity of the Mutapa Kingdom: Towards an Historical Archaeology of Northern Zimbabwe." PhD diss., Uppsala University, 1993.

Pongweni, Alec. *Songs That Won the Liberation War.* Harare: College Press, 1982.

Portelli, Alessandro. "History-Telling and Time: An Example from Kentucky." *Oral History Review* 20, no. 1 (Apr. 1992): 51–66.

Primorac, Ranka. "Rhodesians Never Die? The Zimbabwean Crisis and the Revival of Rhodesian Discourse." In *Zimbabwe's New Diaspora: Displacement and the Cultural Politics of Survival,* ed. Joanne McGregor and Ranka Primorac, 202–28. New York: Berghahn Books, 2010.

Pwiti, Gilbert, and Godfrey Mahachi. "Shona Ethnography and the Interpretation of Iron Age Zimbabwe Burials: The Significance of Burial Location." *Zimbabwea* 3 (Oct. 1991): 57–59.

Pwiti, G., and W. Ndoro. "The Legacy of Colonialism: Perceptions of Cultural Heritage Management in Southern Africa with Specific Reference to Zimbabwe." *African Archaeological Review* 16, no. 3 (Sept. 1999): 143–53.

Ranchod-Nilsson, Sita. "Gender Politics and National Liberation: Women's Participation in the Liberation of Zimbabwe." PhD diss., Northwestern University, 1992.

Randles, W. G. L. *The Empire of the Monomotapa: From the Fifteenth to the Nineteenth Century.* Gwelo, Zimbabwe: Mambo, 1981.

Ranger, Terence O. *"Are We also Not Men?" The Samkange Family and African Politics in Zimbabwe, 1920–64.* Harare: Baobab Books, 1995.

———. "Connexions between 'Primary Resistance' Movements and Modern Mass Nationalism in East and Central Africa." *Journal of African History* 9, no. 3 (1968): 437–53.

———. "The Invention of Tradition in Colonial Africa." In Hobsbawm and Ranger, *Invention of Tradition,* 211–62.

———. "Nationalist Historiography, Patriotic History and the History of the Nation: The Struggle over the Past in Zimbabwe." *Journal of Southern African Studies* 30, no. 2 (June 2004): 215–34.

———. *Revolt in Southern Rhodesia, 1896–97: A Study in African Resistance*. London: Heinemann, 1967.

———. "Traditional Authorities and the Rise of Modern Politics in Southern Rhodesia: 1898–1930." Paper presented at the History of Central African People's Conference, Rhodes-Livingstone Institute, Lusaka, Zambia, 28 May–1 June 1963.

———. *Voices from the Rocks: Nature, Culture, and History in the Matopos Hills of Zimbabwe*. Bloomington: Indiana University Press, 1999.

Ranger, Terence, Jocelyn Alexander, and Joanne McGregor. *Violence and Memory: One Hundred Years in the "Dark Forests" of Matebeleland*. Oxford: James Currey, 2000.

Rhodes, Cecil John. *The Last Will and Testament of Cecil John Rhodes with Elucidatory Notes*. Ed. W. T. Stead. London: Review of Reviews, 1902.

Richartz, Francis. "The End of Kakubi and the Other Condemned Murders." *Zambesi Mission Record: A Missionary Publication for Home Readers* 1, no. 2 (Nov. 1898): 53–55.

Ricoeur, Paul. *Memory, History, Forgetting*. Trans. Kathleen Blamey. Chicago: University of Chicago Press, 2004.

Roberts, Richard. "Introductory Comments: History and Memory; The Power of Statist Narratives." *International Journal of African Historical Studies* 33, no. 3 (2000): 513–22.

Rosaldo, Renato. "Imperialist Nostalgia." In "Memory and Counter-Memory," special issue, *Representations* 26 (Spring 1989): 107–22.

Sadomba, Wilbert Z. "War Veterans in Zimbabwe's Land Occupations: Complexities of a Liberation Movement in an African Post-Colonial Settler Society." PhD diss., Wageningen Universiteit, 2008.

Scarnecchia, Timothy. *The Urban Roots of Democracy and Political Violence in Zimbabwe, Harare and Highfield, 1940–1964*. Rochester, NY: University of Rochester Press, 2008.

Schmidt, Elizabeth. *Peasants, Traders, and Wives: Shona Women in the History of Zimbabwe, 1870–1939*. Harare: Heinemann, 1992.

———. "Review." *Journal of Southern African Studies* 21, no. 3 (Sept. 1995): 539–40.

Schreiner, Olive. *Trooper Peter Halket of Mashonaland*. Leipzig: Bernhard Tauchnitz, 1897.

Selous, Frederick C. "A Recent Journey in Eastern Mashona Land." *Proceedings of the Royal Geographical Society and Monthly Record of Geography*, new monthly series, 12, no. 3 (Mar. 1890): 146–50.

———. *Sunshine and Storm in Rhodesia*. London: R. Ward, 1896.

Shoko, Tabona. *Karanga Indigenous Religion in Zimbabwe: Health and Well Being.* Hampshire, UK: Ashgate, 2007.

Shropshire, Denys. "Native Development in Southern Rhodesia." *Journal of the Royal African Society* 32 (Oct. 1933): 409–23.

Shutt, Allison K., and Tony King. "Imperial Rhodesians: The 1953 Rhodes Centenary Exhibition in Southern Rhodesia." *Journal of Southern African Studies* 31, no. 2 (June 2005): 357–79.

Sinclair, Ingrid. *Flame.* San Francisco, CA: California Newsreel, 1996. Also available at http://www.zimmedia.com/flame.

Sithole, Ndabaningi. *Obed Mutezo of Zimbabwe.* Nairobi: Oxford University Press, 1977.

Smith, Ian Douglas. *The Great Betrayal: The Memoirs of Ian Douglas Smith.* London: Black, 1997.

Sollors, Werner. "National Identity and Ethnic Diversity: 'Of Plymouth Rock and Jamestown and Ellis Island'; or Ethnic Literature and some Redefinitions of 'America.'" In *History and Memory in Africa American Culture,* ed. Geneviève Fabre and Robert O'Meally, 92–121. New York: Oxford University Press, 1994.

Southern Rhodesia, 1890–1950: A Record of Sixty Years of Progress. Salisbury: Pictorial Publication Syndicate, 1950.

Spierenburg, Marja J. *Strangers, Spirits, and Land Reform: Conflicts about Land in Dande, Northern Zimbabwe.* Leiden: Brill, 2004.

Staunton, Irene, ed. *Mothers of the Revolution.* Harare: Baobab Books, 1990.

Steyn, Mellisa. *"Whiteness Just Isn't What It Used to Be": White Identity in a Changing South Africa.* Albany: State University of New York Press, 2001.

Strobel, Margaret. *European Women and the Second British Empire.* Bloomington: Indiana University Press, 1991.

Summers, Roger. *Inyanga: Prehistoric Settlements in Southern Rhodesia.* Cambridge: Cambridge University Press, 1958.

Suttner, Raymond. *The ANC Underground in South Africa, 1950–1976.* Boulder, CO: Lynne Rienner, 2009.

Tawse-Jollie, Ethel. "Southern Rhodesia: A White Man's Country in the Tropics." *Geographical Review* 17, no. 1 (Jan. 1927): 89–106.

Thiong'o, Ngugi wa. *Decolonizing the Mind: The Politics of Language in African Literature.* Nairobi: East African, 1986.

Thomas, Antony. *Rhodes: The Race for Africa.* London: BBC Books, 1996.

Thompson, Leonard. *A History of South Africa.* 3rd ed. New Haven, CT: Yale University Press, 2001.

Trevor-Roper, Hugh. "The Rise of Christian Europe." *Listener* 70 (28 Nov. 1963): 871–75.

Trouillot, Michel-Rolph. *Silencing the Past: The Power and Production of History.* Boston: Beacon, 1995.

Tsomondo, Madziwanyika. "Shona Reaction and Resistance to the European Colonization of Zimbabwe, 1890–1898: A Case Study against Colonial and Revisionist Historiography." *Journal of Southern African Affairs: An Interdisciplinary Research Quarterly* 2, no. 1 (Jan. 1977): 11–32.

Turino, Tom. *Nationalists, Cosmopolitans, and Popular Music in Zimbabwe.* Chicago: University of Chicago Press, 2000.

Tutu, Desmond. *No Future without Forgiveness.* New York: Doubleday, 1999.

Vambe, Lawrence. *An Ill-Fated People: Zimbabwe before and after Rhodes.* London: William Heinemann, 1972.

Vansina, Jan. *Oral History as Tradition.* Madison: University of Wisconsin Press, 1985.

Vera, Yvonne. *Butterfly Burning.* New York: Farrar, Strauss & Giroux, 2000.

Victor, Father. "The Condemned in Matabeleland." *Zambesi Mission Record* 1 (May 1898).

Weiss, Ruth. *Women of Zimbabwe.* London: Kesho, 1986.

West, Lois A. ed. *Feminist Nationalism.* London: Routledge, 1997.

———. Introduction to L. West, *Feminist Nationalism,* xi–xxxvi.

West, Michael O. *The Rise of an African Middle Class: Colonial Zimbabwe, 1890–1965.* Bloomington: Indiana University Press, 2002.

White, Luise. *The Assassination of Herbert Chitepo: Texts and Politics in Zimbabwe.* Bloomington: Indiana University Press, 2003.

———. "Telling More: Lies, Secrets, and History." In "'Not Telling': Secrecy, Lies, and History," theme issue, *History and Theory* 39 (Dec. 2000): 11–22.

Winter, Jay. *Sites of Memory, Sites of Mourning: The Great War in European Cultural History.* Cambridge: Cambridge University Press, 1995.

Wood, R. H. "The 1898 Criminal Sessions." *Heritage of Zimbabwe* 6 (1986): 47–58.

Wright, Howell. "Ex Africa Semper Aliquid Novi." *Yale University Library Gazette* 15, no. 4 (Apr. 1941): 87–88.

Yoshikuni, Tsueneo. *African Urban Experiences in Colonial Zimbabwe: A Social History of Harare before 1925.* Harare: Weaver, 2007.

———. *Elizabeth Musodzi and the Birth of African Feminism in Early Colonial Zimbabwe.* Harare: Weaver, 2008.

Zeleza, Paul Tiyambe. "Gender Biases in African Historiography." In *Engendering the Social Sciences,* ed. Ayesha Imam, 81–116. Dakar: CODESRIA, 1997.

Zilberg, Jonathan. "Review." *International Journal of African Historical Studies* 28, no. 3 (1995): 684–88.

Zimbabwe Women Writers. *Women of Resilience: The Voices of Women Ex-Combatants.* Harare: Zimbabwe Women Writers, 2000.

Zimmer, Bradley. *The Mists of Avalon.* New York: Ballantine Books, 1984.

Zimunya, Musaemura B., and Solomon Mutswairo. "Mother Tongue: Interviews with Musaemura B. Zimunya and Solomon Mutswairo." By Angela A. Williams. *Journal of African Travel-Writing* 4 (Apr. 1998): 36–44.

Index

ationalization of, 78; oral, 17, 116, 138, 139, 142, 158–59, 193, 206, 209; "ours" versus "theirs," 159; past's importance to settlers, 114; political nationalists' version of, 11; re-membered to suit founding myths, 139; reorganizing, 145; the right side of, 219; tensions with memory, 21–22; true, 8; value of, 7

Hole, Hugh Marshall: archive of, 35, 79, 103–15; attitude toward Africans of, 35; conflict with British South Africa Company, 105, 111; death of, 105; histories of Rhodesia of, 79, 105, 107; as key figure in Rhodesia's early administration, 108; on Pollard's disappearance, 34–35; as quintessential imperialist and settler, 103

Hole, Mary (Molly) Marshall-: assists husband's historical work, 107; death of, 113; financial need of, 104, 110, 240n79; greed attributed to, 107, 109; husband's archive sold by, 35, 79, 103–15, 223; hyphenated surname of, 240n65; Sally Mugabe compared with, 190

homosexuality, 178

Honey, W. S., 117, 118

Huggins, Godfrey, 96, 128

human rights, 6–7, 150

Hwata (Chief Chitaura; Wata): among the Ndebele, 175; badge for, 75; court's mercy toward, 61; indictment of, 50; on Mativirira, 70, 71, 72, 73, 164; Nehanda-Charwe's power over, 59, 60; in Salisbury, 102, 103; trial of, 54, 58

Hwata dynasty, 24–25, 38, 69, 72, 145

identity: double-consciousness, 178; as shifting, 172, 173. *See also* gender; national identity

identity papers, 150

Ill-Fated People, An: Zimbabwe before

and after Rhodes (Vambe), 160, 162, 175. *See also* Vambe, Lawrence

imagination, 8–9; blending analysis with, 16; history as, 119; imagined communities, 121

incest, 22, 23, 73

indirect rule, 31

insurrection of 1896–97, 34–39; African heroes of, 139; Africans' bitter memories of, 149; Africans imprisoned after, 154, 155; arrest of Nehanda-Charwe and, 48; in central Mashonaland, 32; colonial postwar policy, 74; complexity of human interaction after, 146; faith in power of ancestors shaken by defeat in, 167; forced labor in, 150; heroes not reinterred, 216; history and memory circle each other in, 21–22; Madzidza wants repetition of, 164; Mazoe Relief (Mazoe Incident), 116–21; memories of humiliation of defeat in, 156–59; nationalist focus on, 188, 193–94, 199, 203, 205; Nehanda-Charwe as skeptical about African chances in, 69, 154; Nehanda-Charwe in, 36–40, 48, 197, 213; Occupation Day reminds Africans of, 195; police brutality in start of, 144; in radio announcement of Zimbabwean independence, 204–5; settler memory founded on, 76; shared African memory of, 168; victors controlled narrative of, 158; war medals in, 42–46, 117; women and historiography of, 54

Jacha, Aaron, 161, 171–75, 223

Jakobo, 165, 166

Jameson, Leander Starr, 82, 231n33

Jennings, A. C., 95

Jesuit missionaries, 164–65, 167–68

Johannesburg, 141

Johnson, Frank, 81, 96

Johnson, Phyllis, 27

present, 205; business relationships with Europeans, 32, 33, 40, 69; as captive spirit, 210; capture of, 48–49, 49, 62; cave of, 38, 39, 62; charge against, 48, 50, 57; chief native commissioner's report on, 37–38; children of, 69–70, 155; Chishawasha shares history and culture with, 162; claims on new regime of keepers of, 205–12; clientele of, 61–63; colonial bureaucracy fears memory of, 70; as "Comrade Nehanda," 6, 203–4; conflation of spirit of legendary Nehanda with, 4, 5, 6, 26, 38, 59, 60, 188, 194, 195–96, 203, 209; cryptic nature of testimony of, 53; death of, 4, 5, 34, 66, 147, 154, 202; death warrant of, 62; early life of, 22; erasure of memory of, 76; gatekeepers of, 206; guns distributed by, 158; hunt for, 47–48; indictment of, 50; innocence maintained by, 59; in insurrection of 1896–97, 36–40, 48, 197, 213; Kaguvi-Gumboreshumba's accusations against, 48–49, 56, 57, 73; Kenny's report ignores, 67; male witnesses against, 54, 55, 58, 146; Mativirira Nehanda and, 68, 69, 71–74; memory alive in Mazowe valley, 211; memory of Nehanda transferred to, 25; Mugabe on, 204; as national ancestor, 4, 188, 195; as ngozi spirit, 5, 19, 210, 212; as nonliterate, 50; as not first Nehanda medium, 21; occupation of, 50; philosophical differences with Kaguvi-Gumboreshumba, 61–62; power attributed to, 59–61; in radio announcement of Zimbabwean independence, 204–5; refuses conversion to Christianity, 65, 163, 196, 246n8; remembered as one and only Nehanda, 26; Richartz visits in her cell, 64–65,

66, 167; on the run from British, 39, 42; self-possession of, 63, 66; separating the spirit from its medium, 3–6; settler nationalist view of, 52; significance in Zimbabwe, 27; skepticism about African chances in insurrection of 1896–97, 69, 154; in solitary confinement, 53, 65, 154; status compromised by insurrection, 39; as symbol, 52, 199, 201, 203, 204; testimony at preliminary hearing of, 50–51, 52–54; trial of, 54, 55, 58–63, 136; two appearances in national history, 19; women nationalists appeal to, 197–203; ZANU-PF adopts, 196

Nesbitt, Native Commissioner, 46, 116, 118

ngozi spirits, 5, 19, 59, 68, 166, 178, 210, 212

Ngũgĩ wa Thiong'o, 175

Nhongo-Simbanegavi, Josephine, 200

Nicholls, James E., 122–24, 125, 126, 128

Noordervliet, Nelleke, 13, 17

Norton family, 33–34, 36

nostalgia: etymology of term, 238n33; imperialist, 6, 90, 101–3; in Occupation Day, 85, 89; postimperial and postsettler, 6; about Rhodes, 81

Nyamhita Nyakasikana, 23–25; Mativirira adopts name of, 67, 69, 71, 72, 73; Nehanda-Charwe conflated with, 4, 5, 6, 26, 38, 59, 60, 188, 203, 209; power of memory of, 37–38

Nyandoro, George, 183, 184, 185

Occupation Day, 78; African presence at, 88; Africans excluded from, 185; class distinctions and, 97; early years of, 82–90; exclusionary memory in, 181; first official celebration in 1930, 78, 94–95,

Reconsiderations in Southern African History